Gendering Organizational Analysis

CHAMOWITZ

Gendering Organizational Analysis

edited by

Albert J. Mills
Peta Tancred

SAGE Publications
International Educational and Professional Publisher
Newbury Park London New Delhi

For information address:

SAGE Publications, Inc.
2455 Teller Road
Newbury Park, California 91320

SAGE Publications Ltd.
6 Bonhill Street
London EC2A 4PU
United Kingdom

SAGE Publications India Pvt. Ltd.
M-32 Market
Greater Kailash I
New Delhi 110 048 India

Printed in the United States of America

Library of Congress Cataloging-in-Publication Data

Main entry under title:
Gendering organizational analysis/ edited by Albert J. Mills, Peta
Tancred.
p. cm.
Includes index.
ISBN 0-8039-4558-2.—ISBN 0-8039-4559-0 (pbk.)
1. Organizational behavior—Research. 2. Gender identity—Research. 3. Feminist theory. I. Mills, Albert J., 1945- II. Tancred, Peta.
HD58.7.G453 1992
302.3'5—dc20 92-12403

93 94 95 10 9 8 7 6 5 4 3 2

Sage Production Editor: Astrid Virding

Contents

Preface

This book originated in a small restaurant in Montreal in the spring of 1987, where we first met and discussed our mutual interest in gendering organizational analysis. We have kept in touch since that time despite the geographic distance between us (usually Athabasca to Montreal), the vagaries of postal strikes and of fax machines, pressure from competing projects, and the need to discuss various drafts of this work in airports or during rushed visits. We were greatly assisted by a series of sessions that we organized jointly at the annual meetings of the Canadian Sociology and Anthropology Association from 1988 onward, where, within the framework of "Critical Approaches to Organizations," we explored diverse facets of gendered organizational analysis.

Despite the distance between us, we consider this book to be a joint and equal endeavor for which, on occasion, we have been hard put to disentangle the authorship of individual paragraphs or sections. Our names are listed in alphabetical order on the basis of convention only and not as an indication of any unequal contribution.

For helping to bring this book to fruition, we would particularly like to express our thanks to the following: Stephen J. Murgatroyd and Terry Morrison for their enthusiasm and financial support; Valerie Delorme for invaluable technical assistance throughout the project; Nora Brown for her patience with the reformatting process and the unending successive versions; Iris Weyenberg for library assistance when it was really needed; Ann West at Sage for her early support; and Harry Briggs, also at Sage, for his commitment, encouragement, and advice.

Because of the geographic distance between us, we are enormously grateful for support in our private spheres, particularly from Julie Mills and Guy Paquette. We would like to acknowledge publicly their patience in taking telephone messages, their tolerance of our unending discussions, and their willingness to allow the "gendering of organizational analysis" to take precedence over private obligations on many occasions. We cannot promise that these experiences will not be repeated in the future—but we want them to know that their help in the past has been an essential element in completing the current volume.

Albert J. Mills
Maastricht
The Netherlands

Peta Tancred
Montréal
Canada

Introduction

Why is it necessary "to gender" organizational analysis? Isn't such analysis a gender-neutral way of understanding how organizations operate? Why should gender matter in organizational settings?

These and other similar questions illustrate the traditional view of organizations based on the fundamental premise that most workers in the public[1] sphere are male—and it does not matter if they are not. In opposition to this perspective, we argue through the readings selected for this book that it matters a great deal whether organizational employees are female or male. For us, traditional approaches to organizational theory are gender blind; because of this, considerable errors have been made in interpreting how organizations operate. The whole of organizational analysis needs to be rethought on the basis that a fundamental gendered substructure (see Acker, Chapter 14 of this volume) characterizes the workplace.

A second reason for gendering organizational analysis is that other perspectives for the study of the work world—particularly an occupational approach—have incorporated gender into their thinking at a much earlier date and, for the past two decades, have attempted to explain women's unequal workplace situation on the basis of their conceptual frameworks. There is clearly a great deal that organizational analysis can contribute to our understanding of women's ghettoized work experience—on the condition that such analysis is gendered.

Through the subsequent selection of readings, we argue that an understanding of the gendered substructure of organizations facilitates our analysis of women's position within the workplace. This emphasis on *women's* reality is, of course, a response to their previous exclusion. A gendered analysis of organizations includes both women and men and places gender at the center of the explanatory framework.

Organizational Analysis: From Weber to the 1980s

The development of organizational analysis has been characterized in various ways, depending on the perspectives of the authors.[2] One main theme that runs through this variety of accounts concerns the development of organizational analysis parallel to the growth of industrial organizations and in collaboration with managerial preoccupation with their greater "efficiency." Thus a major thrust of organizational studies, until very recently, has been to uncover the "preferably-one-but-possibly-more best ways" of managing organizations. A second and not unrelated theme, as already suggested, is the absence of gender from any of the discussions—even in those approaches that place the individual at the center of their analyses. Clearly, managers were not centrally concerned with their female labor force and they encouraged no consciousness of a gendered reality in the questions that they posed to researchers.

At first glance, this characterization does not fit the work of Max Weber, whose classical writings, early in this century, did a great deal to delineate the characteristics of bureaucracy and its historical development over time. But Weber's work, originally designed to analyze how ideal-type bureaucracies worked in practice, was transformed by managerial concerns into a prescription as to how organizations *ought* to operate.[3] Thus we get the so-called Weberian decalogue ([Tancred-]Sheriff 1976) transmitted to generations of managers in a variety of cultural settings, who courted incompetence if their organizations did not fit the Weberian characteristics. It goes without saying that all Weberian "officials" were male—both in the language used and in the representations communicated.

The work of the Scientific Management School of the first decades of the twentieth century illustrates this researcher/management collaboration with particular clarity. In a considerable body of work (for a good overview, see Braverman 1974: chaps. 4, 5) dominated by the work of Frederick Taylor—hence "Taylorism"—researchers explored the way in which the human and genderless machine could be adapted to organizational priorities. The precision of their measurement was allied with very detailed recommendations as to how organizations should be managed, and the influence of their work is still evident in some contemporary management consultancy approaches.

The celebrated Hawthorne studies, initiated in the late 1920s, constituted a clear collaboration between management concerned with the labor unrest of the time and the Harvard researchers who were invited to investigate the reasons for organizational imperfections (Roethlisberger and Dickson 1939). The Human Relations School that developed out of this work and prescribed a humane yet paternalistic concern for the worker has exerted an enormous influence on our thinking about organizations. With devastating results, the worker had no gender—as Acker and Van Houten (Chapter 1) point out in their powerful reanalysis of the Hawthorne data.

Postwar initiatives in organizational analysis included the work of the organizational psychologists (see Silverman 1970: chap. 4), whose central focus on the individual, rather amazingly, did not succeed in ascribing a specific gender to workers. This work *did* succeed, however, in responding to management concerns as to how the worker could be motivated, with a delineation of the factors encouraging optimum performance. The 1950s functionalist paradigm within sociology had its parallel in organizational analysis; the emphasis on the function of organizations was conceptualized within a nongendered framework, with the problems of order and the maintenance of the status quo in the forefront—questions of overriding importance from a managerial perspective. Even the subsequent Contingency Theorists (e.g., Burns and Stalker 1961; Woodward 1965; Perrow 1970), who aimed to describe the combination of technological or environmental factors and certain organizational arrangements, were interpreted as *recommending* "several best ways" of managing organizations, whatever the gendered substructure, in varying circumstances. It should be recognized that the analysts themselves, by linking certain organizational arrangements to optimal performance in particular situations, encouraged this interpretation of their work. For authors such as Woodward (see [Tancred-]Sheriff and Campbell in Chapter 2), the collaboration with management was quite deliberate.

Development of action accounts in the early to mid-1970s shifted attention toward the role of the actor in maintaining organizational reality. The work of people like Silverman (1970) and Child (1972) raised questions about the understandings and meanings that actors bring to an organization. They did so, however, within a framework that failed to challenge the dominant wisdom on the viability and desirability of the capitalist organization. Within this actionalist phase, a number of interpretive accounts took the notion of human meaning and the creation of organization even further. The work of

Bittner, Strauss et al., Emerson, Sudnow (Salaman and Thompson 1965), and others focused upon how organizational realities are "accomplished" and "negotiated." While by no means intentionally managerialist, the focus on the individual's understanding of organizations could certainly be adapted to managerial ends; once again, despite the individual focus, the worker had no gender.

From the mid-1970s on, a number of radical approaches to organization began to appear and finally broke the researcher/management collaboration. These approaches challenged the very nature of organizations as currently constituted within the ethos of capitalism: "radical humanist"[4] works (e.g., Illich 1973; Dickson 1974) focused upon exposing the "ideologically dominating character" of organizations, counterposing alternative, "liberating," ways of life; "radical structuralist" works (e.g., Allen 1975; Benson 1977)—with their focus upon system and structures—sought to expose capitalist organization as "systems of oppression" within a broad framework of domination. While radical approaches to organization shifted attention to the role of organizations in the process of domination and oppression, they very much continued in the vein of "male-stream" (O'Brien, 1981) analysis that has characterized most of organization theory.

Alternative Analyses of Women in the Workplace

The organizational perspective put forward in this volume is concerned with analyzing the workplace at the level of the organizational "totality" (Benson 1977). Ideally, organizational analysis, while cognizant of processes within this totality, is concerned with viewing the organization as a whole, from the "top down," as one would expect from its managerial collaboration.

The considerable body of feminist work, during the past two decades, that has addressed women's segregation within the workplace, is rooted in alternative approaches—in particular, in an *occupational* approach that views women's labor force participation from the perspective of broad societal divisions crossing organizational boundaries. Within this approach, considerable attention has been devoted to the nature of women's remunerated labor—its resemblance (or lack of it) to domestic labor, the extent to which it is biologically or culturally influenced, the role that unions have played in maintaining women in specific occupations, the way in which capitalism has benefited from women's segregated labor, to mention only a few examples.[5]

An illustration of the kinds of concerns that guide this approach is provided by Jeff Hearn (1985c). He illustrates the importance of a gendered focus by exploring the relationships between the development of professionalization and the entry of women into certain occupations:

> Capitalist development entails the shifting of control of different types of emotions or different bases of emotionality from merely domestic labor into socialised labor . . .
>
> Since the development of the "established" professions monopolised by men, this process has continued apace elsewhere. It is in the so-called semi-professions that this second phase of professional development has taken place. Within nursing, health visiting, midwifery, social work and teaching are the emerging structures by which grief, joy, loss and despair are patriarchally socialised. (p. 195)

A second perspective is the focus on *work*—that is, a traditional concern with remunerated labor, broadened by feminists to include domestic labor, that looks at the nature of work historically and "how it connects individuals to the social structure" (Feldberg and Glenn 1979: 527). Always cognizant of the gendered reality of the workplace, this approach has been developed by feminists to make gender a much more central variable in explanatory terms. Feldberg and Glenn illustrate the kinds of recent insights provided. They critique existing approaches to the sociology of work and the way in which different assumptions are made about the relationship of men and women to work. This has led, according to Feldberg and Glenn, to two models of analysis, namely, a *job model* (when thinking about men) and a *gender model* (when women are the focus of attention): "For men, it is assumed that economic activities provide the basis for social relationships within the family and in the society generally. For women, it is assumed that family care-taking activities determine social relationships" (Feldberg and Glenn 1979: 527).

In contrast to these types of preoccupations, organizational analysts focus upon "the multiple, interpenetrating levels and sectors" (Benson 1977) that constitute a given organizational reality. This level of analysis concerns itself with the process and dynamics that create and maintain given organizational realities and, from a radical perspective, the impact of those realities upon the construction of social relationships. Thus feminist organizational analysis would be concerned to understand the contribution of organization per se, and of given organizational settings, to the construction and maintenance of gendered persons.

Toward Feminist Organizational Analysis

The chapters[6] selected for this volume are only a small sampling of the work of feminist organizational analysis during the past decade and a half. Our original selection included nearly a dozen more articles, sadly dropped as the economic realities of publishing impinged on our consciousness but to which we will make reference as we discuss our selections.

It was clear, from the beginning, that the initial part of the book ("Organizational Analysis: A Critique") would be devoted to feminist critiques and commentaries on the traditional literature. For us, the Acker and Van Houten article (1974—Chapter 1 of this volume) initiated the process of gendering organizational analysis, for they were the first to demonstrate—and to do so dramatically—that the inclusion of the gender variable was capable of transforming such analysis. That their work was buried under the avalanche of masculinist organizational work of the period[7] meant that, nearly a decade later, Hearn and Parkin (1983—Chapter 3) were still engaged in a critique of the neglected area of gender and organizations. We have included this latter article as an overarching critique of the state of the field, as recently as the 1980s.

The other article in this first part ([Tancred-]Sheriff and Campbell 1981—Chapter 2) takes a completely different orientation by asking what contributions women scholars had made, up to the 1980s, toward the sociology of organizations. A very different type of critique of the field, it demonstrates the handmaiden role of many women in the field, either to managers and their priorities or to their male colleagues in undertaking specialized tasks within the literature. It would be salient to learn whether the past decade has transformed this role in important ways; the rest of the chapters included in this volume would so indicate, and we leave this mammoth task to an interested researcher of the future.

A major section that had to be dropped from this volume traced the slow development of feminist thinking on organizations through the literature of the late 1970s and early 1980s. We took into account that much of the desirable work was already available in book form; this includes Janet Wolff's (1977) early article emphasizing the gendered context in which organizations are located, Clegg and Dunkerley's (1980) historical approach to women's organizational reality, Kathy Ferguson's (1984) magnificent feminist attack on bureaucracy, and Gareth Morgan's (1986) brief treatment of women in his recent imaginative approach to organizations. Other material that could not be included stemmed from conference and other unpublished papers. This work illustrated the vast effort that needed to be devoted to gendering organizational analysis—sometimes with limited results as we groped our way forward.

To illustrate these efforts to conceptualize organizations from a feminist perspective, we finally selected three works that are included in Part II of this volume ("Toward Feminism as Radical Organizational Analysis"). Burrell's article "Sex and Organizational Analysis" (1984—Chapter 4) exerted considerable influence on a growing literature—*The Sexuality of Organization* (Hearn et al. 1989)—and we include it here as a categorical statement of the sexual reality of organizations—whatever myths might be perpetrated on this subject. The succeeding articles (Mills 1988—Chapter 5; Grant and Tancred 1991—Chapter 6) illustrate two attempts, from the recent literature, to theorize, first, organizations in general and, second, the bureaucracy of the state (but see also Part IV, "Contemporary Voices"). Having run the theoretical gauntlet ourselves, we are aware of and sympathetic with the difficulties posed by the feminist reorientation of organizational analysis. In some ways, we are still at the stage of gendering existing frameworks, with all the disadvantages this entails. Such hobbling of feminist thought merits further discussion.

The empirical chapters included in Part III of this volume ("From Theory to Application: Explorations in Feminist Organizational Analysis") are a wide-ranging attempt to illustrate the kind of data gathering that has taken place in gendered organizational analysis. On the basis of quantitative data (Gutek and Cohen 1987—Chapter 7), qualitative interviews (Sheppard 1991—Chapter 8), historical approaches (Benson 1978—Chapter 9), and case study material (Burton 1987—Chapter 10), we obtain an image of how women are shaped and yet resist such shaping in organizational settings. The masculinist nature of these settings comes through clearly as we follow women managers, department store staff, public servants, and others as they attempt to manage their working reality.

The final part, "Contemporary Voices," contains unpublished material as we present the most recent feminist organizational analysis. Issues of race and ethnicity are in the forefront (Calás 1989—Chapter 11; Bell and Nkomo 1991—Chapter 13) as in feminist analysis generally at the current time. We also present the most recent conceptualizations on the part of feminist researchers (Calás and Smircich, 1989—Chapter 12) and, in particular, Joan Acker's up-to-date commentary on the issue of gendering organizational theory (1991—Chapter 14). Because Acker was part of the early initiative for the current topic, it is only appropriate that we benefit from her most recent reflections.

Taken together, these selections constitute what we consider to be important examples of gendered approaches to organizations. Not only is the gender distinction centrally located throughout the selections, but the guiding assumption is that gender makes an overwhelming difference to organizational reality. We trust that this collection of writings will contribute to invalidating the traditional genderless perspective that has dominated the field of organizational analysis for far too long. In this way, "gendered organizational analysis" will be able to prevent future errors of interpretation as well as contributing to our understanding of women's workplace reality.

Notes

1. We use the terms *public* and *private* to refer not to type of organizational ownership but to the spheres of remunerated and nonremunerated work—or to the *workplace* and the *family* in traditional language. Because all traditional terminology infers that one only "works" in the former sphere and not in the latter, however, we prefer the terms *public/private,* which are used widely in the feminist literature and are intended to indicate that work takes place in both spheres.

2. Excellent accounts of organizational analysis over time are available, for example, in Silverman (1970), Burrell and Morgan (1979), Reed (1985), Perrow (1986), Morgan (1990), and Mills and Murgatroyd (1991). Readers who require a fuller coverage than is possible within this introduction are encouraged to consult one or more of these works.

3. It should be added that Weber, in his political writings, provided some ammunition for this interpretation by emphasizing the "efficiency" of bureaucracy (see Silverman 1970: 74).

4. The categorization of approaches as "radical humanist" and "radical structuralist" comes from the work of Burrell and Morgan (1979).

5. A recent overview of such work, in English Canada at least, is contained in Armstrong and Armstrong (1990).

6. This Introduction presents an overview of the work included in this volume; the introductions to each part present this work in greater detail.

7. One of the editors (Tancred) admits that it took her six years to find the Acker and Van Houten article (Chapter 2, this volume), which only came to light when she was invited to contribute an evaluation of women's contribution to the sociology of organizations for the Quebec journal *Sociologie et Sociétés.*

PART I

Organizational Analysis: A Critique

Until 1974, next to nothing had been written on organizational analysis from a feminist perspective. The field was almost exclusively dominated by "male-stream" approaches and ways of viewing organizational reality. In 1974, the publication of an article in the *Administrative Science Quarterly* by Joan Acker and Donald Van Houten represented a rare challenge to the dominant male-stream paradigm. Nonetheless, between 1974 and 1984, very few feminist works were published in the fields of organization and management theory,[1] but those that were made a valuable contribution to our understanding of the relationship between gender and organization. Rosabeth Moss Kanter (1975a, 1975b, 1975c, 1977a, 1977b) and Janet Wolff (1977), for instance, raised vital questions about the impact of organizational structure upon female opportunity and sense of self. Kanter—in her 1977 book—argued that numbers, power, and "opportunity structure" contribute to the way that women (and men) come to view their worth within an organization. A concentration of women in the lowest clerical or manual grades coupled with an absence of women in management positions send a very definite and negative message about the relative worth of females within the organization. In regard to power, Kanter argued that not only are there fewer women in managerial positions but that those positions often carry less discretion and decision-making powers than those occupied by male counterparts. Disparities of power and numbers, coupled with other factors, contribute to what Kanter calls an opportunity structure that signals to men and women their relative worth within the organization.

In a more critical vein, Janet Wolff (1977: 7) argued that "organization theory cannot account for the differential treatment and experience of the sexes unless its traditional assumptions about the existence, rationale and functioning of organizations are crucially reassessed."

In contrast to Kanter's focus upon the structural causes of inequity *within* organizations, Wolff focuses upon "extraorganizational influences," arguing that, "women's position in any organization is inseparable from women's position in society." She concludes that "the very question of women's role and position in organizations can only be answered by a macro-sociology which situates the organization in the society which defines its existence, goals and values" (Wolff 1977: 20).

Wolff's article appeared in an edited collection by Stewart Clegg and David Dunkerley and was one of the earliest British feminist critiques of organization theory. In 1980, Clegg and Dunkerley, building directly on the work of Wolff, returned to the issue of gender. In a chapter on "people in organizations,"[2] they were concerned to expose the ideological and structural rules that cohere in the formation of dual-labor markets. In so doing, they suggested an approach that, while focused upon structural outcomes, sought answers through analysis of human subjectivity and its gendered construction.[3] And here they indicated the potential of a reevaluated action frame of reference:

> One of the strengths of the action frame of reference . . . was its commitment to an explanation couched in terms of 'the ways in which social, economic and technical aspects of a worker's market and work situations are mediated by his definition of their significance.' It stressed 'the ways in which his actions must be seen as the outcome of his perceptions of the various options open to him and of which alternative best meets his priorities at the time.' . . . We can also apply this to *her* definitions, *her* actions, *her* perceptions of the various options open to *her*, and *her* priorities. (Clegg and Dunkerley 1980: 405)

The following year—1981—an article by Peta [Tancred-]Sheriff and Jane Campbell, in the Canadian journal *Sociologie et Sociétés*, helped to introduce a feminist critique of organizations into the francophone literature. And, by 1983, progress was such that Jeff Hearn and Wendy Parkin were able to provide a substantial overview of developments and, in the process, provide an important springboard for further advancement of feminist organizational perspectives. In this part of the book, we have included three works that made important contributions to the development of a feminist critique of organizational analysis—the work of Acker and Van Houten (1974), [Tancred-]Sheriff and Campbell (1981), and Hearn and Parkin (1983).

The article by Acker and Van Houten represented an important milestone in the development of a feminist critique of organizational analysis, and for that reason we have included it as the first chapter of this book. The article was important in beginning the process of exposing the sexist nature of organizations and of organizational analysis. It provides telling examples of the extent to which sexist thinking has informed the design, methods, results, and analyses of some of the "classic" studies of organization. Reanalyzing the Hawthorne studies and Michel Crozier's work on bureaucracy, Acker and Van Houten reveal how "sex power differentials" were a key element in the design and consequent findings of both major studies and yet were ignored by the researchers involved. The relative power of the male maintenance workers in contrast to the female production workers in Crozier's study, the relative autonomy of the men in the "Bank Wiring Room" compared with the controlled activities of the females in the "Relay Assembly Test Room" at Hawthorne, and the gendered character of organizational power reflected in all-male supervisors were all viewed as normal by the male researchers.

The Acker and Van Houten article was important in encouraging feminist reanalyses of classic studies of organization (Feldberg and Glenn 1979; Mills 1988a; Mumby and Putnam 1990; Martin 1990b), in challenging us to examine our own role as researchers in the processes of gendered realities, and in arguing that "the sex structuring of organizations needs to be taken into account along with organizational factors to arrive at fuller explanations of organizational phenomena" (Acker and Van Houten 1974: 152). It was a message that went unheeded for much of the following decade. Acker herself has since made several important contributions of her own (Acker 1982, 1987, 1988, 1989, 1990).

The [Tancred-]Sheriff and Campbell article was important not only in bringing a feminist critique of organizations to the attention of francophones but in focusing upon the contribution of female organizational analysts. For those reasons, we have included it here as Chapter 2. [Tancred-]Sheriff and Campbell argue that, despite the overwhelmingly male character of organizational analyses, some of the more prominent work in the field was conducted by female researchers—in particular, Mary Parker Follett, Joan Woodward, and Rosabeth Moss Kanter. They go on to argue that a combination of male dominance and the assimilation of females into a managerialist framework led to a downplaying of their contribution.

Mary Parker Follett, for instance, through a recognition of the motivating desires of the individual and of the group influenced a move away from Taylorism toward an emergent Human Relations school of thought. Yet, one would have to look very hard through the literature to find any acknowledgment of her influence in presaging the transition from one major school of organizational thought to the next. Joan Woodward has fared somewhat better. Her development of a technological approach to organizations has been influential. Yet, even here, as [Tancred-]Sheriff and Campbell point out, Woodward's major contribution to the development of the contingency theory of organizations has been greatly overshadowed by the attention given to Charles Perrow's work on technology and to the Aston group's research on structure. More controversially, [Tancred-]Sheriff and Campbell argue that the influence of Kanter derives from the fact that she highlights the situation of women in organizations within a framework of male-stream organizational theory, focused ultimately on managerialist concerns. For [Tancred-]Sheriff and Campbell, the relative success and containment of all three women researchers results from the fact that, rather than challenging the prevailing male definition of the field, they participated in it, in effect sharing the same links with management that have propelled the general development of the field.

In the years since 1981, [Tancred-]Sheriff has continued to develop a feminist analysis of organizations (Tancred-Sheriff 1987, 1988, 1989; Hearn et al. 1989) including work, with Judith Grant, on state bureaucracy (Chapter 6 of this volume).

The work of Hearn and Parkin has been included here (Chapter 3) because it represents an important milestone in the development of feminist critique. It represented at the time of publication—1983—the most thoroughgoing attempt to provide an overall critique of organizational analysis from a feminist perspective.

Hearn and Parkin set out to analyze the "neglect" of gender in organizational analysis using as a framework a "tactical reappraisal of Burrell and

Morgan's typology of organizational paradigms." Their analysis led them to argue that organization theory—across all paradigms—has taken a number of sexist routes, including either a complete neglect of gender or the use of relatively simple descriptive models that treat gender as no more than a variable of which account should be taken. They conclude by outlining a number of key areas of analysis to be explored in the development of a feminist theory of organization—work and the division of labor, authority and power, sexuality, and the interrelationship between work, power, and sexuality. They have since developed these areas of analysis through a number of studies (Hearn 1982a, 1982b, 1985a, 1985b, 1987, 1991; Hearn et al. 1989; Hearn and Parkin 1983, 1984, 1987, 1991; Parkin 1989; Parkin and Hearn 1987; Burrell and Hearn 1989).

Notes

1. This was less true in the case of feminist analyses of work (e.g., Hartmann 1976; Glenn and Feldberg 1977; West 1982), which appeared in growing numbers throughout the period.

2. A title that, according to Stewart Clegg, was designed to parody existing gendered approaches to organizational analysis.

3. Clegg and Dunkerley were subsequently criticized for the fact that their "mammoth work only devotes about 25 pages to gender out of 560" (Hearn and Parkin 1983: 225) but this underplays the fact that they were among the few radical organization theorists to include feminist accounts in their work.

1

Differential Recruitment and Control: The Sex Structuring of Organizations

JOAN ACKER
DONALD R. VAN HOUTEN

Sex differences in organizational behaviour have been recorded in the research literature since systematic research in organizations began (for example, Roethlisberger and Dickson 1939), and the sex segregation of the occupational world is being increasingly recognized as a significant aspect of social structure (Gross 1968; Epstein 1970; Oppenheimer1970). The relationship between these two phenomena has been suggested (Epstein 1970; Etzioni 1969; Marrett 1972), but has been studied primarily within the professions, with other occupations largely ignored. Whyte's (1949) study is a notable exception. Sex differences in

AUTHORS' NOTE: Reprinted from "Differential Recruitment and Control: The Sex Structuring of Organizations" by Joan Acker and Donald R. Van Houten published in *Administrative Science Quarterly* Volume 19, number 2, by permission of *Administrative Science Quarterly*.

organizational behaviour, when they have been commented on at all, have been variously interpreted, but rarely related to sex segregation and differential sex power in organizations

We suggest, along with Caplow (1954: 230-47), that there is sex structuring in organizations, which consists of differentiation of female and male jobs, a hierarchical ordering of those jobs so that males are higher than females and are not expected to take orders from females. As a result males generally have more power in organizations than females; we call this the sex power differential. Furthermore, this sex structuring of organizations may be as important as social psychological factors in understanding sex differences in organizational behaviour and may provide alternative or additional explanations for some well known generalizations in the organizational literature.

The Male Bias in Organizational Research

Organizational theory and research has been heavily weighted toward the study of male society. Studies of top level managerial and professional workers usually focus on men, since men are usually in positions of power and leadership. In industrial sociology and organizational research which focuses on the lower participants of organizations, the samples studied are often entirely male (for instance, Tudor 1972; Goldthorpe et al. 1968); but even when women workers are included, the research has largely ignored or dismissed sex power differentials.[1]

Most organizational analysts attribute sex differences largely to differential patterns in socialization and adult roles outside the organization, such as women's family roles not shared by men (Furstenburg 1968). One cannot rule out the importance of such differences in trying to explain the sex structuring of organizations, but what is disturbing is the neglect of other processes that sociologists have commonly associated with problems of social organization: patterns of selective recruitment and social control mechanisms other than socialization. Specifically what has not been sufficiently examined are (1) differential recruitment of women into organizational roles demanding passivity and compliance, and (2) unique mechanisms employed in organizations to control women. We suggest that these factors are at least as important in explaining sex differences as socialization, role, or biological differences. The necessary data are not available to prove this assertion, but we are going to examine the possible interaction of sex and organizational factors in two well-known studies in the field for questionable or incomplete interpretations resulting from failure to consider adequately the sex dimensions of organizational processes.

The studies to be analyzed are one of the earliest, (1) the Hawthorne studies, and a more recent example, (2) Crozier's study of two French bureaucracies. These particular studies were chosen because they are classics that have had considerable impact upon the field of complex organizations.

The Hawthorne Studies

Textbooks still mention the Hawthorne studies and people still talk about the "Hawthorne effect," which refers to the positive reaction of research subjects resulting from their being selected out and treated as special and interesting in the course of a research project. Another finding of the Hawthorne studies, and one which led to many other studies of organizations, was that workers responded to friendly supervision and increased autonomy in the work situation with the development of group solidarity. In one small group in the factory, output increased. In another group, output was restricted. Commentators on the original research have not noted that the group with increased output was all female, and the group with restricted output was all male. Landsberger (1958), in his lengthy defense of the Hawthorne studies, did point out that many of the workers were unmarried women of immigrant background, but did not explore the implications of this fact. In order to explore the implications of that observation, we examined the original reports of the research (Roethlisberger and Dickson 1939; Whitehead 1938) to determine how the experimental treatment differed with the female group and the male group, and whether there was some relationship between the differential treatment and the effects of the sex power differential. The following discussion deals with only two of the studies, the First Relay Assembly Test Room and the Bank Wiring Room—the studies most extensively referred to and criticized in the literature.

The women in the Relay Assembly Test Room (five assemblers and one layout operator) were individually subjected to a great deal of contact with male supervisors and administrators (Whitehead 1938: 109, 112-14), and there may have been some implicit pressure in these individual contacts. For example, the women subjects were individually and informally selected for the research.[2] They were then interviewed (Whitehead 1938: 26, 103-4; Roethlisberger and Dickson 1939: 32) by the plant superintendent to make sure that they really wanted to participate. Four of them were either 19 or

20; the two others were slightly older. All except one were living at home with their parents in first-generation Polish, Italian, Norwegian, and Czechoslovakian families (Roethlisberger and Dickson 1939: 23; Whitehead 1938: 16-17). These young, unmarried women from traditional families were brought in by the bosses and asked if they wanted to participate; it is not surprising that they all agreed.[3]

The point is not simply that these female workers probably had been socialized to obey males in positions of authority, but that the sex power hierarchy in the home and in the factory were congruent; and when there is such a congruence, sex power differentials outside the organization act as a power multiplier, enhancing the authority of male superiors in the work place. When there are no alternative experiences with different distributions of male and female influence and power, there is little experiential basis for questioning the legitimacy of the existing status hierarchy. Thus, at a social psychological level, we would expect greater acceptance of a given system of authority relationships if there is consistency in these relationships across the main institutional areas in which men and women interact.

There may also have been a power multiplier effect in the economically disadvantaged position of the women. We suggest that an economically dependent position in one domain reinforces powerlessness in other areas of life. At least four of these young women lived at home and gave their wages to their parents, who then gave them a small allowance (Roethlisberger and Dickson 1939: 44). Economically their position was similar to that of children; but, at the same time, their families probably desperately needed their added income. The family situation, then, did not provide a secure economic base from which they could challenge the authority of the male supervisors upon whom they were dependent for their jobs. Furthermore, the work place probably did not provide a base from which they could question parental-paternal authority; their wages were probably too low for them to establish independent lives, even if culturally and psychologically this presented itself as a possibility.

In spite of the effects of socialization and the power multiplier, some of the women in the Relay Assembly Test Room were not compliant or cooperative. In response to this, both researchers and management made strenuous efforts at control. Some elements of direct coercion are implied in the published reports of the research (Whitehead 1938: 111-12). Carey (1967) documents this well. For example, the operatives were told to "work like you feel," "don't make a race out of it" (Whitehead 1938: 26); "The group were assured that the test was not being set up to determine the maximum output . . ." (Roethlisberger and Dickson 1939: 33). However, as soon as the experimental period began, if they did not work hard, or if they slowed down, they were reprimanded and told to work faster. Two of the women objected, and kept saying, "We thought you wanted us to work as we feel" (Roethlisberger and Dickson 1939: 53). In addition, they talked and laughed a lot on the job. They were frequently admonished about this (Whitehead 1938: 116; Roethlisberger and Dickson 1939: 53-55), and the chief offender "was told of her offenses" (Roethlisberger and Dickson 1939: 55) by the test room authorities and later by the superintendent.

These two women also objected to being examined by a doctor every six weeks (Whitehead 1938: 109, 114). The experimenters wanted to control for the effects of physiological changes on productivity, one of which was the periodic effect of menstruation. Their objections were, of course, very disruptive to the experiment, since data collection required the physical examination. This was another reason that the two women who objected were viewed as destructive to the experiment and ringleaders of recalcitrant behaviour. After about eight months the two troublemakers were removed from the experiment and replaced by two other women (Whitehead 1938: 116-19).

The events following the replacement of the uncooperative women seem to indicate manipulation by the researchers of the leadership structure of the group through the granting of special economic rewards. One of the women replacements was providing for her whole family; her sister had died, her father was temporarily unemployed, and she was desperate for work. Soon after she entered the test room, her mother also died (Roethlisberger and Dickson 1939: 62, 171-72; Whitehead 1938: 120-22), and she was given a special loan by management because of her financial difficulties. She was also an ambitious woman who saw in the assignment to the Test Room an opportunity for advancement (Whitehead 1938: 120, 123, 158). She worked very diligently and was furious with the other women if they did not do so also. At the same time that the two new operators were brought into the experiment, "the daily hours of work were shortened by half an hour but it was decided to *pay the operators the day rate for the half hour of working time lost*" (Carey 1967: 309, his emphasis; Whitehead 1938: 121). A little later, further reductions in work time were made, and again the women were paid for the time not worked. The woman who had been given the loan became a leader of the group, and group productivity increased. The interpretation by the researchers was that a very strong leader emerged from the group process. Rather, what seems to have happened is that management inadvertently found a strong leader, put her into the test room, and reinforced her leadership potential with special rewards not only to her, but to the entire group.

There are also hints in the published reports of paternalistic attitudes and manipulation. The paternalistic attitudes of researchers and managers is best documented by the repeated use of the term "girls" throughout the texts of both Roethlisberger and Dickson (1939) and Whitehead (1938) and throughout the excerpts from the research logs published in both books. Examples of paternalistic manipulation are also frequent. Participation by the workers in decisions about the research was encouraged, while the real power was always retained by the male researchers and supervisors. Although the women were asked for suggestions and comments throughout the experiment (Landsberger 1958: 9), some comments were incorporated in the research procedures, but some of the more strenuous objections, such as the opposition to the physical examination, were not. Even on relatively minor issues, the unanimous opinion of the subjects was not followed if the researchers did not agree. Also, in a situation of great power differentials, efforts by those with power to maintain a friendly atmosphere or to get comments or suggestions can be seductively co-opting. For example, the male observer stationed in the room had as one of his tasks to "create and maintain a friendly atmosphere in the test room" (Roethlisberger and Dickson 1939: 22). To reduce objections to the physical examination, the women were treated to a party with ice cream and cake after each physical (Whitehead 1938: 109, 114). These parties were attended by the male doctors, researchers, and supervisors. Finally, on repeated occasions during the study, the "girls" were called into the superintendent's office to discuss changes in the study (for instance, Whitehead 1938: 112). It is possible that such special and unusual contacts with high status and authoritative figures may not only have been coercive, but may also have had a particular reward value.

In summary, it appears that the cumulative effect of coercion, paternalistic treatment, and special rewards resulted in a rise in productivity.

In contrast to the female group, the members of the male group in the Bank Wiring Room (Roethlisberger and Dickson 1939: chap. 17), the group which restricted its production, were not selected and interviewed individually; only the group as a whole was under pressure to participate in the research (Roethlisberger and Dickson 1939: 397, 398). That is, a preexisting work group was designated as a research group and "nothing was to be said or done in selecting the group to be studied, in explaining the study to them, or in removing them from the department which might alter their status in any way" (Roethlisberger and Dickson 1939: 388). In addition, methods of observation which might make the workers apprehensive were avoided and "the observer was stationed with the group in the role of a disinterested spectator" (Roethlisberger and Dickson 1939: 388). Types of worker activity which were viewed as disruptive to the experiment in the Relay Assembly Test Room were seen as only data to be observed in the Bank Wiring Room. No one was replaced during the course of the research, and no one was reprimanded even though there was slowing down, laughing, and talking.

Group norms relating to productivity did develop in both work groups, but they developed in relationship to the external environment of each group and the external demands in regard to increasing production were different for the two groups.[4] Furthermore, the immediate external environment was controlled by males in both experiments. But male control constitutes a different kind of external environment for a female group than for a male group because the effect of the sex-based hierarchy of the larger society is added to the structuring of control in the organization. For the women's group, the relationship was between powerful males and weak females; that is, the females, being weak, had to please the supervisors if they wished to stay in the test room, so they adopted the norm of increased production. Their attempts at developing some self-protection resulted in reprimands and eventually exclusion; compliance led to special rewards.

Since the research treatment was very different for the males and for the females, there still remains the question of whether the group of males would have responded similarly to the same combination of rewards and punishments. Of course, we do not know. However, having refined their hypotheses and their methodology, the investigators chose a group of males as subjects for further investigation. It is obvious that the researchers were not aware of the possible effects of the sex of their subjects on the outcome of the Relay Assembly Test Room experiment. They also seem to have taken no notice of the possible effects of variation in research procedures and the interaction of those variations with the sex of the subjects.

It is clear from our reexamination of the Hawthorne Studies, that the experimenters' treatment of the men in the Bank Wiring Room was very different from their treatment of the women in the Relay Assembly Test Room. The women were carefully recruited and closely supervised, and in numerous subtle ways were told that their productivity should rise. This is an amplification of Carey's analysis, which has already pointed to the coercive elements in the research procedures in the Relay Assembly Test

Room. The men, on the other hand were recruited as a group and were allowed considerable autonomy in developing their own production norms. We argue that these differences in experimental treatment account to a considerable extent for the increase in productivity of the women's group and the restricted productivity of the men's group. Furthermore, we contend that the differences in treatment are at least partially attributable to the sex differences of the two groups. This reexamination of the Hawthorne researches suggests organizational processes related to sex based power differentials, which may be found in other organizational settings.

Crozier's Studies

In 1964, Michel Crozier reported on his studies in the preceding decade of two French bureaucracies, which employed a large number of women: the Clerical Agency employed 4,500 persons, most of them women[5]; and the Industrial Monopoly had women in 2/3 of its production jobs. At only one point (which we will identify later) does Crozier comment at all extensively about these facts of organizational life, and there he essentially argues that those facts are relatively insignificant. His neglect of the sex of employees is important in itself, but it gains in importance when one notes that there is considerable occupational segregation by sex within the organizations. We will discuss that occupational recruitment by sex, but also draw attention to portions of Crozier's data that refer to differential socialization histories as well as differential control patterns of women.

In the Clerical Agency located in Paris, although the majority of nonsupervisory employees were women,[6] most of the supervisors were men, most of the supervisors' bosses were men, and most of the union representatives were men. Women held jobs as strawbosses but these were not supervisor's jobs. Of the few men in nonsupervisory positions, all worked in auxiliary services, mail rooms, printing shops and maintenance work. Quotations suggest that this occupational and status segregation by sex was important and contributed to antagonism; for example, one woman commented: "Supervisors have no skill in human relations. They do not know how to deal with women" (Crozier 1964: 42). Another woman complained about union representation: "But we are defended by men who do not understand the situation of women workers very well and are not able to talk the language of the average girl" (Crozier 1964: 42). Crozier largely ignored the possible female-male basis of conflict and argued that the antagonisms were a function of a bureaucratic system that began with centralization and impersonality and developed a vicious circle which was dysfunctional for organizational effectiveness. He did not point out that sex differences may exacerbate the effects of the bureaucratic system and account for a substantial portion of the antagonisms.

The backgrounds of many of these women resembled those of the women in the Hawthorne studies. Most of them were "daughters of farmers, rural shopkeepers and craftsmen" (Crozier 1964: 16). Crozier contrasted these women with rural backgrounds with the few with more urban backgrounds: "Parisian girls with the required schooling now very rarely accept the salaries and terms of employment of the lower grades of the civil service. Only girls who come from under-developed areas with few employment opportunities will accept them" (Crozier 1964: 16-17). It isn't clear what Crozier means by the "terms of employment," though they might include the traditionally submissive role of women. Some support can be found for that in Crozier's discussion of the male supervisors who have been with the Agency for some time and who came from the same rural backgrounds as the women: "Twenty and thirty years ago, the southwest was sending its boys to Civil Service jobs in Paris. Now when its girls seem independent and are looking for employment, they in turn are going; *but the old network of relationships has not, in fact, changed very much*" (Crozier 1964: 17, emphasis added). Crozier ends a section with that sentence and it isn't at all clear what he is referring to by the "old network of relationships." We suggest that he may be referring to traditional authority relationships between men and women that are more characteristic of rural families. The Clerical Agency, then, exhibits a high degree of occupational and status segregation by sex, which appears overladen with traditional power relations between the sexes.

Besides recruitment and socialization differences by sex, there was some evidence of coercive control patterns. Crozier described a harsh discipline imposed by managers of the agency:

> It is sufficient to hold in check a woman employee whose feelings are easily manipulated by threats of public humiliation, such as official reprimands and insertions of criticism in the personal files. No kind of absenteeism is tolerated; mistakes are traced to the girls administratively responsible for them, and written excuses are demanded from each of them. (1964: 20)

There were some male nonsupervisory personnel and these control patterns may have been used on them as well, but there was no mention of that, and Crozier referred specifically to women employees. Some of the controls were reminiscent of the treatment of children. For example, one woman commented about one of the managers: "I never saw him and I like it better that way, since one sees him only to get a scolding" (Crozier 1964: 44). Whether or not the control tactics seem more appropriate to children or adults, they are still clearly harsh and the question remains whether male employees would have long endured them. Again, the impression is of a male group constituting the external, governing group for a female one and the controls being sex-based.

The bureaucratic system Crozier described certainly contributed to the antagonism and frustration characteristic of the Clerical Agency, but much of the conflict pattern may have been based on the oppression of women. The sex differences would at least seem to have amplified the effects of the bureaucratic system, or vice versa. And both patterns may have been a function of the French culture. Crozier suggests that the bureaucratic pattern is a reflection of that culture. We suggest that the sex power revealed in the organization may also be a part of the French culture, although certainly not restricted to it.

In the study of the Industrial Monopoly, Crozier argued that uncertainty in organizations cannot be eliminated, yet the achievement of organizational goals requires some degree of certainty; consequently, those individuals and groups who control important uncertainties have a basis for power in the organization. Principally because the Industrial Monopoly faced no competition from other organizations, the major uncertainty for it was at the production level. But production was highly routinized, and had few uncertainties. The principal uncertainty was around machine breakdown, and that uncertainty was the basis of considerable power for the men who maintained the machines. We suggest, however, that sex differences amplified their organizationally derived power.

The major disruption of the production work was machine stoppage. Production workers were "held personally responsible for all stoppages of less than one hour and a half and must compensate for the loss of production; if the stoppage is longer, they will be displaced or may be sent around to do menial jobs if there is no possibility of bumping less senior workers" (Crozier 1964: 109). Only maintenance personnel were allowed to cope with the machine stoppage. The maintenance personnel were all men and the production workers were almost all women. Crozier (1964: 97) stated:

> Production workers, mostly women, behave as if they were dependent on the maintenance men and resentful of it. The sex difference, of course, is probably an important element in shaping the situation. But this influence

> should not be exaggerated. No comments were ever made about it, and there is a complete lack of differentiation between men servants and women product receivers.

This is the only point at which Crozier acknowledged that sex differences shape the work situation, but he was quick to deemphasize that factor. The fact that no comments were made about the sex differences is not altogether surprising. His second justification may be more convincing. If sex differences were operative in the general work situation, one would expect differences in resentments of women and men in the more auxiliary production roles, the men servants and the women product receivers. But, there were no differences in expressed complaints between men and women in these auxiliary roles, and both men and women in these roles made more complaints than the women machine operators. The problem is to explain the differences in open resentment in two groups of women. The women product receivers may have been a deviant group, who selected themselves out of work positions which had for them, excessive constraints against complaints. The product receiver job acted as a sort of safety valve for those women who could not tolerate the degree of dependence demanded in the machine operator's work. If a machine operator found her work intolerable, she could transfer to the product receiver job and many did, even though the pay was somewhat less. Women who remained as machine operators might be expected to be more compliant and submissive. Thus there seem to have been organizational mechanisms for accommodating contradictions between the demands of work positions and the personality orientations of particular workers.

The monopoly the maintenance men had over machine repairs was defended up the organizational hierarchy. For example, a new foreman did not accept a maintenance man's judgment that a particular machine breakdown was serious. He attempted to fix the machine himself, and found that the breakdown was not serious and was due to poor maintenance. Furious, he complained to three different superordinates, including the director of the organization, and received no satisfaction other than some sympathetic murmurs (Crozier 1964: 127). That case testifies to the power of the maintenance men within that organization, but it is not altogether clear whether that power is solely based on the organizational uncertainties that they controlled, or partly on the fact that women were in the dependent role and controlled by men.

In his discussion of power and uncertainty, Crozier (1964: 156) noted: "Each group fights to preserve and enlarge the area upon which it has some discretion." One might add that they also struggle to manage the impressions others have of how large that area is; that is, groups struggle to control the objective bases of their power, but also others' perception of that area of uncertainty and therefore others' perception of their power. The maintenance men's ability to manage others' perception of their power may have been enhanced by the presence of women rather than men as machine operators. As long as women are mechanically less competent than men, or at least most persons believe they are less competent, the maintenance men have fewer problems managing others' perception of their power. Crozier (1964: 77) himself said that women are significantly more hostile to mechanization. In addition, quotations from the maintenance men showed that they believed women were not mechanically inclined or competent. "Workers do not care about technical problems. . . . Workers do not understand anything beyond the narrow requirements of their own job" (Crozier 1964: 97). The accuracy of these judgments is really irrelevant, for they need only to be believed to have important consequences. As long as the machine operators were felt to be too incompetent to understand let alone to repair machine breakdowns, maintenance men could maintain their position of power. Any complaints the women might have raised about maintenance men's judgment and performance would be discredited by male superiors. Male machine operators might challenge the seriousness of machine breakdowns, as the new foreman did, making the foreman's complaints credible. The degree of dependence may not, then, be due just to the character of the technology.

The dependency also tended to be personal. One maintenance man was responsible for the machines of three to six women machine operators; that is, women machine operators had continually to deal with the same maintenance man, who came to talk of "their machine operators." Also, maintenance men were allowed to intervene regularly in the work of "their machine operators," apparently because they thought their operators "rather careless" (Crozier 1964: 97). And although they realized that the machine operators did not usually take their advice, about half of them continued to give their advice quite often (Crozier 1964: 97). The picture one gets is of each woman machine operator being subjected to fairly close control by a single maintenance man.

We would agree with Crozier that machine breakdown was a critical uncertainty for the Industrial Monopoly, but the degree and character of dependence experienced by the machine operators seem to have been shaped significantly by sex differences. If the machine operators had been men, the dependency might have remained but might have been weakened considerably. Crozier is essentially correct, then, in stating that technology creates a dependency relation. However, the severity of the relation in this case was aggravated by the differential recruitment of women as machine operators. It may even be that the technology created a relationship of such dependency that only women could be recruited to such jobs and controlled in them.

The bureaucratic vicious circle, the influence of French culture, and the relations between objective organizational uncertainty and power remain as important variables in Crozier's analysis; but if our suggestions carry weight, Crozier's analysis is only a partial one. He neglected the impact of sex differences in socialization, occupational recruitment, and organizational control patterns.

Conclusion

Our reexamination of the Hawthorne studies and Crozier's work seems to support our contention that organizational structures and processes are influenced by sex. Specifically, sex differences in organizational participation are related to (1) differential recruitment of women into jobs requiring dependence and passivity, (2) selective recruitment of particularly compliant women into these jobs, and (3) control mechanisms used in organizations for women, which reinforce control mechanisms to which they are subjected in other areas of the society.

These suggestions lead to specific research questions. For example, from the differential recruitment of women into jobs requiring dependence, one may expect that technologies, as well as occupations, are sex segregated, highly routinized technologies employing disproportionately women, and less routinized technologies such as craft and continuous process ones, mostly men. A related question would be whether women are disproportionately recruited to highly routinized jobs where machines largely control the work, which might be a better explanation of the frequent assumption that women are more antagonistic to mechanization, than early socialization.

It is not possible to suggest all the dimensions on which control mechanisms might vary with sex. Control mechanisms for women may more often resemble those used with children, as indicated by both studies analyzed in this paper. Also in these studies, adult women were frequently referred to as girls. The use of this word shaped the construction of reality for both the men and the women, and allowed for control. Also, organizational rewards offered women may be often products or services stereotypically thought to be preferred by women, while rewards offered men are not so sex-linked. For example, women may be frequently rewarded with such things as flowers, trinkets, and so forth.[7] Women may be subjected to more personalized control arrangements than men. Men may usually face impersonal rules and regulation that are fairly universalistic for men occupying similar positions, while women may more often be required to adjust to rules that are particular to their relationship with a male supervisor.

Converse to sex-differentiated controls are possibilities of sex-differentiated power strategies. The power strategies which are available to participants in organizations are certainly shaped by the nature of the structure. But, it may also be true that individuals are differentially socialized to the appropriateness of different power strategies, and/or are differentially penalized for using different power strategies. Those differences may fall along sex lines. For example, women may be frequently proscribed from forming coalitions as a power strategy. The proscription may be communicated through primary socialization, or severe penalties may be imposed upon women if they try that strategy as organizational members. Similarly, women may be constrained more from complaining particularly about specific male coworkers or supervisors, and again this constraint may be internalized in early socialization or may be differentially penalized in organizations.

If women do experience different controls than men, those controls may be particularly effective if they are consonant with controls women experience outside of organizations as indicated in our analysis. For example, we expect that women who come from fairly traditional families with patriarchial arrangements would experience as employees the power multiplier and probably respond with greater conformity than women from less traditional families. If power distributions in organizations multiply larger patterns of power by sex, perhaps organizations with more sex segregated occupations are more hierarchical.[8] Also, in sex segregated occupations involving both men and women, one might expect that the sex power differential would be greater between male groups controlling female groups, than male groups controlling male groups, or female ones with female subordinate groups, or any power arrangements involving integrated groups.

We tentatively suggest, also, that organizations with occupational segregation by sex and embedded in traditional societal contexts may exhibit less intergroup conflict. March and Simon (1959: 121) suggest a number of factors that may contribute to intergroup conflict. These factors may be dampened in organizations where males control female occupational groups. One factor, the need for joint decision making, may be felt less with such arrangements because the stereotyping of sex roles in the larger society would tend to imprint clearly separated domains for decision making. Conflict between the maintenance men and the production workers is a case in point. Women production workers did not challenge the decisions of the maintenance men; if the production workers had been men, there might have been more conflict. Consonant sex power hierarchies would tend generally to clarify goals and perceptions of reality, two other factors March and Simon referred to as possible sources of intergroup conflict. However, these relationships could be expected only where occupational sex segregation and power differentials correspond to patterns in the larger society and which continue to be viewed as legitimate by both men and women. Occupational segregation by sex may increase intergroup conflict where women have begun to question such arrangements. The segregation by sex would facilitate the sharing of such questionings, and provide greater opportunities to organize within the group to combat the power arrangements.

It may be that sex power differentials have a more profound effect in some cases than the organizational variables. In any case, sex power differentials can at least be used together with organizational factors to develop a more thorough explanation of variation in organizational phenomena.

Notes

1. Mechanic (1962) in a very perceptive analysis of the sources of power of lower level participants in organizations, describes a number of mechanisms used for enhancing personal power. Some of these would seem to be used more often by women than men, although Mechanic does not point to this possible sex differentiation.

2. It is not clear exactly how the women were selected. They seem to have had some part in the selection. The accounts of Roethlisberger and Dickson (1939) and that of Whitehead (1938) differ on this point.

3. Carey (1967), in a critique of the Relay Assembly Test Room research, discussed in much greater detail many of the problems with the research, but did not take account of the sex hierarchy variable.

4. Economic conditions were also different for the female and male groups. The Relay Assembly Test Room studies began in 1927 before the Depression and continued into 1932; the Bank Wiring Room experiment took place during the bottom of the Depression, 1932. This undoubtedly was a factor in the differences in group behaviors. Landsberger (1958) gave a detailed discussion of this problem.

5. Crozier does not provide the exact proportion of men and women.

6. Again, Crozier does not provide the specific figures.

7. Elinor Langer gives some excellent examples of gifts received by women in the New York Telephone Company (1970: 16, 17).

8. Marrett (1972) examines the evidence for and against the hypothesis that female predominance in organizations encourages centralization. She concludes that the question cannot be resolved with the data presently available.

2

Room for Women: A Case Study in the Sociology of Organizations[1]

PETA [TANCRED-]SHERIFF
E. JANE CAMPBELL

In assessing the contribution by women to the sociology of organizations,[2] one is immediately struck by the pervasive "maleness" of this field. The male fact exists in a double sense: Men have produced a body of organizational theory and research in which men are assumed to be the primary objects of study. Dorothy Smith's (1975: 366) description of the academic discipline of sociology applies with particular force to the sociology of organizations that has been developed by male academics and consultants from the perspective and positions in male-dominated authority structures, focusing on the organizational networks of control and authority that underlie those positions (Acker and Van Houten 1974; Crozier 1964). Thisrelationship between men as subjects and men as objects in the context of organizational sociology has been reflected in the dominant orientation

AUTHORS' NOTE: This chapter, in a slightly longer version, was originally published in French in *Sociologie et Sociétés* (1981) under the names of Peta Sheriff and E. Jane Campbell.

toward management concerns and interests that characterizes much of the work in this field.

During the past 50 years, the development of a distinctive sociology of organizations has been heavily influenced by the historical growth in scale and complexity of industrial organizations and the managerial preoccupation with productivity and control. This fact accounts in part for the tendency of organizational sociology to be characterized by a largely ahistoric, monocausal, and systematic view of organizational structure and processes. In fact, the view of the organization as a system—whether "closed" or "open" is of little importance—is so pervasive not only within sociology but also as a lay image of organizations that we tend to forget that such an essentially employer viewpoint serves to minimize the role of workers, including women, and encourages the formulation of managerial questions with preferably monocausal explanations for an easy solution. A more historical view of organizations, focusing on changes in the labor process over time, would invert the organizational image, highlighting workers' concerns rather than those of management.

Women and the Sociology of Organizations

In light of this general stance within organizational sociology, it is not surprising that, at first glance, women's contribution to the area appears to be more remarkable by its absence than its presence. Nevertheless, it is worth devoting some time to the *character* of women's contribution,[3] which is congruent with our argument concerning the overall development of the field.

The Innovators

It has been rare for women to be responsible for major departures in organizational sociology, but a few women are remarkable for putting their imprint on the direction of the field. Of these, the earliest is Mary Parker Follett, who wrote and lectured in the early 1900s and whose writings bridge the transition from the Scientific Management School to the Human Relations School. While hardly a household name among organizational researchers, her emphasis upon "a recognition of the motivating desires of the individual and of the group" (Metcalfe and Urwick 1941: 9) distances her from the preoccupations of the Scientific Management School, although she continues to share the importance according to "principles" of management, which, in her case, consist of a frequent repetition of the principles of coordination (Follet 1937: 159-69). Kanter cites her as "among the influential figures in generating this more human approach to management and one of the only important female organization theorists" (Kanter 1975a: 67-68). Despite an active lecture circuit in Britain and North America and a very respectable publication record (Metcalfe and Urwick 1941: 315-17), however, her influence does not appear to parallel the way in which she presaged the transition from one major school of organizational thought to the next, and the Roethlisberger and Dickson (1939) study, which finally succeeded in reorienting the field, makes no reference to her work. It is only in retrospect that one appreciated her pioneering role.

More appreciated and much more influential was the work of Joan Woodward, who, starting in the early 1950s (Woodward 1958, 1965, 1970), was the first to formulate the so-called technological approach to organizations. With meager resources and a small research team, she undertook an exhaustive study of 100 firms in the South East Essex area of Britain, and this led to the delineation of the characteristic structure of industrial firms engaged in batch, mass, and process production. Looking at such factors as the number of levels in the hierarchy, the ratio of administrative to nonadministrative personnel, the span of control, and so forth, Woodward formulated the principle of *optimum coherence* between the type of technology and the type of management structure for maximum efficiency to be achieved. It remained for her successors, particularly Charles Perrow, however, to broaden the definition of technology to facilitate the inclusion of nonindustrial structures as well and thus derive the full significance from the tenets of the technological school.[4]

Finally, the most recent period has witnessed not the development of a new paradigm but a departure, led by Rosabeth Moss Kanter, toward the study of women in organizations (Kanter 1975a, 1975b, 1975c, 1976, 1977a, 1979; Kanter and Zurcher 1973). In a relatively scant literature, Kanter's contribution is all the more remarkable for its emphasis on the "masculine ethic" of rationality and reason in the early image of managers, the relegation of women in the organizational setting to the "office housework" (Kanter 1975b: 49), and the effects of the "skewed" representation of men and women at higher organizational levels, which produces a very different interaction context for women than for men (1977a: 206-42). A few others have participated in this examination of women in organizational settings (Fennel et al. 1978; Marrett 1972; Milward and Swanson 1978; Wolff 1977), but the approach remains at the stage of a sociology *of* women rather than a sociology *for* women (Smith 1975: 367), and it is of course the latter rather than the former perspective that would be required for a major reorientation of the field.

It is of interest to note that these three women, who have marked the field of organizational sociology more dramatically than any of their female colleagues, are also women who have had strong links with management. Follett held no academic position but appears to have acted among other guises as a freelance management consultant in close contact with managers for whom she had an enormous admiration (Metcalfe and Urwick 1941: 17-18). Woodward (1970: vi) was a strong advocate of close cooperation between researchers and management; in her research, findings were "accepted and absorbed into the thought processes of those concerned with organizational problems," enabling "the research workers to reach a deeper understanding of the situation." Following a period at a technical college, she joined the management section of the college of engineering of the University of London, where she remained until her early death. Of the three, Kanter has perhaps gone furthest in her links with industrial management. She sees her work as extremely practical, from which "leaders, policy-makers or managers can take away a number of useful insights," and she has founded an organizational consulting firm, Goodmeasure Inc., "to . . . straddle the worlds of academia and action" (Kanter and Stein 1979: xiv).

In effect, all three women share the same links with management that have propelled the general development of the field. Through participation in the dominant model of the dissemination of ideas on organizations and through the mutual respect that is evident between management and researchers, their ideas have been welcomed and influential. Academically, however, they have stopped short of deriving the fullest implications from their work, providing leads, directions, or guidelines but surpassed in their own mode of thought by succeeding researchers. This is clear in the cases of Follett and Woodward, and Kanter's work, despite a voluminous production, may be used more fully by a successor concerned with a critical reorientation of the field based on the study of women.

The Service Workers

The nature of the contribution made by the majority of female writers on organizations is perhaps best characterized as consisting of work that "rounds out" the theories, themes, and theses emerging from the efforts of male contributors to the field. This is not to suggest that the work of most male authors is not also of the same type, for the development of research and theory in academic disciplines proceeds in fairly mundane fashion on an incremental basis. Rather, this depiction of the contribution made by women points out the implicit hierarchy of work within the sociology of organizations in that most widely recognized contributors to theory and research have been predominantly male, while the overwhelming proportion of female students of organizations have fulfilled the "drone" functions of assessing and testing the previously developed insights.

The types of contribution made by female authors to this field fall basically into two categories: first, literature reviews that synthesize and extend work done by others in a specific area and, second, empirical tests of derived hypotheses. Terreberry's (1968) outline of the ideal-types of environment proposed by Emery and Trist falls into the first category, suggested above. Although her extension of their model offers a seminal direction for further development of the area of interorganizational relations, it appears to have suffered from relative neglect. Working in the same area, Cora Marrett (1971) has proposed, on the basis of a review of the relevant literature, four dimensions characterizing the cooperative relations among organizations to yield two alternative models of interorganizational relations. Similarly, Karen Cook (1977: 63) synthesized this literature to "present an extension to the exchange model for the analysis of interorganizational relations, incorporating into the model recent developments in exchange theory." On this basis, Cook develops a number of propositions for further research. On a larger scale, Renate Mayntz has a very useful, if now somewhat dated, summary of most of the significant literature in the field of the sociology of organizations in a 1964 issue of *Current Sociology*. In a more recent issue of the same periodical, one of the current authors ([Tancred-]Sheriff 1976) has brought together the somewhat scattered writings on public bureaucracies in a wide-ranging review of this field. Both Mayntz and [Tancred-]Sheriff provide comprehensive annotated bibliographies that constitute distinctive contributions. Finally, Brenda Danet has coauthored a valuable survey of theory and research on relations between bureaucracies and clients, and her jointly edited book dealing with this area contains extensive overviews of the various topics represented by the collected articles (Katz and Danet 1973a, 1973b).

In the second category, women writers on organizations have contributed to empirical work in a number of areas. Research on the nature of client-organization relations has been carried out in the Israeli context by Danet and by Harriet Hartman. Focusing on the tension between the bureaucratic norms of universalism and particularism, this research has explored some of the implications for treatment of clients as well as the variables that influence bureaucratic decisions. Some of this research used the innovative approach of analyzing the content of letters to officials, relating this to the writers' backgrounds, while other studies have been based on a nationally drawn sample of more than 1,800 adults to survey attitudes and reported behavior in their contacts with Israeli government bureaucracy (Danet 1971, 1973; Danet and Hartman 1972a, 1972b; Katz and Danet 1966). Several other female authors have also taken the issue of the conflict between particularism and universalism derived from Weber's ideal-type as a starting point to examine empirically the forces influencing discretionary treatment of clients by bureaucratic officials (Gordon 1975; Kroeger 1975; Shuval 1962).

Female students of organizations have *not* contributed to any great extent to the burgeoning research on the causal relations among the internal structural variables of organizations. By and large, the participation of women in this area has been in collaboration with male researchers. Diana Pheysey has been involved with the Aston group in their research on the influence of technology on structure and the effects of structure on groups within the organization (Hickson et al. 1969; Payne and Pheysey 1971; Pheysey et al. 1971). Marrett has collaborated with Hage and Aiken in one of the series of studies based on their research in 16 health and welfare organizations (Hage et al. 1971). Janice Beyer appears as the major author in a joint effort replicating Blau and Schoenherr's research on the relationship between the variables of organizational size and complexity (Beyer and Trice 1979). Cecilia McHugh Falbe has contributed to Peter Blau's research on the relation between plant technology and several dimensions of internal structure in a sample of manufacturing firms (Blau et al. 1976). Dominique Schnapper has collaborated with Alain Darbel in studying the characteristics of French administration (Darbel and Schnapper 1969, 1972, 1974). Other studies in this area in which women have participated have examined variation in the dimension of technology and the effects of size and structural complexity on innovation (Blau and McKinley 1979; Overton et al. 1977).

The dominant methodology used by women in the sociology of organizations has been the exploration of organizational processes through the use of case studies based on one or a combination of data collection methods such as observation, interviews, and analysis of written documents and records. Some of these have been undertaken on a relatively large scale, such as Eckstein's (1976) study of co-optive processes in a squatter settlement, a center city slum, and a subsidized housing development in Mexico; Rianne Mahon's (1977) analysis of the unequal structure of representation within the Canadian state structure; Nancy DiTomaso's (1978a) examination of the development of the U.S. Department of Labor; Nicole Biggart's (1977) research on organizational change in the U.S. Postal Service; and Antoinette Catrice-Lorey's (1966) work on the French system of social security administration. Other case studies look at single organizational units of smaller dimensions, for instance, schools, colleges, and universities (Gerôme 1969; Kanter 1972; Rader 1979), hospitals (Bucher 1970; Goss 1963; Query 1973), churches, and other organizations (Brown 1954; Brown and Shepherd 1956; Spencer and Dale 1979).

In reviewing the kinds of activities undertaken by female writers, it would seem appropriate to attribute to women students of organizations a "housekeeping" role in relation to this field. They "tidy up" work done by others, usually male researchers and theorists, by bringing together the literature on specific topics and evaluating its significance; they assemble and rearrange the pieces to develop additional hypotheses for other researchers to test; they carry out the time-consuming and relatively menial tasks of piling up the building blocks of knowledge through individual case studies that test derived hypotheses. These functions are congruent with the role women are traditionally expected to perform in the household setting. This should not be surprising because it has been noted elsewhere that the work carried out by women in the labor force in general parallels their typical work in the home. The supportive and integrative aspects of women's domestic role are extended into other spheres of their social and economic lives (Armstrong and Armstrong [1978] 1984: 46-50). The fact that the predominant setting for much of the research undertaken by female authors consists of service organizations reinforces the accepted image of the proper concerns of women as being the nurturing and serving functions. This extension of the "mothering" role also can be seen in the kinds of work context and occupations in which women are concentrated such as teaching, nursing, clerical, and service jobs. As a result, the focus of women writers on organizations of this type fits predictably with the structural and ideological position of women in general.

The Oppressed

A dominant theme that emerges from much of the work of female authors is the treatment of power and its distribution among subgroups within the organization and its environment, whether this consists of other organizations or of clients. One might speculate that there is a parallel between the position of women as a dominated group and their apparent sensitivity to issues revolving around the unequal distribution of power and authority in the organizational context. This can be seen, for instance, in the willingness of female researchers to search for explanations of structural and relational outcomes in terms of power processes. Beyer and Trice (1979), for example, reject the monocausality of accounts relating organizational complexity to independent variables such as size or technology. Instead, they argue for a perspective based on the decisions and actions taken by those in authority as explanatory factors determining the ways in which size or technology may be related to various aspects of complexity. Other writers have imported analogies from political science to treat organizations as political systems within which power relations are central to an understanding of organizational structure and processes (Biggart 1977; Weinstein 1977). In a recent book, Patricia Marchack (1979) looks at the much larger issue of power in multinational corporations and their impact on society. In other works of such authors as Rianne Mahon (1977, 1979) and Nancy DiTomaso (1978a, 1978b, 1980), the explicit focus is on the internal structure of the state as a condensation of power relations among class forces. In this respect, state structure and the relations among the subunits represent the outcomes of class conflict, which is institutionalized in a hierarchy of authority that mirrors class relations of domination and subordination.[5]

Women writing in the more traditional areas of the sociology of organizations have also concerned themselves with the implications of the unequal distribution of power. Some of this research has taken the issue of internal control structures and patterns of influence among groups within the organization as its main focus (Beyer and Lodahl 1976; Bidwell and Vreeland 1964). Much of the work on the situation of professionals within bureaucracy deals explicitly with themes regarding the power of professional groups in relation to other occupational groups within the organization or with the impact of bureaucratic structures on professional autonomy and authority (Bidwell and Vreeland 1964; Blau 1979; Brown 1954; Bucher 1970; Bucher and Stelling 1969; Coser 1958; Daniels 1969; Davies 1972; Engel 1969; Goss 1963; Noble and Pym 1970). Analysis of interorganizational relations almost inevitably requires that some attention be paid to patterns of domination and influence among organizations (Cook 1977; O'Sullivan 1977; Provan et al. 1980).

A large proportion of research by females working in the sociology of organizations has been concerned with the relations between organizations and their clients, as has been mentioned in the preceding section.

Coming out of studies of social service and health organizations, this has been translated into an emphasis on the relative powerlessness of clients vis-à-vis bureaucracies. Katz and Danet treat this relationship of organizations and clients as a societal issue stemming from the nature of bureaucracy itself. Bureaucracy, they argue, is a social problem with certain dilemmas inherent in its structure and the norms under which it functions (Katz and Danet 1973a). Much of this research has examined the ways in which clients can attempt to manipulate or influence bureaucratic decisions to their benefit.

"Persuasive appeals," petitions, "proteksia," aggressiveness, and "bureaucratic competence" are strategies and characteristics by which clients can obtain particularistic treatment from officials and thus partly redress the balance of power in their favor (Danet 1971, 1973; Danet and Hartman 1972a, 1972b; Gordon 1975; Katz and Danet 1966; Kroeger 1975). Other female writers have examined the internal processes through which organizations establish or maintain control over client groups. Co-optation and integration of powerless groups (Eckstein 1976), shaping patient social systems (Galinsky and Galinsky 1967), and control of resources (Rader 1979) are some of the ways in which the subordination of certain client populations is reinforced. Catrice-Lorey's research on the French social security system points up a paradox of relations between clients and bureaucratic organizations. Despite the fact that the client population was able to control the administration of the system through elected representatives, the development of a bureaucratized structure resulted in alienation of the beneficiaries of the service and the feeling that they were controlled by an anonymous authority (Catrice-Lorey 1966).

The analysis of power relations by women writers takes the structure of power as a given. Thus, instead of concentrating on power holders and wielders, women are led to focus on powerless groups. This orientation toward the situation of the oppressed tends to produce an emphasis on examining the qualitative ways in which those without power experience and deal with their oppression. The vantage point from which women have explored questions of power is congruent with their own situation as a subordinate social group. Deprived of significant opportunities to exert direct control over the condition of their material and social existence, women, in common with other oppressed groups, rely on indirect forms of power to attain their ends. Familiarity with the necessity to resort to strategies of manipulation has perhaps made female students of organizations more aware of the subtle kinds of manoeuvres that may be employed by relatively powerless groups. It is therefore not improbable that this implicit understanding of the "view from the bottom" has conditioned the approach taken by women to analyses of power processes within the organizational context.

The Optimists

As if propelled by the mute recognition that classical models of bureaucracy are "masculine" models, women researchers have explored the nature of alternative modes of organization, making this one of the main areas for their original contribution to the organizational field. Women's contributions have included a theoretical refinement of Weber's model of bureaucracy (Constas 1958; Satow 1975) in which the alternative professional type of organization is linked to Weber's fourth type of value-rational authority. The main thrust of the discussion, however, has centered on the type of organization in which professionals predominate. Bucher and Stelling (1972) must be credited with having formulated the main characteristics of such an organization, which they delineate as (a) continuing role creation and negotiation, (b) spontaneous internal differentiation, (c) competition and conflict for resources, (d) integration through a political process, and (e) constant shifts in the locus of power. Running through the discussion is a preoccupation with conflict both between bureaucratic and professional norms and also between different groups of professionals (Brown 1954; Bucher 1970; Daniels 1969; Goss 1963). There is a strong emphasis on the underlying theme of the power of professionals, as indicated above. Finally, there is a rather curious concern with the organizational effects on professionals (e.g., Engel 1969) and with the effect of professionals on the organization (Davies 1972; Goss 1963), based on the assumption that all organizations operate mechanistically, divorced from participating groups. A more contemporary formulation does not talk of professional organizations but literally of "alternative" organizations, focusing on myriad collectivist organizations that arose in the 1960s and that survive in a number of domains. Joyce Rothschild-Whitt (1976, 1979) has gone furthest both in contrasting the characteristics of such alternative organizations with the classical model and in delineating those conditions that facilitate the emergence of collectivist organizations. Because the defining characteristic of such organizations is the devolution of power, it is not surprising that this theme should recur in various discussions of alternative organizations (Chesler 1973; Johnson and Whyte 1977; Query 1973; Valentine 1978), thus continuing this leitmotif of the women's literature.

There is one intriguing question that is raised in the literature on alternative organizations but that is not examined in detail, and this concerns the position of women in professional or alternative organizations. The question is pertinent, for the characterization of the classical model as "masculine" rather simplistically suggests that alternative models must, at least, be "less masculine," in which case women's socialization might be more relevant and women's role in such organizations might be enhanced. Such an interpretation is supported by a consideration of the nature of housework, viewed as a small-scale family firm (for which women are still implicitly if not explicitly socialized) in contrast both with the classical Weberian model and with the organic model that was developed in the 1960s. There can be absolutely no doubt that, in most instances, the housework enterprise can be considered an "organic" rather than a "classical" form of organization, as shown in Table 2.1. Are we arguing, then, that a "feminine ethic" predominates in alternative organizations if the Weberian model is masculine?

In an early response to this question, Simpson and Simpson (1969) argue the opposite—that semiprofessional organizations are more bureaucratic in their organizational assignments than professional organizations and that one reason is the prevalence of women who are more ready to follow directives than males, who lack long-range ambition, and who have compliant dispositions, among other factors. Marrett (1972) disagrees, suggesting that this stereotyped view at least requires investigation. Kanter, following her insistence on a "masculine ethic" in the earlier image of managers (1975b: 43), embarks on a discussion of traditional management from which she concludes that women differ from men in according greater importance to satisfying peer relationships and in limiting their levels of aspiration. She does not confront the question of women's role in nontraditional organizations. Finally, Wolff (1977: 19) takes a macro-sociological approach to the issue of women's role in organizations such that women's traditional societal role is the determining factor and "no amount of equality of pay, training or opportunities will actually make women equal with men in the work situation." Given that she defines women's societal position very broadly to include prejudice against women in the workplace, the attitudes and expectations of women workers, the differential socialization of the sexes including female propensity to underachievement, the predominance of the male working pattern, and the expectation of *women's* and not men's two roles, it is clear that most of these factors apply equally to alternative organizational

Table 2.1. Organizational Models

Classical Model[a]	*Organic Model*[a]	*Housework Enterprise*
1. Specialization of tasks	Contribution of expertise to the overall task	Minimal specialization of tasks
2. Coordination of tasks through the hierarchy	Spontaneous coordination through interaction	Coordination is part of the general task
3. A precise definition of rights and obligations	No precise definition of rights and obligations	No precise definition of rights and obligations
4. Rights and obligations translated into responsibilities	Broad commitment to the overall goal	Broad commitment to general goals
5. A hierarchy of control	A network structure of control	No rigidly defined hierarchy
6. Vertical communication and commands predominate	Lateral communication and consultation predominate	Lateral communication and advice predominate

a. Based on Burns and Stalker (1961: 119-21), which remains the clearest formulation of the mechanistic/organic contrast.

settings as to traditional ones. In other words, despite any apparent congruence between a "feminine ethic" and alternative organizations, subsidiary factors in alternative organizations reinforce the usual status difference between the sexes to the advantage of the male.

But do micro-structural factors have *any* effect? Given the unfortunate societal baggage with which women are surrounded in the workplace, does it make any difference to modify organizational arrangements to facilitate women's contribution? Kanter would presumably answer in the affirmative because she argues forcefully (Kanter and Stein 1979) that system-level change is required to modify women's position in organizations (p. 241) and that opportunity shapes behavior (p. 159) such that women's attitudes and orientations should be viewed as "*human* responses to blocked opportunities" (p.159; emphasis in original). Sheer common sense would also suggest that minimizing at least some negative factors might be preferable to leaving the unfortunate baggage in place. But we don't know, and the literature on alternative organizations provides few guidelines. This is at least in part, one can hypothesize, because the question of facilitating women's participation in organizational settings has not yet become such an important issue to management that it overrides all questions of efficiency on which organizational structures have been based up to the current time. In other words, after decades of being told by organizational researchers that the most efficient organization is based on coherence between environmental characteristics and/or technology and organizational structure, modifying organizational arrangements to benefit women would be of secondary importance to employers. A much stronger thrust toward affirmative action would be necessary to overtake these paramount questions of efficiency—assuming that such a thrust is conceivable within a capitalist framework.

The other theme running through women's contribution to this area of alternative organizations is that such organizations are literally *alternates*, that is, subsidiary to the dominant organizational model of capitalist society. This perspective emerges clearly from presentations of alternative organizations, which follow statements that they do not fit the Weberian model (e.g., Bucher and Stelling 1969), that they are throwbacks to the past or possibly future thrusts (Kanter and Zurcher 1973), or even that they are "deviant" (Davies 1972). Implicit is the view that the masculine model of rationality and reason has come to dominate our view of the optimal organization. Despite any lip service paid to the value of organizations in which power is shared, the force of Weberian ideology is sufficient for researchers to view them as unusual pockets or undesirable manifestations within an efficient capitalist society—to be tolerated at the margins of society but unlikely to predominate in the foreseeable future. From this perspective also, whether women's role is enhanced or not in alternative organizations thus becomes a question of minor importance in a society dominated by Weberian organizations, and women researchers are probably realistic in not treating the question too seriously.

Room for Women

It is our view, shared by a number of researchers, that the nature of organizational sociology can best be grasped through an appreciation of the collaboration between organizational researchers and employers, directed toward the concerns of the latter. Given the "maleness" of management, issues of interest to women are unlikely to be raised and one would expect women's contribution to be minimal in this male area.

This survey of women's contribution to the sociology of organizations has confirmed the broad outlines of this image to some extent. This is not an area in which women have taken the lead, and the subsidiary role of women researchers to male colleagues is very evident. At the same time, we have been agreeably surprised to note that women researchers have carved out various domains for their contributions, and we view these domains as a reflection of women's position in general and in the workplace. In other words, it is not surprising that female research has emphasized those issues that are familiar to women through their own personal experience or through their aspirations for change.

In particular, the service role of women within the field emerges clearly from a variety of work, the role including not only the refining or synthesizing of previous work but also the emphasis on service organizations in contradistinction to the industrial sector. A sensitivity to power differentials also guides much of the work accomplished by women; there is an interesting emphasis on the more subtle manifestations of power, espoused by the powerless, and the general orientation is to the problem of the oppressed rather than of the powerful. Finally, the aspiration toward change is reflected in the concern with alternative modes of organization; without examining the question of women's role within such contexts, there is an optimistic note to the preoccupation with modifying the classical organizational model with its "masculine ethic."

As indicated, a few women have escaped the organizational mold and genuinely can be considered to be innovators within the field. Their work has been expressed in terms that have appealed to employers, and these women have maintained a very real respect for their managerial colleagues. This collaboration has resulted in some influential work that has marked organizational sociology and, at least in the case of Joan Woodward, has heralded a major new development in the field. But, as noted, such contributions are rare on the part of women.

If our assumptions are correct, the changing position of women, in society and in the workplace, must have repercussions on their contributions to the organizational field. As women experience a wider range of organizational realities, their definition of the familiar will automatically be extended. At the same time, we anticipate that issues concerning women's place within organizations will take on an added concern for employers, which will constitute a major impetus for raising questions formulated by women for women. A similar approach to women's contribution to the field, carried out by the next generation of researchers, should reflect women's more varied position in the workplace and a much wider range of domains of endeavor.

Notes

1. Our experience in writing this chapter has underlined the difficulties involved in disentangling the contribution of coauthors. For this reason, and particularly because our collaboration results from a former professor/student status, we would like to provide a brief outline of our division of labor to avoid any impression of a secondary role for either one of us: Campbell undertook the initial literature search and was responsible for writing the first draft of the introductory section and the sections on "the service workers" and "the oppressed"; [Tancred-]Sheriff made a particular search of the French-language journals and wrote the first draft of the sections on "the innovators" and "the optimists," as well as the Conclusion. Later drafts resulted from a collaborative effort, and we, of course, take joint responsibility for errors of omission and commission. We would like to acknowledge the assistance of our colleague, Thelma McCormack of York University, who, during a particularly busy period, agreed to read and comment on an earlier draft.

2. In the context of the current chapter, the field has been defined to exclude research dealing with individual-level phenomena, concentrating on system-level structures and processes in both the public and the private sectors. In defining the area in this way, we are reflecting a generally accepted approach to the field; however, we do recognize that such an approach does not serve to highlight women's role in organizations, and this point is discussed further in the text.

3. The definition of "literature by women" is not completely straightforward. Some journals and bibliographies have adopted the tiresome practice of using initials rather than complete first names and even the latter are sometimes misleading. In addition, there is the problem of joint authorship across gender lines where the woman is often a junior author with a number of male colleagues. We have adopted the rule of thumb of considering joint-authored articles where the woman concerned has published elsewhere as the main author or perhaps independently—in other words, where her contribution can be distinguished. We apologize if our procedures have unintentionally included or excluded inappropriate persons. We would like to note the dominant contribution of anglophone women to this field. Despite particular efforts to seek out the work of francophones, this chapter bears witness to the very limited number of items that can be cited.

4. One might add that Perrow was considerably influenced by some seminal work by Rose Laub Coser in which the contrast between the surgical and medical wards of a hospital formed the basis for a nonindustrial formulation of the technological perspective (Perrow 1967, 1970; Coser 1958, 1963).

5. DiTomaso (1980) has attempted to create a bridge between the sociology of organizations and research on community power structures by arguing that much research within organizational sociology has necessarily dealt with issues of power implicitly if not explicitly.

3

Gender and Organizations: A Selective Review and a Critique of a Neglected Area[1]

JEFF HEARN
P. WENDY PARKIN

One of the major developments within sociology over the last decade has been an increased concern with the sociological analysis of women and of gender issues (e.g., Stacey 1981). This can be seen largely, though probably not wholly, as a response to the impact of feminism and feminists and the related greater attention to sexism and sexual discrimination throughout many spheres of society.

Organizational sociology and organization theory, like general sociology, have suffered from a neglect of gender issues. If one searches the index of most of the standard textbooks or readers on organization, one finds few references to sex and gender. Taken at random, although we trust

AUTHORS' NOTE: This chapter originally appeared as J. Hearn and P. W. Parkin (1983) "Gender and Organizations: A Selective Review and a Critique of a Neglected Area," *Organization Studies* 4(3):219-42; reprinted by permission of *Organization Studies*.

not unrepresentatively, from our own bookshelves, three very different works on organization—Blau and Scott's (1963) *Formal Organizations,* Salaman and Thompson's (1965) *People and Organizations* and Allen's (1975) *Social Analysis*—provide no references to "men," and "women," "sex," or "gender" in their indexes. Admittedly, in *People and Organizations*, one of the readings (Emerson 1970) concerns "sustaining definitions of reality in gynaecological examinations," but even here the prime focus is on the issue of definitional maintenance, not gender relations. The point is reaffirmed in one of the most recent general surveys of the study of organizations, Burrell and Morgan's (1979) *Sociological Paradigms and Organizational Analysis*, which also has no specific reference to these issues. In addition, it must be said that the other obvious source of material on gender and organizations, that is, feminist and Women's Movement literature, is useful in an indirect rather than a direct way of critically examining the topic. Such literature has tended to stress either general societal processes and means of oppression of fairly specific issues and experiences which concern women. Accordingly, it also has tended to neglect the middle-range questions on what happens in particular organizations or types of organizations. The reasons for this state of affairs are complex. Some might argue that attention should be directed away from formal organizations and work organizations at least because such organizations are so dominated by men that thinking along that particular level of reality has become "corrupted." The fact is that the social arrangements labelled "organization" occur almost exclusively within the public sphere of life rather than the private sphere. A number of feminist writers, and especially O'Brien (1981), Elshtain (1981) and Stacey and Price (1981), have critically attended to the public-private divide. Such studies point out that not only do men dominate particular public situations but they also dominate what might be called "public thinking," including social and political theory, and thereby organization theory. In contrast, women's exploration of their personal experience may tend to begin by concentrating on the private sphere, but this division is not sacrosanct, and may be increasingly threatened. Most organizations remain patriarchal, if only by virtue of their domination by men. There are very few, if any, organizations composed of more men than women, yet managed by women. It should be added that even all-women organizations can indirectly serve the interests of men (Cohen 1979). Although there is a clear disjunction between mainstream organization theory and feminist critiques, both may at times focus on the same or similar social phenomena and may attempt to describe, explain and act on similar tensions and conflicts.

Interestingly enough, the recent upsurge in critical approaches to the study of organizations (e.g., the "Organizational Analysis" special issue of *Sociological Quarterly* 1977; Clegg and Dunkerley 1977) has concentrated more upon class division than sexual division within organizations. Similarly, the European Group for Organization Studies (EGOS) has done much to further comparative approaches to organizations, the study of organizational power, and the interrelation of structuralist and managerialist perspectives, but relatively little on gender issues.

Here we attempt to continue work within this general critical tradition whilst shifting analysis more explicitly to questions of gender. As will be seen below there are signs of an emerging emphasis on gender within organization studies, but these concerns are by no means well established as yet. For example, these first two issues of the *International Yearbook of Organization Studies* (Dunkerley and Salaman 1980, 1981) each contain but one relevant contribution, while the first two editions of *Research in Organizational Behaviour* (Staw 1979; Staw and Cummings 1980) fail to assist. Sadly the first three volumes of *Organization Studies* are also lacking in this respect.

The purpose of this article is therefore to contribute to the process of necessary consolidation of the topic by reviewing the major contributions to the study of gender and organizations.

The need for greater coherence in the topic also arises from the scatter and variety of relevant material, some of it esoteric and difficult to obtain. As is often the case, working in relatively novel areas also brings with it an essential multi-disciplinarity, with material informed by a wide range of social science traditions. We hope that this necessarily selective review will assist in making the available literature more accessible, and indeed more fully read. In producing this review, however, a second overlapping project has arisen in terms of the possible application of the typology of organizational analyses developed by Burrell and Morgan (1979). These authors consider the range of debates within the social sciences as a preliminary to the study of organizational analyses. Two main types of debate are described—those about the nature of social science and those about the nature of society. On the first count four main strands are considered—around ontology, epistemology, human nature (psychology?), and methodology. Subdebates within each of these strands are eventually conflated to give one broad dimension of subjectivist versus objectivist assumptions about the nature of social science. On the second count, the nature of society, consideration is given to the order-conflict debate, and subsequently a classification of sociological approaches in terms of the broad dimension of the sociology of regulation versus the sociology of radical change. These two broad dimensions, that is, subjectivist-objectivist and sociology of regulation-sociology of radical change, in turn define four major sociological paradigms. These paradigms, functionalist, interpretive, radical structuralist, and radical humanist, are represented in Figure 3.1.

We have already noted how in their extensive survey of organization theory, Burrell and Morgan have neglected questions of sex and gender, at least in *explicit* terms. Furthermore, their work has subsequently been criticized for using the notion of paradigm too loosely (Cox 1979; Harvey 1982). Even so, the framework of the book can be of use as a basis for clarifying major approaches to the topic of gender and organizations. In this sense Burrell and Morgan's work provides an *implicit* account of different treatments of gender and organization. This review therefore presents another application of a typology that, despite methodological and other shortcomings, has already proved to be creative and productive (e.g., Burrell 1980; Whittington and Holland 1981).

The literature reviewed is arranged in the following way. The next section considers four basic positions on gender and organizations: functionalist, interpretive, radical structuralist, and radical humanist. This is followed by a consideration of the nature and orientation of feminist critiques. The following section focuses on more particular issues; work and the division of labour, authority and power, sexuality, and their relationships. These particular issues are selected as they allow a more detailed investigation of organizational process. The first two, work and authority, in many ways represent the two predominant themes of organization theory (e.g., Bendix 1956); the third, sexuality, is much neglected within organization theory, but is raised as an obvious subtopic within the general topic of gender and organizations. The final section considers some theoretical and other implications of these questions.

Basic Positions

The setting out of "basic positions" underlying the analysis of women and men in organizations can appear a somewhat arbitrary process. Writers and researchers rarely record their own underlying assumptions about gender in a precise or coherent way, so that the elucidation of "basic positions" is in itself an exercise in interpretation. Nevertheless, the detailing of the major "basic positions" that seem to underlie debates about gender and organizations is seen as useful for two reasons: firstly, to begin to stake out the terrain within which we are working, and secondly, to

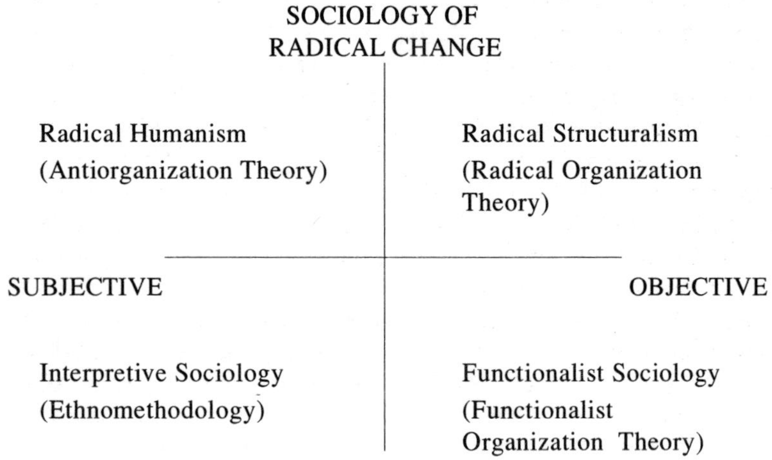

SOCIOLOGY OF
RADICAL CHANGE

Radical Humanism (Antiorganization Theory)	Radical Structuralism (Radical Organization Theory)
SUBJECTIVE	OBJECTIVE
Interpretive Sociology (Ethnomethodology)	Functionalist Sociology (Functionalist Organization Theory)

Figure 3.1. Burrell and Morgan's Paradigms

avoid repetition in the subsequent consideration of the more specific issues of work, authority and sexuality.

We will now briefly consider the basic position on gender represented within the four paradigms outlined, together with a review of feminist critiques.

Functionalist

Within this paradigm the most usual approach is either to neglect gender completely or to use relatively simple descriptive, sometimes stereotyped, models or somewhat more critically to see gender as no more than a variable of which account should be taken. Many texts conform to what Feldberg and Glenn (1979) refer to as the job model within the sociology of work. According to this the work (by which they mean largely paid or organizational work) that people do is the primary independent variable in explaining workers' behaviour both on and off the job. There are numerous examples of this sort of approach within the functionalist literature. Most importantly they argue that the job model is usually applied to men, while in contrast a gender model is more often used to explain women's behaviour. The latter model emphasizes personal characteristics and relationships to (paid) employment. Thus while there are many texts, some of them significantly considered to be "classics," within organization theory which focus on men in the manner described above there are few that have a similar approach to women in organizations. The list of the former would include *Man on the Assembly Line* (Walker and Guest 1952), *Organization Man* (Whyte 1956), "Bureaucratic Man" (Kohn 1971), and *Corporation Man* (Jay 1972), while the interestingly entitled *Organization Woman* (Stott 1978) has a rather different project in presenting the history of the National Union of Townswomen's Guilds in the United Kingdom and remains largely unnoticed within organization theory, functionalist or otherwise.

In addition to these relatively explicit texts, there are a large number of texts which treat gender questions in a more implicit way (e.g., Perrow 1970; Silverman 1970; Hall 1977). Such mainstream texts can usefully be re-examined, particularly in their treatment of male roles and masculinity (Acker and Van Houten 1974; Morgan 1981). Discussions of, say, organizational goals, hierarchy or management function can often be seen as euphemisms for discussions of men.

It is important to note that the underlying assumptions of many treatments of gender and gender relations within the functionalist paradigms are dominated to a greater or lesser degree by Parsonian structural functionalism. Parsons, together with such coworkers as Bales (Parsons and Bales [1955] 1975) and Shils (Parsons et al. 1951), has provided mainstream organization theory with a set of "background assumptions" (Gouldner 1971) about women and men, that bear a close approximation to conventional, commonsense wisdom on sex differences. Generalized distinctions on role differentiation between the instrumental and the expressive have been translated to sex role differentiations within nuclear families and small groups (Bales and Slater [1955] 1975; Zelditch [1955] 1975). Although this approach is now much less dominant than it was twenty years ago, the general instrumental-expressive division remains implicit within much organization theory, and particularly systems theories. An interesting example of an application of open system thinking to the organization of "men" is Dunkerley's (1975) work on the foreman.

Such structural functionalist and systems approaches have a continuing significance in the development of psychological and social psychological perspectives on gender and organizations. Although there are certain difficulties in matching dominantly psychological standpoints with Burrell and Morgan's sociological framework, studies focusing primarily on differential socialization and sex differences between women and men often have a strong objectivist basis. The interesting point is that many of these texts combine a psychological interpretation of women and sex differences with a managerialist perspective (e.g., Stead 1978; Fenn 1978; Henning and Jardin 1978), which places them firmly in the functionalist camp. The orientation of such texts varies from Jacklin and Maccoby's (1975) exploration of the implications of "sex differences" for developing more "female" management styles, to McLane (1980) on corporate strategies of attracting, selecting, positioning and developing women executives, to Henning and Jardin's (1978) advice for the aspiring careerist woman in management, as if "going to a foreign country for an extended stay" (1978: 184).

Most of such work on women in management is written in the American context and implicitly accepts a functionalist standpoint. It is open to criticism on both empirical and theoretical grounds (Eichler 1980). Meeker and Weitzel-O'Neill (1977) have comprehensively argued against the underlying sex differences approach and instead propose an analysis of sex roles that is more specifically context-based. Above all, the literature on women in management can actually be seen as reinforcing patterns of organization and management that neglect women's interests.

Interpretive

The majority of work on organizations that has been attempted within an interpretive framework has neglected questions of gender. At first sight this may be surprising, for if the phenomenological tradition has accomplished anything, it is an assertion of the imperative to attend to the subjective realities of individuals. One might reasonably expect such subjective realities to include members' sense of gender. In any event, most interpretive work has looked at organizations or organizational situations that are almost exclusively male, without attending to the issue of male-male relations (e.g., Bittner 1967) or what are probably mixed organizations, whilst still neglecting the gender issue (e.g., Zimmerman 1970). The most promising exceptions are when the starkness of male-female relations is such that the issue cannot be avoided, as, for example, when women clients face male professionals. Thus there are relevant interpretive studies of the abortion clinic (Ball 1967), gynaecological examinations (Emerson 1970) and childbirth itself (Shaw 1974).

There remain, however, a number of problems with most interpretive treatments, or lack thereof, of gender. It may be that the researchers have been careless or that fixed gender distributions are often so taken-for-granted that they fail to be "worth mentioning" by the actors themselves. Alternatively, and much more critically, it might be possible to place the very notions of "maleness" and "femaleness" themselves in brackets, in suspension. More likely is it that it is men's rather than women's accounts of organizational reality that dominate most interpretive analyses. This is an issue to which we will return in examining the feminist critique.

Radical Structuralist

Within the radical structuralist paradigm the gender issue is still neglected, although for different reasons than in the functionalist and interpretive paradigm. Orthodox Marxism, as represented within much Russian social theory, places class struggle first and concern for the position of women secondary, on the assumption that liberation of the sexes follows class liberation.

Contemporary Mediterranean Marxism is both less rigid in its analyses and, particularly following the work of Althusser (for example, 1969), more willing to acknowledge the relative autonomy of ideology, and thus the reproduction of ideas and labour power. Most organization theory that is radical structuralist in orientation tends to be influenced more by this latter, more open-ended form of Marxism than the former more dogmatic form. Even so, the place accorded to gender is usually not great. Class divisions are seen as having far greater significance than sexual divisions. Benson (1977), for example, in his dialectical formulation of organizations, describes four major factors: social construction of reality, totality, contradiction, praxis, but not gender. More generously, we see some attention to the *type of work* done by women in the studies by Braverman (1974) and Salaman (1981), with a particular emphasis on subordinate clerical work. Clegg and Dunkerley's mammoth *Organization, Class and Control* (1980), which is probably the most comprehensive review of organization theory from within the radical structuralist paradigm, devotes about 25 pages to gender out of about 560. Here the emphasis is placed fairly and squarely on the dual labour market, a theme developed further by Martin (1981) in her analysis of labour markets and employing organizations.

Radical Humanist

The radical humanist paradigm, the fourth of Burrell and Morgan's paradigms, is premised upon a sociology of radical change and a subjectivist orientation to social reality. In this sense it is the most unfamiliar and undeveloped of the four paradigms, and is in clear opposition to mainstream functionalist sociology and organization theory. Although Burrell and Morgan (1979: 306-8) argue, as with the other paradigms, for the underlying unity of this paradigm, there is inevitably within this particular standpoint an inherent variety and variability. The range extends from texts, such as those by Clegg (1975) and Beynon (1973), which examine the subjective and linguistic experience of paid work albeit within a structuralist framework, to less academically conventional texts on the perception of alternative realities, such as those by Pirsig (1976) and Castaneda (1970). There is if anything an important tension within the radical humanist paradigm between the alternativism of, say, 1960s thought, represented by the work of Roszak (1969) and Reich (1972), and the Critical Theorizing of Habermas (for example, 1971) and others, representing a continuation of themes explored by the young Marx and a coming together of Marxist and Freudian thinking.

The main implication of this broad approach is perhaps a wholesale critique of work, the work experience and the work ethic, and a striving to both understand and change the conditions of work. In fact much of this critique of work can readily be reinterpreted in terms of a critique of men. Virtually all the radical humanist thinkers quoted by Burrell and Morgan are writing implicitly about men; some, such as Beynon, largely about men at work. A more explicit text, which draws on aspects of this tradition, is that by Willis (1977) on *Learning to Labour,* in which perceptions of young people about work, sex, class, and race are interrelated at both structural and subjective levels.

Another feature of this paradigm relevant to gender and organizations is an increase in interest in small-scale, alternative forms of organizing, such as communes. Such arrangements may change perceptions and experience of work, but not necessarily the sexual division of labour. Finally it is necessary to take note of an inherent ambiguity in the term "antiorganization theory" between opposition to organization theory as usually constituted and opposition to (certain types of) organization. This connection and relationship is also crucial within feminist critiques, to which we now turn.

Feminist Critiques

By their very nature, feminist critiques are varied. In this respect, along with a number of other more detailed points, there are clear links with the radical humanist paradigm described above. However, it would be misleading to equate the radical humanist paradigm and feminist critiques, partly because the latter has had an impact within all four paradigms, and partly because in their own terms feminist critiques are likely to be critical of all four paradigms, constructed as they are in universalist terms. Analytically it may be useful to distinguish those feminist positions which orientate themselves towards or away from the four paradigms, so giving reactive academic feminism, phenomenological feminism, Marxist (or socialist) feminism, and yet more autonomous radical feminism. However, such differentiations are more clear-cut in analysis than in practice, due to their common interest in the political liberation of women. Such issues point up again some of the limitations of Burrell and Morgan's universalist typology.

Mitchell's statement in 1966 of the fourfold oppression of women, through production, reproduction, sexuality, and socialization, remains a very useful working brief for a feminist analysis of organizations. Not only does this sort of approach point to the dangers of reifying organizations and so ignoring (the variety of) structural determinants beyond, but it also raises the possibility that each of these four realms is inhabited by organizations that are themselves male-dominated. Much more specific attacks on male dominance of both work organizations and organization theory, and the link so between, have been put forward by Wolff (1977) in Britain and Kanter (1975c) in America. The former has accordingly written: "Within the perspective of organisation theory, we can see how long hours and inflexible working time mitigate against the employment of women with 'two roles,' but we cannot discuss the basic question of *why* women have two roles" (Wolff 1977: 20).

Kanter, if anything, takes a more radical (humanist) position still in urging attention to the ideological underpinnings of modern organizations, a theme more self-consciously taken up by the anarchist and radical feminists (Farrow 1974; Kornegger 1975; Siren and Black Rose 1971; Ehrlich 1978). Here the idea and practice of organization itself is held to be dominated by men, and so to be subject to critical theory and practice. Attention is therefore to be directed to women creating feminist organizations (Charlton 1977; Gould 1980), with "non-patriarchal, non-hierarchical structure . . . no stars and no drudges" (Toynbee 1982). Within these situations there may be continuing debates on structure and structurelessness (Freeman 1970), which themselves shift according to political exigencies and practice. Such shifts are very much in keeping with that aspect of feminism that promotes practice as a basis of theory, a feature itself compatible with anarchist, existential, and certain critical traditions.

More specifically, we may note several implications of such feminist critiques; firstly, the link between critiques of organizational practice and organization theory, deriving from the general concern to relate theory and practice; secondly, the way in which this tension itself affects the research process, the organizations studied and the purpose of such research on organizations; and thirdly, the way in which feminist studies of organizations highlight the tension and connection between understanding women collectively "as a class" and women's individual experience and situation.

Particular Issues

The following four sections consider three particular organizational issues, and their interrelationship, in more detail: work and the division of labour, authority and power and sexuality.

Work and the Division of Labour

The majority of literature that deals specifically with the sexual division of labour within organizations has been from a functionalist perspective, with more recent contributions from radical structuralist and feminist perspectives. The classic British studies of women and men workers have tended to focus on manual occupations (Cunnison 1966; Lupton 1963). Lupton compared a predominantly female clothing factory with a predominantly male engineering factory and concluded that differences were not so much sex-based as the result of market forces and the seasonal variations in work. Much rarer have been studies of subordinate clerical workers, and particularly secretaries. Mills (1951), Lockwood (1966a) and Crozier ([1965] 1971) all make some reference to gender, but it is not central to their theses. It is only in the last few years that we have seen more extended and specialized treatment of women secretaries (McNally 1979; Vinnicombe 1980). There are now a number of well-documented accounts of both sexual discrimination at work and of the historical development of the sexual division of labour (e.g., Davies 1975; Mackie and Pattullo 1977; Lewenhak 1980).

The problem with most of these accounts of women, men, and work is that they fail to take the doubly difficult step of linking the nonorganizational division of labour and the organizational division of labour, and then linking these two structures to the development of internal organizational dynamics. This general project clearly fits very much with the concern to broaden the analysis of organizations, as seen within studies of women's work and class divisions (Garnsey 1977; Blackburn and Stewart 1977; Gardiner 1977), reserve army of labour theory (Braverman 1974), and the detailed operation of the labour process (e.g., J. West 1977, 1982; Pollert 1981).

The second stage of this double challenge of linking with internal organizational dynamics remains more problematic. In this respect Simpson and Simpson's (1969) study of the semi-professions represented something of a landmark in linking societal divisions of labour, organizational divisions of labour, and organizational structure. The study suffers somewhat from its Parsonian heritage, a descriptive and at times overly simple style that appears to attribute intrinsic qualities to women and men. The same criticism cannot be voiced against Beynon and Blackburn's (1972) study of a food factory. Divisions examined here are not only between women and men, but also between day shift and night shift, and full-time and part-time workers. This study can be usefully read in conjunction with Kanter's (1975c) attempt to relate the division of labour and the nature of mixed and single sex groups in differing organizational contexts.

The most comprehensive statement on this double-levelled project has to date been produced by Martin (1981), who concludes:

> The position of women in labour markets and employing organizations reflects their position in the broader society. Subordinated inside the patriarchal family, women find themselves subordinates in economic and organizational spheres as well. . . . Since paid work in modern societies is, with few exceptions, conducted in the context of formal organizations, a fundamental change in the fate of women at work . . . will require change in the family and educational systems, and in the institutional arrangements around religion, welfare, law, politics and government as well. (pp. 145-46)

A variety of recent studies have gone on to examine the complexity and contradictions of specific organizational changes in detail. For example, Bruegel (1979) notes how in Britain the reserve army of labour seems to be generally applied in recent years, with women's greater "disposability" in many sectors, and yet in certain service sectors women's labour continues to be sought due to its relative cheapness. Thus contradictory changes may occur within given organizational contexts, especially large, wide-ranging corporations. Such debates are closely tied to form of and change in work process. The feminization of clerical labour (Davies 1974) has in many instances been accompanied by a process of proletarianization that can have unexpected effects and inefficiencies particularly within larger organizations (Glenn and Feldberg 1977). The introduction of word processing has recently been seen as a specific instance of the transformation of patriarchal relations of control to more explicitly capitalist relations. Barker and Downing (1980: 96) specifically suggest that the "traditional, previously effective forms of control in the office which have their roots in patriarchy, are within the context of the present crisis in the accumulation process, becoming redundant." Many of these particular issues are also examined in an American case study by Hacker (1979) that also draws out the interplay of sex and race.

Finally, in this section it should be noted how much of this literature on work and the division of labour has helped to dispel various gender-based myths. Fenn (1976) has codified and dismissed many of these myths of women and work. She accepts that women enter into organizations with different backgrounds and experience from men as their socialization has produced a different orientation from that of men. However, once in organizations, they are not found to be taking jobs from men, not working any less, not prone to absenteeism or illness, and are just as capable as men of taking responsibility.

Authority and Power

While debates about gender, work, and the division of labour have ranged far and wide, drawing on economics and sociology as well as organization theory, debates about gender, authority, and power in organizations have been much more localized within organization theory.

An early classic study that raised the issue of gender and authority in organizations was that by Whyte (1949) on the social structure of the restaurant. He noted men are often more comfortable in a relationship in which they take responsibility for originating initiatives for women. The male kitchen staff had much to gain by "containing" orders (in both senses) from female waitresses by physical barriers, use of written slips, and generally controlling their own work rate. The relative authority of women and men in working situations is clearly illuminated by the reviews of Kanter (1975c) and Meeker and Weitzel-O'Neill (1977) of status differences between the sexes.

In shifting attention from the informal organization and its group dynamics to the formal structure of organizations, the work of Simpson and Simpson (1969) is again important. They postulated that the differential work orientation of women and men was a major contributory factor in female-dominated organizations, such as are found in the semi-professions, becoming more bureaucratic and more centralized. The hypothesis, though imaginative, has brought considerable criticism from empirical researchers (Marrett 1972; Grandjean and Bernal 1979).

Kanter (1975b) has gone further and has suggested that work attitudes and behaviour are a function of the location of a person in organizational structures and not a function of sex differences. Men, as well as women, are in disadvantaged positions both in society and in organizations but women are more disadvantaged. It is the structure of the power within an organization which explains the concentration of women at the bottom rather than gender attributes or characteristics. Wells (1973) pursues a similar line of thought by suggesting that women were "late entries" into organizations where the structure and power already emanated from masculine values and male prerogatives. Women often find the covert power of men, reinforced by the power structure of organizations, influences the way in which the power is experienced by them. Fighting competition and power in hierarchical organizations will help men and women, concludes Wells, but will help women more.

This raises the yet more subtle issue of the way in which power itself is thought of as essentially male (Korda 1976). Not only do men dominate within organizations, but they dominate the currency by which domination is maintained. The issue is expressed by Kanter as "preference for men = preference for power" (1977a: 197).

In the light of the deeply embedded nature of male power, it is not surprising that alterations from the norm in the behaviour of women leaders can arouse considerable fear and insecurities amongst men (Mayes 1979). It is the ubiquity of male power that suggests an analysis of patriarchy is necessary to appreciate the nature of authority and power in organizations. Thus we are brought to the question of how men relate to *each other* in their domination of women, a subject that has been examined more by a number of men (e.g., Korda 1972), though not necessarily from a position sympathetic to feminism (Tiger 1969; Jay 1967, 1972).

A promising line of inquiry into this phenomenon is the investigation of "male homosociability": "the seeking, enjoyment and/or preference for the company of the same sex" (Lipman-Blumen 1976: 16). Interestingly enough, homosociability does not necessarily mean that homophobia—fear of close contact with members of the same sex—may not also be present among male workers at the same time. This brings us on to consider the issue of close contact, actual or potential sexuality.

Sexuality

We have already noted that, despite being the most obvious gender issue, sexuality is perhaps the most underresearched area of organizational dynamics affected by gender. Although there is a considerable amount of general theoretical work on the social construction of sexuality, from both functionalist and feminist perspectives, this is rarely related directly to organizational processes. Moreover, most mainstream organizational theory either ignores the issue of sexuality or uses crude formulations thereof.

A more promising contribution from outside organization theory but with clear implications for organizations is that by Zetterberg (1966) on "the secret ranking." According to this hypothesis status and power are seen to derive partly from physical attraction between individuals although this fact of life is rarely explicitly acknowledged. "The secret ranking" may or may not coincide with the official hierarchy of an organization, with important repercussions either way.

One basic problem in the study of sexuality and organizations is the shortage, not surprisingly, of empirical information. Quinn (1977) has attempted to rectify this by using third party reports of romantic relationships in organizations. The variety and location of, as well as management responses to, these relationships is examined with a number of important implications and conclusions.

At the general level there is the contradictory nature of sexuality and much organizational life; "organizations are a natural environment for the emergence of romantic relationships," while often being deemed inappropriate in particular cases. More specific is the way in which organizations provide the social structure for the social construction of sexuality, just as they may do for the development of friendship in general. Most important here is the way in which organizations create conditions of dependence and interdependence which themselves may provide the basis of romance (Huston and Cate 1979). Two organizational arenas of dependence that deserve special mention and have indeed taken on almost legendary significance are the relationships between bosses and secretaries (McNally 1979), and the selection of staff (Rose and Andiappon 1978; Schuler and Berger 1979). In both these sorts of situations dependence and sexuality may become intimately combined, at least in thought if not in action.

The move from this dominantly functionalist perspective on sexuality to a more critical position has been eased by several studies that may loosely be described as interpretive in flavour. Bradford et al. (1975) have charted the intimate association of sexuality and work success, and its implications for management, drawing on Kanter's (1975a) work on sexual stereotypes. These may exist primarily in peoples's minds, but as such they may constitute a significant part of organizational reality. This perspective had if anything been elaborated more fully and more critically by Korda (1972) in his discussion of the magnitude of sexual energy circulating in the workplace, and the way a good deal of ambiguity may therefore bedevil workers' perceptions of each other. Korda's conclusion is that "sex in the office remains, even in its more innocent forms, a male chauvinist institution, until such time as women gain a working equality in business" (1972: 116).

This leads us to more explicitly feminist critiques of sexuality and organizations. Two studies which respectively illustrate more socialist and more radical feminist analyses of the situation, but which in so doing show something of the arbitrariness of the socialist-radical division, are those by MacKinnon and Rich. MacKinnon's (1979) study *The Sexual Harassment of Working Women* is a major work that is important both in demonstrating how the high level of sexual harassment is consistently overlooked or treated with a lack of concern, and more generally in noting the interplay of sexuality and capitalist organization. Subordination of women at work is in effect "eroticized" or "sexualized," so that women both market their sexual attractiveness and find their sexual attractiveness considered by men a relevant factor in their evaluation as workers. With other recent work and campaigns (Farley 1978; Sedley and Benn 1982) it has helped to put sexual harassment on both the academic and political agenda.

Rich (1980) agrees with much that MacKinnon writes, but places the question of heterosexuality and lesbianism more centrally. She argues that women are given "compulsory heterosexuality" through organizational and other practices. While the study of both male and female homosexuality is well established with specific, usually closed institutions, such as prisons (Giallombardo 1966; Ward and Kassebaum 1965), it is hardly recognized at all as an issue in most organization theory. For this reason the interrelation of organizational dynamics and dominantly heterosexual institutions, such as marriage, seems a necessary area for research. Kanter's (1977a) study of *Men and Women of the Corporation* significantly also has a section on women outside the corporation, the wives of the male managers. This may presage similar wide-ranging studies.

Interrelationships

It will now be apparent that these three realms of work, authority and sexuality, are dealt with very differently within each of the paradigms outlined earlier, with different causal links between the realms in each case. In very general terms, authority is emphasized, even reified, in both the functionalist and interpretive paradigms. In the functionalist, authority is held rigid in the functions and structures of organizations, while in the interpretive, authority is fixed in individual interactions. Work is given a more basic causal place within the radical structuralist and radical humanist paradigms. This, however, only gives the broadest of overviews.

A more specific set of relationships can be drawn between work and authority, the division of labour, and the distribution of power. Indeed one can often recognize a reciprocal relationship between work and authority, with each reinforcing the other. Mennerick (1975), for example, in a particularly interesting study of travel agencies, notes how women tend to enter less prestigious organizations even within nonstereotyped sectors of work, and how they are more likely to occupy management positions there than in the more prestigious units. In effect the structuring of sex roles, in terms of both work and authority, is reproduced both *between* organizations and *within* organizations.

The interrelationship of work and authority with sexuality is less easy to disentangle and is indeed one of the themes running through many feminist critiques. In contrast, Rubenstein (1978) has surveyed the assumed antagonism between love and work, expressed particularly in the effect of modernization on the quality of social relationships. This assumption is challenged by much feminist writing; for example, Bland et al. (1978) argue for the connection between the organization of production and social definitions of masculinity and femininity.

These connections have recently been the subject of study in the context of the professions, the "semi-professions" and "people work" (Hearn 1982; Stacey 1981). The complication in these fields is that the process of the work, with people, often has a strong emotional component of its own. Such issues are partly structural, but are also observable in the minutiae of organizational life. Korda (1976) has analysed how power and sexuality in organizations may be related, down to the arrangement of office furniture and the subtlety of nonverbal cues. The micropolitics of interactions between women and men in organizations have been studied by, amongst others, C. West (1982), with the conclusion that changes in the structure of organizations alone will not alter women's experience "in a man's world," unless interactions are also transformed. Language itself remains largely man-made (Spender 1980), and organizational language especially so. More interesting still is the interrelation of power and heterosexuality, so that threats to men's power may also be construed as threats to heterosexuality (Mayes 1979). The possible long-term effects of gender-based changes in work, authority, and sexuality in organizations may indeed be drastic (Torrey 1976).

Conclusions and Implications

This selective survey of gender and organizations raises numerous issues, most unresolved, some perhaps unresolvable. In conclusion, we will therefore limit ourselves to a few general points, before individually considering implications for women and men, from our own different positions.

General Implications

Firstly, we should reiterate the great extent of male domination of organization theory. This applies particularly to the functionalist and interpretive paradigms, but also to a large extent to the radical structuralist, and to a lesser extent the radical humanist. It is no wonder that a recent critical review of sexism in the study of organizations produced by the British Sociological Association concluded in the following way: "If organizations are defined as collections of individuals who come together to carry out transactions with the environment which they would find impossible to carry out separately, then it is the 'collectivity' of women that sociologists have failed to identify" (British Sociological Association n.d.: 29). The study of women, men and organizations clearly remains contested.

Secondly, there are the implications of feminism for organization theory. In some respects this resurrects some familiar debates, for example, that of structure and structurelessness has certain parallels with "classical" versus "human relations" theories, or the "technical" versus "socio-." Here again Burrell and Morgan's typology is useful in organizing these debates in terms of their objectivist and subjectivist dimensions. However, feminist approaches may often go further in examining the impact of gender relations on organizations, for example, on questions of sexuality. Even the very way in which the idea of "organization" is thought about in our everyday lives is thus related to gender, leading to the conclusion that dominant notions of "organization" are themselves patriarchal.

Thirdly, there are a number of important methodological problems raised for research into gender and organizations. Male domination of organizations may often depend upon the perpetuation of closed or even secret decision making which in turn leads to observations and theories of organizations being male dominated. A feminist theory of organizations premised as it would be upon a high level of openness becomes almost a contradiction in terms. Movement towards a more explicit consideration of women in organizations may be facilitated by research into all-women organizations but only up to a point. Even all-women organizations, such as Women's Aid, may depend upon other existing organizations, which are themselves male-dominated, for funding or other assistance. Many attempts by women to organize autonomously may persist in the short term or for small-scale projects but attempts to move beyond this will usually lead to encounters, and probably conflicts, with male-dominated organizations. This is not to diminish the potential of such alternative ways of organizing as the nonhierarchical group (Jenkins and Kramer 1978), network, or telephone tree, it is simply to recognize the difficulty within a male-dominated society of researching alternatives to male-dominated organizations in isolation.

There are also linked to this problems around the organization of research itself. Just as there are questions about the police investigating themselves and the unlikelihood of outcomes being free of bias, similarly there are questions of in-built bias in research done by men in organizations and by women who suffer least from discrimination. It is not that such research is invalid but rather that there are omissions in its concerns and very little that might be called feminist organization theory. Until those most discriminated against can themselves research and theorize, or at least have their concerns brought more centrally into organization theory, then the male domination of organization theory is likely to continue.

Implications for Men (by J. Hearn)

All of the general conclusions just noted have considerable implications for men engaged in the study or organizations. First, there is a need to reconstruct the objects of organizational research, to attend to such issues as the construction of sexuality within organizations, the relationship of power and gender, of maleness and management, and so on. Many texts on organization theory fail to give even the most basic information on gender division within the organizations studied, let alone analyse the implications of such division. Secondly, and more specifically, there is the problem of how to research either all-men organizations or cliques of men within organizations. There is an urgent need for men concerned about sexism to begin to unearth some of the ways in which men control and "fix" meetings, use the pub or the golf club to exclude women from organizational discussions, and generally relate to each other as men. Of particular importance is research into the way men may seek out each other's company yet be fearful of trust and intimacy with each other. This project clearly raises personal, ethical, and political problems for research strategy. Above all, organizational research of this nature is no longer likely to be a distanced academic exercise, but one where the boundaries between the objects of research, research method, and personal life begin to break down.

Implications for Women (by P. W. Parkin)

The feminist movement has raised awareness of women about our place in male-dominated organizations but in spite of legislation for equal pay and opportunities women continue to predominate at the bottom of mixed organizations. Legislation can be circumvented by, for example, organizations being unwilling to employ women likely to require maternity leave. Feminist theory will thus remain nebulous until women can themselves research organizations, effectively involving the moving from observing and accepting their position in the hierarchical structures to examining and understanding the power, both overt and subtle, which excludes them from creating theory and change. Women are not discriminated against equally and mothers are an example of a group most discriminated against and least likely to be doing research on and theorizing about organization. Thus, none of Burrell and Morgan's paradigms represent a feminist view as certain women (not feminists) will be seen to subscribe to all four. Research completed by a woman does not automatically have a feminist perspective. "Successful" women will inevitably have experienced discrimination but surmounted this at the cost of having to find the time to penetrate the secrecy of the "closed doors," difficult meeting times, hidden agendas and nondecision making. This type of organizational woman will not necessarily be radical or feminist.

A feminist view of organization is more an overview of male organizational power than a separate paradigm, theory, or typology. Male power is constantly perpetuated, for example, in avoiding equal pay and opportunities legislation; in strengthening the "old boys" networks of schools, pubs, clubs; in the arrangement of meetings at times when women with family commitments need to be at home. The mere fact of accepting a job outside the home does not liberate a woman or begin to make her equal with men. Rather it usually means coping with two jobs with her position in the work organization being little different from her position in the home or any other groups in society to which she might belong. She will rarely have the energy, time, or facilities to research her position or be an activist for change. Most of the apparently generous provision for women workers by organizations is little more than tokenism and does not alter power relationships. Provision of creches and paternalistic attitudes towards women taking leave to care for sick children will not enable women to attend board meetings or union meetings at 5:00 p.m. Similarly, flexi-hours, part-time work and job sharing offer maximum time to the organization but seldom a route to powerful organizational positions. Instead, the chance of being discriminated against may be increased, as with many part-time teachers who do not have contracts. Women seeking flexibility of hours are often those needing the time to fit in heavy child-care commitments.

The future for women in organizations is not an optimistic one. Word processing will possibly lead to more factorylike offices with male engineers replacing female typists. Microprocessing is more likely to result in job losses for women and as the unemployment figures rise men will increasingly be seeking traditional women's jobs at lower levels provided they have different names, for example, "cleaning agencies" rather than domestics. The political climate of "back to the home," union indifference to women's roles in organizations, high unemployment, and reactionary moves against legalized abortion, for example, all seem to be strengthening the male domination of organizations. How change can be achieved is a subject in itself but a feminist theory or overview must look beyond the tokenism and beyond the antiorganization movement to the power relationships that need to be changed before women can achieve equality with men in organizations.

Note

1. We would like to thank *Organization Studies* and its reviewers for their helpful comments on an earlier draft of this paper. We have explored these issues further in a number of more recent publications, including Parkin and Hearn (1987), Hearn and Parkin (1987, 1991), Hearn et al. (1989) and Hearn (1991).

PART II

Toward Feminism as Radical Organizational Analysis

In the mid-1980s, conference papers by Anne Balsamo (1985) and Linda Smircich (1985b) made important contributions to the development of feminist organizational analysis. The papers occupy a pivotal point between feminist critique and the flowering of feminist organizational analysis. The paper by Balsamo set out to "construct a feminist perspective on organizational analysis," laying out a series of ideas for the development of feminist organizational methods and concerns, while Smircich's paper focused on the development of a "women centered organization theory."

The emergent feminist organizational analyses of the 1980s focused attention upon a number of key aspects of the relationship between gender and organization—including sex (Burrell 1984), sexual harassment (Gutek 1985), and sexuality (Hearn and Parkin 1987); organizational culture (Mills 1988b) and subculture (Lamphere 1985); bureaucracy (Ferguson 1984), the state (Grant and Tancred-Sheriff 1986), and public service (Morgan 1988); and numerous other aspects. In this part of the book, we have included articles that helped to open up a particular aspect of analysis and that cover a range of topic areas.

The work of Gibson Burrell on "sex and organizational analysis" (Chapter 4) occupies an important temporal and intellectual point in the development of feminist organizational analysis. Burrell's analysis is complex and far reaching and, although its central concern is not informed by feminism, it provides a wealth of ideas and understandings that are informative to an emergent feminist organizational analysis. He is crucially concerned with the interrelationship between organizational control and sexuality and the light that this sheds on our understanding of organizational reality. In many ways, it is an exercise in Foucauldian logic—an exploration of Foucauldian themes for an analysis of organization. In effect, Burrell's study concentrates upon a historical charting of, what he calls, organizational desexualization—the purging of sexual relations and emotions from organizational life.

Burrell's view of sexuality "as incompatible with labour power" has been contested by Hearn and Parkin (1987) and by Pringle (1989). Pringle argues that sexuality is very much a feature of organizational life as witnessed in her study of secretaries. Secretaries, according to Pringle, stand apart from the bureaucratizing trend of modern organization and, in fact, are expected to exude emotionality, inhabiting an organizational discourse in which sexuality plays an important definitional role. Hearn and Parkin, similarly, contend that sexuality—when approached from feminist concerns—permeates organizational life and the very construction of organizations: They nonetheless pay tribute to the breadth of Burrell's work on the relationship between sexuality and organizational life.

Burrell (1984), in attempting to argue for a more central concern with the problem of sexuality and organizations, recognizes the impending difficulties involved in such an analysis divorced from feminist concerns:

> It is the lack of resistance to desexualization and the need to eroticize our academic labour which have struck me as key features of the myopia of the contemporary sociology of organizations and perhaps of social science as a whole. But what a non-myopic (and one suspects male-dominated) eroticized sociology would look like and how it would relate to feminist scholarship remains, to say the least, a considerable problem. Nevertheless, one can only hope that it is a problem to which we, as organizational analysts, will soon turn. (p. 115)

Burrell's contribution to the development of a "non-myopic eroticized" theory of organizations can be seen in Burrell (1987) and Hearn, Sheppard, Tancred-Sheriff, and Burrell (1989).

Albert Mills's work is concerned with the development of a "feminist materialist" concept of organizational culture as a model for exposing discrimination. By way of a feminist adaptation of Clegg's (1981) rule focus, Mills argues that the gendered character of organizations needs to be understood through analysis of the major rule configurations that compose specific organizations. It is through the process of "rule enactment, mediation and resistance," he continues, that gendered relationships are maintained and developed. Mills's rules approach contributed to a feminist reappraisal of the concept of organizational culture and is included here as Chapter 5. Mills has since developed the rules approach through a number of works (Mills 1988a, 1989; Mills and Murgatroyd 1991; Mills and Chiaramonte forthcoming; Mills and Simmons forthcoming).

In the final chapter of this part, Judith Grant and Peta Tancred set out a feminist perspective on state bureaucracy. Aware, following MacKinnon (1983), that there is a vast task ahead in developing a feminist approach to understanding the state, Grant and Tancred begin the process through a focus upon selected issues: power differentials, unequal representation, "women's issues," adjunct control roles, and bureaucracy as male centered. Through analysis of the Canadian state, they argue that the related bureaucracies have grossly unrepresented women in all but the lowest rungs of the ladder. Quantitatively (e.g., number of officeholders) and qualitatively (e.g., the type of power and authority that goes with the office), males occupy by far the greatest number of positions of authority. Grant and Tancred go on to argue that this association of maleness and bureaucracy has led to a situation where male interests are inherent throughout bureaucratic thinking (i.e., policymaking). Concerns arising out of the experiences of women, on the other hand, have been mediated through male understandings and marginalized in the form of "women's issues." It cannot be assumed, they continue, that women's interests are represented throughout policymaking areas but are more likely to be restricted to those areas so designated "women's" areas. Building upon Tancred's earlier work, they go on to argue that the growth of bureaucracy has involved the development of adjunct control positions designed to control relationships between state and clients, state and employees, but without placing any real authority in the hands of the personnel concerned, a process that has been achievable through the use of female employees. Within organizational analysis, the work of Grant and Tancred was one of the first of several feminist studies of the state (Findlay 1987; Morgan 1988; MacKinnon 1989), and, along with the other contributions in this part, made an important first step toward the development of feminist organizational analysis.

4

Sex and Organizational Analysis[1]

GIBSON BURRELL

Despite the fact that many people spend much of their waking lives in organizations thinking about sex, very little attention has been paid by organizational psychologists and sociologists to the issue of sexuality. The relative absence in social scientific literature of any detailed consideration of this fundamental dimension of human action, frustration, motivation and decision making is made all the more remarkable by the emphasis placed upon it in the humanities. Poetry, novels and biography are all redolent, for the most part, with sexuality and its manifestations. In this regard, at least, novels and fiction do present this feature of organizational life much more readily than much of organization theory. Few could or would deny the existence of sexual relationships in organizational settings but yet their presence is not described let alone explained by much of the sociology of organizations. Chatov (1981,

AUTHOR'S NOTE: This chapter originally appeared in G. Burrell (1984) "Sex and Organizational Analysis," *Organization Studies* 5(2):97-118; reprinted by permission of *Organization Studies*.

498-99) has recently maintained that

> little attention has been given to the influence of the unconscious motivation and sexuality on business or organisational behaviour . . . organisation theorists seem to have overlooked the ubiquitous human pre-occupation with sexual activity. Between 1970 and 1979 not one article explicitly dealing with sexuality appeared in the Academy of Management Journal, A.S.Q. or Organizational Behaviour and Human Performance. About 15 articles discussed sex difference problems in organisations, most of them dealing with employment relationships. In general, articles dealing with sex differences seem to have become more abundant in the sociology journals, a reflection of the women's liberation movement, but no attention has been given in these articles to the subject of sexuality.

In the face of such neglect an attempt will be made in this paper to elevate "sexuality" to a position of theoretical relevance in the analysis of organizations.

The essentialist view of sexuality stresses that *it* (singular) is a driving instinctual force derived from the biological features of the human animal and is therefore ever-present, ever-potent. In linguistic terms, such a view sees sex as "a single signifier and a universal signified" (Sheridan 1980: 194). But in fact what is meant by sex, whether or not it is conceptualized as something distinctive, and the ascribed normality of forms of sexual relations and activity are all culturally relative (Brake 1982). Sexuality is not a given; it is a social construction. The body possesses a whole variety of erotic possibilities, only some of which are morally prescribed by given societies at given points in time. Other possibilities are labelled as delinquent and deviant. Sexuality is thus an historical construct which needs to be understood historically (Foucault 1979; Gagnon and Simon 1974). Although there may well be a universal attribute we choose to name sex, the forms which this takes in given social structures are in actuality varied and heterogeneous. But having said this, how are we to recognize *sexual* activity? Are we to restrict ourselves only to that genital sexuality which goes beyond the point of orgasm; or should we include a more generalized eroticism of touch and phantasy? Clearly there is the possibility of conceptualizing a continuum of sexual relationships in which full genital sexuality involving penetration is near one end of the scale whilst the other end is marked by a plurality of polymorphous pleasurable sensations and emotions. In this paper, most consideration will be directed towards the former end of the continuum bcause the acts found there are more "clearly" sexual in terms of contemporary definitions. This should not be taken to imply that many other activities are not sexual, at least in some respects, and I have no doubt that a *full* treatment of the issue of sexuality in organizational life should address these forms of action too.

Here, however, the aim is a more limited one. Rather than treat organizations as sexual markets as Quinn (1977) does (*pace* Chatov 1981) I wish to suggest that sexual relations, understood in this "extreme" way represent a major "frontier" of control and resistance in organizational life (Goodrich 1975). Note that concern here is not only for relationships between men and women but for homosexual, lesbian and bisexual ones too. Bearing this in mind let us turn first to the issue of *control*.

If an historical perspective is adopted, which Foucault and others seem to imply is necessary, what do we find revealed? Certainly one can see that the origins of the modern bureaucratic organization as a form lie buried deep in history, but it is possible nevertheless to reconstruct early rule-formulations in these organizations. From this reconstruction it is permissible to deduce that the suppression of sexuality is one of the first tasks the bureaucracy sets itself (Bede 1907). Moreover, in modern times, individual organizations inaugurate mechanisms for the control of sexuality at a very early stage in their development. For example, the suppression of sexual relations is one of the initial tasks the early factory employers set themselves (Factory Commission 1833). Indeed, the complete *eradication* of sexuality from bureaucratic structures has been a goal which many top decision makers have pursued. Some have even sought to remove sexuality from human existence altogether. For example, John Fothergill, an 18th century Quaker reformer of, and management consultant to, those institutions which dealt with the poor (prisons, workhouses, hospitals and dispensaries) claimed with some pride on his deathbed that he remained a virgin (Ignatieff 1978: 50). He saw celibacy as a key principle of organizational efficiency and good management; though as a strategy, significant numbers of bureaucrats saw this as a dead end. It was realized in some quarters that because "new" labour was always required such a regime was not universally applicable. So whilst eradication of sexuality was sought in the work situation, many managements contented themselves with the incorporation and close containment of sexual relations in the nonwork sphere. Suppression of sexuality, therefore, involved both eradication and containment, inside and outside work respectively. And these twin processes have continued to influence the lives of the worker since that time to this. Today then, we are presented with a situation in which human features such as love and comfort are not seen as part of the organizational world. In popular ideology, rightly or wrongly, they are associated with the home and the family. But this translocation is not accidental. Human feelings including sexuality have gradually been repulsed from bureaucratic structures and have been relocated in the non-organizational sphere—the world of civil society. Their expulsion back into the family, into *private* life and away from the world of work has been achieved by a whole variety of organizational forms. The *desexualization* of labour, for this is what is entailed, involves the repulsion and expulsion of many human feelings out of the organization and out of its sight. It is a process which has come to shape all our lives to a greater or lesser extent.

Faced with such a curtailment of their activities significant numbers of men and women *resist*. Of course, it is debatable to what extent organizational subordinates of whatever gender perceive the suppression of sexuality as an identifiable managerial control strategy since this suppression is mediated and refracted by many features of social change within civil society as a whole. Nevertheless, there is widespread resistance to such suppression in organizational contexts. Acts of intimacy have taken place in the past and will continue to take place in the future in all those organizations where such activity is subject to harsh punishment. Thus, the "control" of sexuality is usually associated with forms of "resistance" to it. But these notions of control and resistance remain crude and undertheorized. In the growing body of literature on the labour process and cognate areas from which we seek to borrow, this lack of theorization is particularly noticeable (Cressey and MacInnes 1980; Storey 1983).

Resistance and Sexuality: Some Conceptual Difficulties

Although it is not apparent from the literature that this is the case, in fact it is very difficult to isolate an activity which is specifically one of "control" and one which is specifically an example of "resistance" in personal relationships. Similarly, exemplars of "control" and "resistance" between superordinate and subordinates within organizations are not as clear-cut as one might believe at first sight. Indeed, when looking at power relationships in organizational contexts it is difficult to recognize who is resisting what control emanating from which direction. Although these kinds of issues are all too rarely raised, the beginnings of some theoretical solutions are now available. The work of Foucault is of some use here.

Let us be clear that Foucault's conceptualization of *power* is not an advance on existing theorizations (Poulantzas 1978; Fine 1979; Minson 1980). This is largely because, as Poulantzas correctly maintained, his theorizing is very reflective of American political science and its articulation of pluralism. In other words, his view of power is a well-established, if not a hackneyed one. Nevertheless, I think he has a contribution to make on "resistance."

Foucault says that "where there is power there is resistance." But he avoids the view that pervades so much of contemporary theorizing on the labour process which seems to see resistance and control as Newtonian billiard balls. "Action and reaction are equal and opposite" may be a putative law of physics but its implicit utilization in social science is woefully inadequate. Richard Edwards, for example, in *Contested Terrain* (Edwards 1979) has a very simple view of resistance as reaction to management techniques. Burawoy's *Manufacturing Consent* (1982) de-emphasises resistance (Peck 1982) whilst Craig Littler's recent work (Littler 1982) also regards resistance as reaction to specific management proposals. Paul Edwards (with Scullion) is no better in his treatment of *The Social Organization of Industrial Conflict* (Edwards and Scullion 1982). They see absenteeism as shaped and formed by the system of control of the labour process. For them absence stands in relation to, but not as part of control. Now, Foucault is much more correct in his theorizing when he says: "Resistance is never in a position of exteriority in relation to power" (Foucault 1979: 95). For him, the very existence of power is seen as relying on a multiplicity of points of resistance which play a role of adversary, target, support or handle in power relations. Seen thus, absence is part of control. It takes its cue from and owes its existence to the control attempt. Resistance can be incorporated and utilized and displaced so that it is never in a position of exteriority. In this way, absence is control and control is absence. They are part of the discourse of each other. Similarly Braverman's supposed neglect of a consideration of resistance to deskilling (Wood 1982; Littler 1982) can be partially explained as a belief that resistance itself becomes deskilled. But of course the opposite is also true: deskilling itself becomes resistant to complete implementation.

As will be evident, a dialectical view of resistance and control is more difficult to theorize and much more difficult to operationalize than conventional formulations (Peck 1982). But ultimately, such a formulation has the capacity to be more persuasive and more sophisticated in the understanding it gives us of crucial organizational processes; processes in which sexuality plays a key role.

A Dialectic Approach to Sexuality

In recent feminist scholarship little attention has been paid to "organizations" per se, but where they are given consideration (Wolff 1977; Kanter 1977; MacKinnon 1979; Hearn and Parkin 1983) certain features of organizational life such as discrimination and power inequalities are recognized to be of key importance.

In recent years, however, attention has also been given to the issue of sexual harassment at work, usually defined as "unwelcome sexual advances, requests for sexual favours and other verbal or physical conduct of a sexual nature" (Cooper and Davidson 1982: 101). Here organizations are viewed as sites of women's oppression in which sexuality and sexual relations figure prominently. Conventional heterosexuality is quite rightly seen as being imbued with a commodification process in which women become seen by men as commodities to be used, abused and exploited in the day to day business of organizational life. For *The Organization Man* (Whyte 1952) embedded in a structure of patriarchy (Beechey 1979), women are the objects of sexuality. And there is no question that some male theorists of organization are unreflexively patriarchal (Checkland 1981: 217-18).

Organizations then, whether located in economy, polity or civil society can be understood fruitfully as sites of sexual harassment in which patriarchy and the control it gives men over women is reflected in, and enhanced by, sexual harassment. There are now some quite detailed investigations of this problem, of which Catherine MacKinnon's *The Sexual Harassment of Working Women* (1979) is a good example. She maintains that "the problem is not epidemic, it is pandemic—an everyday, everywhere occurrence" (MacKinnon 1979: 3). Certainly it has been reported by large numbers of women in British and American surveys (Collins and Blodgett 1981; Cooper and Davidson 1982).

But what of the other side of the dialectic? Sexuality and sexual relations are beset by contradictions as Coote and Campbell recognize. They say:

> And what about men, who have caused us so much trouble, our brothers, lovers, fathers, workmates, comrades, oppressors. There are no simple answers to this one, for sure. We shall need to fight with them and against them at the same time, often at the same moment. (Coote and Campbell 1982: 239)

Every relationship between men and women contains contradictory elements. There is no doubt that patriarchy and power are present in cross-gender interactions but this does not mean that it is impossible for the sexes to co-operate in the face of common problems. Surely it is not overly optimistic to permit a role for love, affection and comradeship. Coote and Campbell tell their audience that: "We need to recognise that men as individuals can be economically oppressed, socially impoverished and psychologically cramped by the system which sustains the power of men in general" (Coote and Campbell 1982: 239). Faced with organizational control systems which oppress, impoverish and cramp men *and* women, we may expect that amongst subordinates of both genders there would be evidence of the development of conflict towards superiors and resistance to their managerial strategies. In its crudest form my argument is that men and women sometimes acting collectively, sometimes alone, are capable of resistance and of exhibiting conflict towards those organizational control systems concerned with the imposition of discipline and the control of the body. Sexuality is at "the frontier of control" (Goodrich 1975; Cressey and MacInnes 1980: 30). Without being overly "romantic" it becomes possible to say that *sexual relations at work may be expressive of a demand not to be controlled*; but Goodrich's notion of "frontier" of control has more to offer than this. In line with Foucault's position it suggests fluidity, interpenetration and reversals. It is a processual notion suggesting ambiguity and flux. At the same moment in time in sexual affairs, resistance and control interpenetrate one another in a unity of opposites moving on, in the next moment, to a new fusion which is both unpredictable and unstable. If we are to use the concepts at all then, we would do well to see "resistance" and "control" in this dialectical way rather than as fixed independent entities (Cooper 1982).

Having said this, however, we are faced with the problem of presentation of substantive material. It is somewhat easier to outline the basic argument by presenting material on control attempts in the next section and then to turn attention to resistance in a subsequent section. In so doing, however, we separate the inseparable: we do violence to the essential synchronicity of control and resistance and tear the intertwined from one another. We must remember, as we consider organizational desexualization, that it engenders resistance to it from the outset—but our discussion of this resistance is postponed for a little while.

Organizational Desexualization

Many questions are begged if one assumes that *history* reveals itself to us as an unrolled carpet, and many writers have recognized the difficulties of interpreting the past in terms of the present. For example, Foucault maintains that he is concerned for genealogy and for locating traces of the present in the past; the reconstruction of the past is not what he seeks (Foucault 1979; Weeks 1981). An analysis of the contemporary state of organizational desexualization to which we will turn presently thus depends upon an investigation of the historical roots of this process. In this task, let us consider four basic and in some ways interrelated approaches to explaining the suppression of sexuality.

1. "The civilising process"
2. The development of religious morality
3. The development of calculative rationality
4. The development of control over time and the body

(1) First, let us consider the work of Norbert Elias on *The Civilising Process* (Elias 1978). By analysis of aristocratic table manners and rules of etiquette in medieval times, Elias has sought to show that European societies were characterized by a civilizing process which develops more or less unilinearly, although occasionally subject to setback and reversal. As far as sexuality is concerned he maintains that "the feeling of shame surrounding human sexual relations has increased and changed considerably in the process of civilisation" (Elias 1978: 169). For example, in the Middle Ages, wedding guests were invited into the nuptial bed chamber to see the married couple undressed and laid together. Private books for use in the education of the children of nobility were quite explicit in their discussion of sexual matters. At this time, says Elias, the concealment and segregation of sexuality was relatively slight. Cleugh, in *Love Locked Out* (Cleugh 1963), tells us that the idea of obscenity, hitherto unknown in Europe, was born in the 15th century. By 1500, public nudity was also becoming unusual. We are told by Elias that only very gradually "does a stronger association of sexuality with shame and embarrassment and a corresponding restraint of behaviour spread more or less evenly over the whole of society" (Elias 1978: 179).

In the course of the civilizing process the sexual drive is subject to ever stricter control and transformation. The development of social *con*straint is matched by individual *re*straint in these matters. Pressure is placed on adults to privatize all their impulses, there is a conspiracy of silence when children are present; words dealing with sexual matters become emotionally charged and the monogamous marriage takes on the form of a social institution. Sexuality, which previously had taken a number of socially acceptable forms, such as chivalric love and knight-squire homosexuality, becomes confined more and more exclusively to a particular enclave—socially legitimized marriage—and takes place behind closed doors as an intimate and private affair.

However, it is disconcertingly easy, following Elias and Freud, to fall into a naive *teleology* in which the desexualization of labour, and life itself, are given some ultimate purpose connected to the rise of civilization or culture. Descriptions of the process may be informative but the process itself remains tantalizingly unexplicated. For teleology and causal explanation are not easy companions. We need to ask *why* shame, delicacy and self control should develop (Stone 1979).

(2) Here then it is necessary to analyse a second set of considerations, namely the religious and moral dimension and particularly the role of the Catholic Church. In early Catholicism, certain doctrinal beliefs had stressed that human sexual appetites were derived from the animal kingdom and were therefore base and unbecoming to mature adults. These beliefs received tremendous impetus and support from the Church as it became bureaucratized.

Many organization theorists, if pressed, might name the medieval church as the first historical example of a bureaucratic organization. In this context, one of the earliest writers on organization structure was the polymath (and suggestively named) Catholic bishop of Lincoln, Robert Grosseteste (Cleugh 1963; Kiel 1965). It is of more than passing interest that as a paleo-organization theorist of the 13th century, Grosseteste was very keen in his writings to stress the need to suppress sexuality in the monasteries and convents of his time. Sexual relations amongst the clergy were seen as part and parcel of the problem of the breakdown of social order. Rioting, drunkenness, lack of discipline, and sexual activity of various kinds were treated as synonymous in threatening both civil obedience and those church activities which were taking an organizational form. Grosseteste's diagnosis was not an idiosyncratic nor original one, however. For example, Damiani informed Pope Leo IX in 1070 of "the frightful excesses epidemically prevalent among the cloistered crowds of men, attributable to the unnatural restraints imposed upon the passions of those unfitted by nature or training to control themselves" (Cleugh 1963:

87). In the absence of self-control a large number of feast days and holidays were allowed in which drinking, rioting and sexual relations were seen as legitimate activities for clerics of both sexes to engage in. These were not, however, enough to stem the worries of the Catholic bishops and the new pope Gregory VII. For in these times, clerics took holy orders not for reasons of "a calling" but often because of familial pressures on them to leave home and reduce the level of the family's material needs. Thus, at this time membership in the clergy was often involuntary. Little wonder then that lewd behaviours spread from the streets *into* the monasteries and convents.

Faced with a recalcitrant membership, various solutions were attempted to stem the rising tide of indiscipline:

(a) Damiani and Gregory tightened up discipline in the monasteries by referring to the threat of Islam from the south and east. The militarization of large numbers of monks rapidly took place thereafter and various orders were set up and encouraged to cultivate male comradeship as a principle of organization (e.g., Hospitallers, Templars, and Teutonic Knights). This only succeeded in encouraging homosexuality of course, which was seen to require other repressive measures at a later date. As Christie Davies tells us (1982: 1032): "The growth of hostility toward homosexuality that followed the transformation of the Catholic Church into a centralized bureaucratic hierarchy of celibate priests from the later medieval period onward indicates the importance of strongly bound hierarchical organizations of this type as upholders of strong sexual taboos." Unlike Davies however, my point would be that the Catholic Church was in some senses the *creator* of these strong sexual taboos rather than their mere upholder. Since the maintenance of good order and discipline in organizational contexts may well depend upon the existence of sexual taboos and, if Elias and Cleugh are to be believed, these taboos did not exist in the wider society at this time, then the Catholic hierarchy would find it necessary to *create* such a set of sexual taboos. Seen in this light it is easy to appreciate the relevance of the second strand in Catholic management strategy of the period.

(b) There was a papal call for "real" celibacy to be practised by monks and nuns. The institutional day was to be filled with work and prayer, prayer and work. The copying of manuscripts, for example, which Robert Grosseteste was to advocate strongly, was a useful time filler. The same bishop also developed a series of tests for nuns before they took their final vows. They were to sleep naked with young monks to ensure that they could withstand a life of celibacy (Cleugh 1963: 95). Whilst the development of agapetism (nonsexual love) was an organizational principle clearly advocated by Grosseteste, it is sadly lacking from usual treatments of his contribution to organization theory (Kiel 1965).

(c) The use of coercive punishment in the form of castration for men and the scourge for those of both sexes who broke the rule of celibacy was an early favourite of the papal hierarchy. But far and away the most popular forms of repression were legal "Penitentials," which provided a somewhat less severe code of punishment for sexual activity. In a classic discussion, the Venerable Bede (672-735) gave much time and consideration to penitential punishments for sexual activity (Cleugh 1963: 275-77):

Simple fornication (with unmarried persons)
—monk: 1 year fasting on bread and water
—nun: 3-7 years fasting
Adultery (with married persons)
—monk/nun: 2-7 years bread and water
—Bishop: 12 years bread and water

25 paragraphs were devoted to the problems of masturbation which for some reason in Bede's time seemed particularly prevalent in church itself.

Masturbation (in church)
—lay people: 40 days fasting
—monks and nuns: 60 days psalm-singing

22 paragraphs are given over to sodomy and bestiality which ends with
—Bishop fornicating with cattle
(1st offence) 8 years fasting
(subsequent offences) 10 years fasting

From all this, it is clear to see that much time and effort was expended in eradicating sexuality as far as possible from the medieval Catholic Church. The widespread promulgation of desexualization was undertaken by the Catholic hierarchy in an attempt to emphasize good order and discipline in its membership as well as within its flock.

The development of more sophisticated attempts to repress sexuality in organizations at later points in time often involved religious ideas and appeals to a more rigid code of morality. Although very different from Catholicism doctrinally, the Quakers in particular (in the British context) were very keen to use religion and its precepts to suppress sexuality from a whole range of then existing organizational forms: the prison, the factory, the workhouse, the hospital and so on. The Society of Friends interested themselves in pacifism, the fight against slavery, and the advocacy of penal reforms, of universal education and of industrial welfare (Child 1964). To these ends great emphasis was put on avoiding waste and sloth and attaining efficiency and improved effort in the wide variety of organizations with which they became concerned. Elizabeth Fry's attempts at reforming prisons, Cadbury's and Rowntree's zeal for social welfare and worker education, and changes in nursing and hospital administration all came in some sense from Quaker ideology. Their interventions could be seen, at least in part, as resulting in the removal from productive and administrative areas of sexuality and sexual relations. They succeeded in using forces already in existence to remove the family from those organizations in which they intervened and to replace it with bureaucratic, professional structures. For example, Elizabeth Fry's disgust at Newgate Prison had the attenuated effect of removing the prisoner's family from the building. Once this was achieved prisons could be seen, not as a place where one was held before being punished, but as a place where one was punished (Ignatieff 1978). Overall, the Quakers saw the variety of organizations in which they interested themselves as sufficiently homogeneous to merit universal solutions; solutions which involved professionalization and bureaucratization and above all the development of *discipline*. In his analysis of despotic, disciplinary power Foucault (1977) sees all organizational forms as representing a unified power in the sense that "prisons resemble factories, schools, barracks, hospitals which all resemble prisons" (Fine 1979: 83). In each of these, discipline is based upon the perpetual observation and surveillance of its subjects without the surveyed being able to survey the surveyors. Within these organizations each individual becomes a "case" whose activities become minutely disciplined. Organizations function, therefore, as technical instruments of the rulers for disciplining the ruled—irrespective of their stated organizational goals. The "reforms" instituted by the Quakers and those of like mind did nothing save improve upon the level of technical efficiency in maintaining discipline in the institutions with which they concerned themselves.

(3) A third major type of explanation of the decline of sexuality in organizational settings, linked to the civilising process and bureaucratization, might revolve around the development of purposive rationality and its concrete expression in legal rational bureaucracies. The work of Reich and Marcuse is particularly relevant in this light (Reich 1962; Marcuse 1966; Robinson 1972). For Reich, the patriarchical family supported by the institution of monogamous marriage served as a "factory" for authoritarian ideologies and conservative structures. Legal rational

bureaucracies, particularly the state, had a simple direct relationship to sexual repression. They required a character structure in which sexuality was sublimated in the interests of calculative rationality. Marcuse greatly illuminates the process of desexualization by his work on the replacement of the pleasure principle by the reality principle (Freud 1948). Of course, he never believed that repression of sexuality could or should be abandoned entirely, even in a postcapitalist world. Marcuse's complaint was against *surplus* repression which operated in the interest of the "dominant classes" within the technocratic society. The necessity of "work" was never questioned by him but he argued that in the postrevolutionary society the *erotization of labour* would be possible—given a new division of labour and new organizational rationalities, particularly the rationality of gratification. Thus, erotized labour would look remarkably like *play* or *joy* (Agger 1979). In linking the alienation of labour with the suppression of libidinal freedom, Marcuse quite clearly adopts a political view of sexuality. Sexual relations become increasingly controlled within the specific mode of production we call capitalism since capitalists require the harnessing of human energy for production. But what Marcuse neglects is any consideration of the crucial other side of the politics of sexuality—namely, the economics of sexuality. Whilst the former may ask the question "*how* is it that labour becomes converted into labour power?" the latter inquires "*why* does labour become converted into labour power?" It is answering the economic question that one must look to the issues of valorization and the extraction of surplus value (Braverman 1974; Elger 1979).

Thus, whilst Freudianism in the Marxianized form advocated by Marcuse is of utility, a less Freudian tack is probably necessary when we are faced with the problem of why desexualization in the *capitalist labour process* takes place. A fourth type of theorizing in this attempt to find a political economy of sexuality might revolve around two related elements: (4a) control of time and (4b) control of the body.

(4a) *Control of time*. Many social historians have recognized the alternation in the pre-industrial workforce between intense periods of activity and long periods of inactivity. But this was not acceptable to early capitalists. As Hill has noted: "The Puritan horror of waste of time helped not only to concentrate effort, to focus attention on detail, but also to prepare for the rhythms of an industrial society, our society of the alarm clock and the factory whistle" (Hill 1964: 30). Similarly, Mumford's view that the key invention of the Industrial Revolution was a reliable clock (Mumford 1946) or the commodification of time to which E. P. Thompson and Sohn-Rethel point (Thompson 1968; Sohn-Rethel 1978) all indicate that time-wasting was inimical to efficient capital accumulation. Of course the time "spent" in domestic production in the family home at this period was not fully controllable by merchant capital. It was possible to spend time in long periods of leisure activity or in sexual play or in a bingelike consumption of manufactured goods and foodstuffs. The atomization, standardization and utilization of time, developing to serve the interests of improved capital accumulation, required that better control of production be developed and led to the decline of the putting-out system and the domestic mode of production (Marglin 1974). Although it was a long drawn-out process in Britain in particular (Littler 1982), once the workforce was out of the home and into the factory, tighter time discipline was possible. The time for sexual relations was very firmly seen as out of working hours. Sex had its place but not within the walls of the factory (Perkin 1969; Gaskell 1836; Factory Commission 1833; Weeks 1981). Surveillance, discipline and good order were not improved by sexual activity during work time, therefore much emphasis was put into their eradication. In the same way as the Catholic bishops externalized into both *time* and *space* problems of sexuality, drinking and riotous behaviour (into numerous feast days and outside the religious house), the early capitalist employers externalized the same problems (out of the factory and into the time allowed for rest and recuperation outside normal working hours).

(4b) *Control of the body.* According to Donzelot in *The Policing of Families* (1979), in the middle of the 18th century there developed "an economy of the body" to prevent its wasteful use. The economic theory of the Physiocrats that attempted to minimize waste was paralleled by 18th century medicine and the theory of fluids. Although predated by injunctions against "onanism" (Brake 1982), medical opinion of the time had it that masturbation "left the other humours weak and feeble"; the deterioration of muscular control we know as epilepsy was seen as the result of overloss of fluids which comes from overindulgence in sexual activity. For the employer then, it became possible on the best medical advice to attempt to minimize the sexual activity of his/her workforce. Puritan accountancy, which emphasized savings and discouraged consumption, thus found itself reflected in the balance sheet of the body. Coordinated muscular activity such as that expected of the industrial worker required good fluid retention and hence little sexual activity. In this light, one does not have to be a semiologist to appreciate that the "esprit de corps" so beloved by managers (Reddish 1975) may well have a double meaning!

In any event Foucault makes the point very well that by the early 19th century "the body is . . . directly involved in a political field; power relations have an immediate hold upon it; they invest it, mark it, train it, force it to carry out tasks, to perform ceremonies, to emit signs" (Foucault 1977: 27).

Because of this, sexuality is seen as of central importance in the disposition and utilization of power. Sex is conceptualized as the pivot of two axes along which bio-politics develops. One axis is the life of the body and control over it; the other axis is the life of the species and its regulation and domination. Thus, sexuality is the prime target for control. The control of sex becomes control of populations and control of individual bodies. Foucault does *not*, it should be noted, maintain that sexuality has become repressed. Instead of a "repressive hypothesis" he argues that "there was a steady proliferation of discourses concerned with sex . . . a discursive ferment that gathered momentum from the eighteenth century onward" (Foucault 1979: 18). There was analysis, stock-taking, classification and specification of sex derived from the growth of rationality. Moreover, in the 18th century sex became a police matter—in the full and strict sense. It became a matter for administration calling for management procedures (Foucault 1979: 18). As such, of course, it drew upon those institutions where administrative procedures were well developed: the state bureaucracy and its military arms. There was discourse on and action against four types of human subject—the hysterical woman, the masturbating child, the Malthusian couple and the perverse adult (Foucault 1979; Weeks 1981). Put simply, bio-power was taken from existing organizations and transplanted into a social setting which was becoming more organizational. The growth of asylums, prisons, schools, hospitals, and universities was founded upon the development of bio-power and control of the body and the population. And in turn this growth of bio-politics was fostered by the establishment of several of the "professions," and the proliferation of control institutions.

The links between these various institutions were really quite close in the 19th century and they remain so perhaps even today. The linkages, for example, between the early penitentiaries and the early factories are strong and clear. The present Japanese word for "labour turnover" has a clear translation as *escape*—a reflection perhaps of the difficulties encountered in leaving early 20th century Japanese factories. In their book, *The Prison Factory*, Melossi and Pavarini (1981) attempt to relate control strategies in prisons and factories to periods of labour shortages and surpluses (Dobash 1983). The method used for controlling workers was essentially that which was to hand and had been tried before—the *militarization of labour*. The method Trotsky was to use in the 1920s had been used much earlier in Italy, France, the U.K. and the U.S.A. (Gombin 1978). In France, for example, barracks housing was rapidly built from around 1850 in Paris and Lille. Within these edifices much effort was put into privatizing worker communal life. Rooms were designed in effect to be the "grave of the riot" (Donzelot 1979). In Japan too the factory dormitory was favoured as a means of retaining labour (Littler 1982), whilst another architectural solution to bad discipline and sexuality was Bentham's famous Panopticon. Prisoners or workers or inmates (for the Panopticon was amenable to the demands of all customers) would work and sleep in full view of a central observation tower. Sexual activity was minimized by use of solitary confinement. Self abuse was restricted by the use of controlled lighting which meant surreptitious activity was always in danger of discovery (Foucault 1977; Melossi and Pavarini 1981; Melossi 1979). In addition, the villages of Bourneville, Port Sunlight, Saltaire and others were monuments to the eradication of free time and private lives. The Quaker factory owners would not allow one waking moment of their workers to be spent in unproductive enjoyment. As late as 1933, Japanese textile workers were lucky to be allowed two rest days in each month. Ford's Sociological Department in the 1920s in Highland Park in Detroit kept a wary eye out for those who were unworthy of the $5 day. Unworthiness was marked of course by the escape attempts of the lower orders everywhere—namely sexual promiscuity, drunkenness and indiscipline (Beynon 1974; Cohen and Taylor 1976).

In all of these ways, serious attempts were made to create *total institutions* around the body of the worker where none had existed and where they had existed, to make more total the institutions of the prison, the workhouse and the factory. The body of the inmate and his or her time were controlled in great detail. And within total institutions, as Gilbert reminds us, "the line between public and private behaviour evaporates. While in civil society the individual can maintain a private life—even one that involves acts unacceptable to the mores of society safely and successfully, he [*sic*] cannot do so in total institutions" (Gilbert 1976: 87).

In the 19th century, a vast number of organizations in different institutional forms attempted to militarize their membership and become total institutions. Often, their command structures were taken from the military. However, had but they been aware of it, the managements of these institutions were using organizations as exemplars in which *resistance* to control was well developed by this stage. And it is to these forms of resistance, engendered by control strategies and dialectically intermeshed with them, that we now turn.

Resistance to Organizational Desexualization

Goffman's analysis of total institutions (Goffman 1968) demonstrates quite clearly that resistance to all forms of control is possible and is to be found, generally speaking, in the *underlife* of the institution. A small number of examples of underlife will suffice here.

(1) *The British Navy.* In Gilbert's eloquently titled paper "Buggery and the British Navy, 1700-1861" (1976) it is made quite clear that tremendous penalties existed and were used against those found guilty of engaging in homosexual relations on ships at sea. Whereas the Navy was relatively tolerant towards men who killed in a moment of passion (provided the dead man was not an officer), sodomy was not tolerated. It was seen as a threat to the structure of naval hierarchy and to good order and discipline (Gilbert 1976: 87). Yet sodomy took place, frequently. Montgomery Hyde (1970: 159) maintained that "to my knowledge, sodomy is a regular thing on ships that go on long cruises. In the warships, I would say that the sailor preferred it." Moreover, it is apparent that homosexual rape does not explain the major portion of cases tried by the Navy (Gilbert 1976: 97). In the majority of such cases the act was consensual. Thus while there were strong coercive penalties available for use against offenders, large numbers of the naval community engaged in consensual homosexual practices. In the total institution which is a ship at sea, the underlife contains large elements of sexual activity which the rule system is designed to eradicate.

(2) *The Nazi concentration camps.* Punishment for engaging in sexual relations within the wartime concentration camps was usually long and painful death. Male and female wings of the concentration camps were widely separated and it was dangerous to negotiate a path between them. Yet inmates did so and engaged in sexual activity thereafter. All in the face of starvation and death (Fenelon 1977; Keneally 1982: 241-46). Of course, there are those who argue that the prospect of death increases the sexual appetite. Bataille's *Death and Sensuality* (1962: 86) raises this point well that "sexuality has always been one mode of affirming life in the face of death."

(3) *Contemporary women's prisons.* Ward and Kassebaum's discussion of a women's prison (1965) devotes much attention to the issue of lesbian

relationships and the difficulties faced by those who engage in them. They say (1965: 99-100):

> One might wonder where and under what circumstances it is possible for inmates to engage in such intimate sexual activities. Staff surveillance and punitive sanctions are designed to discourage illicit meeting. Opportunities for intimacy are limited and usually require co-operation and silence of fellow inmates. . . . The usual practice is for the lovers to utilise a close friend or a trusted inmate to act as a lookout.

The authors asked staff of the institution how institutional homosexuality should be handled. Twenty-eight per cent called for improved control and stronger penalties for offenders whereas another 28 per cent required segregation and solitary confinement for those known to be lesbian. The advocacy of such methods clearly has strongly historical precedents.

(4) *Contemporary U.S. coal mines.* Vaught and Smith in their study of a coal mine (1980) maintain that this is a context in which "sexual themes and dramatic performances were enacted." Their argument focuses on the mechanical solidarity expressed in what they call *encapsulated enclaves.* As a notion these have much in common with Goffman's total institution, but one suspects they are more commonly found. The underlife of the colliery had a large sexual component with strong homosexual overtones. The arrival of women miners into the colliery after the passage of legislation on discrimination led to a severe disruption of normal sexual themes. Women were "initiated" into the workforce as men had been previously but such was the sexual component of the ceremonials that the women felt they had been sexually assaulted. On the one hand this appears to support the feminist position of harassment at work. On the other, it may reflect the miners' acceptance of women and co-operation with them in this particular setting. In actual fact, probably both facets are reflected in this case. In either event, the paper shows the centrality given to sexuality in encapsulated enclaves despite formal proscription by the organization.

In conclusion then, it seems that resistance is to be found where control over sexual relations would appear most developed. It was remarked by a contemporary of Grosseteste that "virginity is least kept where most constrained" and Cleugh reinforces this aspect of the underlife's desire for that which is expressly forbidden when he says "the fanaticism, real or pretended of the clerical hierarchy in its repression of sexual indulgence led directly to an unprecedented pre-occupation with such matters" (Cleugh 1963: 16). Thus, for Cleugh, "sexual continence enjoined by dogma or convention tends constantly to break down" and to result in outbreaks of the very activity one is desperate to eradicate. This is a clear expression of a dialectical perspective on sexuality and is reflective of a view that men and women in contemporary organizations continue to express the frustrations and gratifications connected with sexuality, despite the severe penalties for engaging in it, and despite other great difficulties.

Sexuality in the Contemporary Organization

The 1960s wave of permissiveness supposedly made sexual relationships in organizations less prone to surveillance and punishment. But the end of repression and the rise of permissiveness may have impacted the universities and colleges much more than commercial, industrial and custodial organizations. Within *these* kinds of organizations the pressures towards desexualization still exist.

At the present time, for example, many organizations separate men and women into geographically distinct areas, where their activities are monitored and surveilled throughout the working day (Kamata 1983). The processes of feminization and masculinization of occupations (Kanter 1977) have a spatial dimension too. In 1980, 45 per cent of women and 75 per cent of men worked in totally segregated jobs (I.F.F. Research Ltd. 1980). It was unnecessary to see or talk or interact with a member of the opposite sex in their working lives. Also, many contemporary organizations impose real not hypothetical penalties on sexual offenders. Moreover, many men and women live in total institutions where the deprivation of comfort and heterosexual relations is enshrined as an organizational goal. Though less severe, encapsulated enclaves are also well distributed in contemporary industrial societies. Between them, these features of geographical separation, punishments for miscreants and enclaving of activities all suggest that "permissiveness" is not of universal validity as a description of modern organizational practices.

Yet, within many contemporary organizations one suspects that much activity of a sexual nature takes place. If we are going to comprehend and analyse such behaviour we must first recognize in our theorizing that it exists. A key to understanding lies in the probability that sexual relations do not take place uniformly in time and space. There are organizational *locales* for sexual activity such as "behind the bike shed" and there are organizational *episodes* conventionally allotted for heightened sexual activity such as the "Christmas party." As Giddens (1981) has recently maintained, we may learn much from the time-space movements of individuals. Investigation of locales and episodes in the sexual underlife of the organization is probably a useful starting point for any full analysis of this issue.

Then, we must appreciate that some activity involves control and power, violence and sadism, oppression and harassment. It is no use thinking that all sexual activity represents resistance to control. This is to overromanticize sexuality beyond all recognition. Homosexual rape and the sexual harassment of women by men are examples of sexual activities that take place in organizational contexts and which are extremely difficult to conceptualize as subordinate expressions of resistance to imposed control mechanisms. On the other hand, there are examples of sexual relations taking place, in the face of the suppression and oppression of subordinate organizational members which are clear expressions of human feelings of love and affection. We should also be aware that in some exceptional circumstances sexual feelings may be utilized rather than suppressed by management to attain higher levels of efficiency in their workforces (Geraghty 1981: 4). Overall, we may surmise that many contemporary organizations contain a variety of sexual dimensions involving control *and* resistance. In the majority of cases, it will be difficult analytically to separate control *from* resistance. Most sex acts involve both dimensions in a dialectical interrelationship. Sexuality is nothing if not complicated—but that is no excuse for ignoring it.

Conclusion

The focus of this paper has been on the process of organizational desexualization, which has taken place over a long historical period and upon the resistance that this process engenders amongst organizational subordinates. It is difficult to know precisely why this process has been supported by organizational decision makers. One suspects the reasoning is complex, variable and differs over time. For some, the de-emphasis on sexuality may have sprung from a moral stance which advocated the enticement of rough peasant stock away from the "natural crudities" of rural existence and towards a more civilised life style. Added to this, the legitimation for desexualization offered by many religious beliefs was based upon a rejection of the "baser animal instincts" within human beings. In later periods, the development of a Puritan calculative rationality emphasized a view that sexuality was expressive of nonrational, uncontrollable emotions which must be suppressed in the interests of efficiency and good order. Finally, under capitalism, desexualization is encouraged because both time and the human body become commodified and therefore exploitable. Sexuality and labour power are not compatible. Indeed, they may well be antithetical. Sexual relations are wasteful, in terms of commodity production, of both the body and of time (Rubenstein 1978).

Notice here, that organizational superordinates—top decision makers—are not themselves totally immune from the effect of desexualisation. For example, critics of the "dominant ideology thesis" have maintained that such ideologies are first and foremost for ruling class consumption and are not specifically directed at the workforce as control attempts (Abercrombie et al. 1982). Meaghan Morris, following Foucault, tells us that as far as sexual controls are specifically concerned, "The most rigorous techniques were formed and applied most intensely first of all in the economically privileged and politically dominant classes" (Morris 1982: 269). Although this argument is probably overstated it is fair, nevertheless, to say that organizational managements may be controlled by ideologies over which they themselves have no control. To see top bureaucrats exclusively as controllers and never as the controlled is to miss a factor of some importance in the control-resistance debate. In addition by defining sexuality as a problem which requires strategic choices to be made about how it will be suppressed and eradicated, it becomes possible to conceive that "bad" choices will be made. If any area is seen as problematic requiring decisions to be made, this area, by definition, then becomes vulnerable to achieving the status of *more* rather than less of a problem. Sexuality as an issue may be exacerbated rather than solved by particular and specific managerial decisions. Moreover, to begin to see the labourer's sexual relations as problematic is to become vulnerable in that moment to subordinate sexuality. By recognizing the latent power of labour as a problem, the ruling classes make this power more manifest. It is an interesting contradiction then, that in attempting to control another, one ends up by resisting oneself. And in attempting to resist another, one ends up by controlling oneself (Lazonick 1979).

For these reasons, I do not subscribe to a "conspiracy theory" that effectively attributes omniscience to the propertied classes in developing an approach to the suppression of sexuality for consumption solely by their workforces. On the other hand, however, desexualisation has not persisted and continued to spread simply because it is useful and functional. Human beings have to reproduce their day to day lives within structures of power. Functionality is no guarantee of survival. Only human agency can provide that (Giddens 1979). Thus desexualization is to be found not simply because it has functional aspects for capitalist production but also because it is conceptualized and pursued as a more or less conscious strategy by representatives of capital. In other words both function and *agency* need to be considered when looking at control and resistance (Smith 1983).

Finally, let us return to Chatov's (1981) survey with which we began. If it is accurate, it appears to raise questions about Foucault's view that there has been tremendous growth over the last hundred years in discourses concerning sexuality. One would expect that the "incitement to discourse" about sexuality, linked as it is in Foucault's writing to the bourgeoisie's development of its own sexuality from the mid-19th century on (Foucault 1977), would be well reflected in theorizing about the capitalist enterprise and its functionaries. In other words one would expect that organization theory would be redolent with bio-politics. As a form of discourse relevant to the bureaucracy in a capitalist society, organizational analysis should contain (if Foucault is correct) not a repression of sexuality but its stocktaking, calculation and assessment. A proliferation of discourse on sexual relations is what one would expect to find in the academic literature on organizational life.

But one does not. One finds an absence of discourse; a yawning void of disincitement to discourse. One finds that sexuality is repressed. But why should this be the case? Is it that as "servants of power," the control of our time, our bodies and our discourse has reached a stage that desexualization in our writing has occurred without our noticing? Why have we ignored what novelists and playwrights and organizational members know only too well—that sexuality is a major driving force behind human endeavour? It is the lack of resistance to desexualization and the need to eroticize our academic labour which have struck me as key features of the myopia of the contemporary sociology of organizations and perhaps of social science as a whole. But what a nonmyopic (and one suspects a male-dominated) eroticized sociology would look like and how it would relate to feminist scholarship remains, to say the least, a considerable problem. Nevertheless, one can only hope that it is a problem to which we, as organizational analysts, will soon turn.

Note

1. I wish to acknowledge the helpful comments and criticism received from friends and colleagues in the University of Lancaster, particularly a staff seminar group in the Department of Sociology, David Smith from Social Administration and all those in the Department of Behaviour in Organizations. Finally, comments received from the *Organization Studies* reviewers on an earlier draft of this paper were of particular value.

5

Organization, Gender, and Culture

ALBERT J. MILLS

This paper pursues the argument that gender is a crucial, yet neglected, aspect of organizational analysis, and puts a case that organizational culture provides a critical, but undeveloped, focus for the analysis of gender considerations. In developing this argument, a materialist, but woman-centered approach is proposed as an alternative to existing, functionalist and interpretive, accounts of organizational culture.

Concern with gender is a central aspect of social life (Barrett 1980) and yet it has been seriously "neglected" in analyses of organization (Hearn and Parkin 1983). Given that so much time is expended in defining and refining sexual differences and their consequences it is remarkable that this is ignored when it comes to organizational analysis. Very few studies have sought to analyse the relationship of gender to organizational behaviour (e.g., Wolff 1977). Instead, the practice has been to reflect, rather than

AUTHOR'S NOTE: This chapter originally appeared in A. J. Mills (1988) "Organization, Gender and Culture," *Organization Studies* 9:351-69; reprinted by permission of *Organization Studies*.

consciously address, processes of gender differentiation: a variety of organizational studies have been pursued from a male oriented perspective which at best treats aspects of organizational behaviour as typifying men and women alike (e.g., the Hawthorne studies) and, at worst, treat women as periphery to organizational life (e.g., Blauner's [1967] study of alienation). The ignoring and marginalization of gender, although not limited to any particular approach within organizational analysis, is inexcusable in the face of a growing concern with the experiential aspects of organizations, particularly in regard to the current interest in organizational culture.

The case for linking gender and culture in analysis of organization is a compelling one. The argument has long been made that gender is culturally determined. Oakley (1972), for example, distinguishes between sex and gender, arguing that sex refers to basic physiological differences between men and women while gender refers to culturally specific patterns of behaviour which may be attached to the sexes. In other words, gender refers to a set of assumptions about the nature and character of the biological differences between males and females; assumptions that are manifest in a number of ideas and practices which have a determinant influence upon the identity, social opportunities, and life experiences of human actors. They are assumptions, however, that have tended to be developed and refined in contexts dominated by males and, hence, have been disadvantageous to females. Male dominance in practice has been maintained and developed through a system of ideas, reflecting "asymmetrical cultural evaluations of male and female" (Rosaldo 1974). A central characteristic of this process, across various societies, has been an association of female with "domestic" and male with "public" spheres of responsibility. In modern society the "public" domain is very much an organizational domain. Organizations are ubiquitous, confronting us as "cultural forms" (Smircich 1983a), not only as manifestations of social values—what Denhardt (1981) calls the "ethic of organization"—but also as transformers (Weber 1967) and generators (Deal and Kennedy 1982) of cultural phenomena. Complex organization bears on gender discrimination in at least three vital ways: (1) cultural values associated with maleness are favoured characteristics of many organizations (Morgan 1986); the assumed distinctiveness of males and females according to respective traits of reason and emotion is often mirrored in organizational processes which emphasize rationality and bureaucracy while seeking to suppress emotions associated with home and family (Burrell 1984); (2) certain organizations play a direct part in the socializing processes in which people acquire gender identities, e.g., schools (Deem 1978), sports

(Clarke and Lawson 1985), and state activities (Land 1976); and (3) organizational practices, e.g., recruitment (Barron and Norris 1976), induction (Dubeck 1979), and promotion (Broverman et al. 1972), more often than not, conform to and extend sex-biased values. Hence, I would argue, sexual discrimination is not only evidenced in a number of overt organizational practices but, more significantly, is embedded in cultural values that permeate both organizations and the concept of organization itself.

Interest in gender (Clegg and Dunkerley 1980; Ferguson 1984) and, more specifically, in its relationship to the cultures of organizations (Riley 1983; Crompton and Jones 1984; Smircich 1985a) has only recently emerged within organizational analysis; raising critical questions not only about the focus of enquiry but of its epistemological basis (Glennon 1983; Burrell 1984). Feminist critiques of organizational analysis have begun the important first steps of highlighting and detailing the problems of sexist or gender-blind analysis within studies of organization. Moving beyond that point, Hearn and Parkin (1983) argue for an approach that

> take[s] the doubly difficult step of linking the non-organizational division of labour and the organizational division of labour and then linking these two structures to the development of internal organizational dynamics. (Hearn and Parkin 1983: 228)

This paper, while agreeing with Hearn and Parkin on the level of analysis required, identifies a *materialist* approach as the appropriate method of analysis. It is argued that a materialist account of organizational reality provides the potential for bridging the structure-agency divide that has dogged the organizational culture debate. In developing a materialist approach to organization, gender and culture strategic use is made of Stewart Clegg's (1981) concept of "rules" as a framework for discussion.

The paper proceeds through discussion and critique of studies of gender and of culture within organizational analysis to the case for a materialist approach and the application of that approach to an analysis of culture and gender.

Gender Neglect Within Organizational Studies: Some Implications

Classic, no less than other, studies of organization provide examples of the way gender considerations have been ignored and the implications of that for the development of organizational analysis. The Hawthorne studies are a case in point; key areas of research involved study of a group of females ("test room") and a group of males ("bank wiring room") and, despite the fact that output was increased by the women and restricted by the men, the overall findings were presented as an explanation of the behaviour of employees per se. An almost identical problem is evidenced in the work of French and his colleagues on the effects of "participation." The idea that employee participation in decision making could be an important factor in the altering of work practices (Coch and French 1948) has had a considerable impact upon the field of organizational behaviour despite the fact that the original results were not replicated in a subsequent study (French et al. 1960). The fact that the original study was based on female workers while the replication study was based on male workers was not taken into account: unlike the females the male subjects were less willing to accept the legitimacy participation schemes, were more attached to group norms of restricted output and, as a result, working practices were not "improved." The error in studies of this kind is an ignorance of the fact that gender may be a critical dynamic in the outcomes detailed. Acker and Van Houten (1974), for example, suggest that "sex power differentials" may be an important factor in accounting for differences in outcomes between groups; pointing out that while the male group at the Hawthorne Works was observed under normal working conditions the female group was pressured, by male supervisors, into an experimental situation.

Where organizational studies have taken gender into account more often than not it has been done in a way that has limited its impact to non-organizational considerations. Blauner's (1967) study of "alienation" takes such an approach. Here men's statements of dissatisfaction are recorded as valid expressions of alienation from their working conditions. Women's discontent, on the other hand, is explained by reference to their "weaker physical stamina" and "family commitments." Feldberg and Glenn (1979) refer to this as a "job model" versus a "gender model" of explanation; with men's activities being interpreted as primarily *job* related and women's as being primarily related to their *gender* (in the biologically reductionist sense).

The widespread "neglect" of gender issues within organizational analysis has been reviewed by Hearn and Parkin (1983). *Functionalist* treatments of gender, they argue, have provided mainstream organization theory with a set of background assumptions about men and women, accepting gender divisions as a given or as functionally necessary. Moving on to *interpretive* accounts Hearn and Parkin argue that while a focus upon subjectivity offers potentially useful insights into gender divisions it is a potential that has not been realized due to a "telling it like it is" type of methodological approach. As a result gender distributions have, at best, been taken-for-granted and, at worst, recorded through men's accounts of reality. In any event interpretive accounts have failed to come to terms with the problem that reality is "negotiated" or mediated between actors of unequal power—with females disproportionately occupying the weaker negotiating positions.

Accepting Burrell and Morgan's (1979) division of radicalism into two separate paradigms, Hearn and Parkin go on to an analysis of *radical structuralism.* This approach, it is argued, places class struggle first and concern for the position of women second, on the assumption that liberation of the sexes will follow class liberation. Focusing upon contradictions within the economic structures of capitalism, change is envisioned as being effected by those located centrally within those contradictions, i.e., the producers of surplus value, the proletariat. As these are identified as being largely male workers, women are perceived as being peripheral to the class system. *Radical humanism* is an "anti-organization" theory, concerned with actors' subjective definitions of reality within contexts of structures of power and domination. Concern is with "discovering how humans can link thought and action (praxis) as a means of transcending their alienation" (Morgan 1980: 609). It is an approach which involves "a wholesale critique of work, the work experience and the work ethic, and a striving to both understand and change the conditions of work": as such, "much of this critique of work can readily be reinterpreted in terms of men" (Hearn and Parkin 1983: 226); i.e., organizations, in the way they are understood, reflect male thinking and purpose that have implications not only for less powerful men but also for women. Despite recognition that it, in common with the other three paradigms, is "constructed . . . in universalist terms," Hearn and Parkin (1983: 226) see clear links between radical humanism and feminist critique. The similarity, they argue, is in the radical challenge that both pose to the resolving of social problems by way of a destructuring of organizations and their replacement with "small scale, alternative forms of organizing" (Hearn and Parkin 1983: 226). But, they add, there is a need to go beyond changing perceptions and experience of work to a restructuring of the sexual division of labour itself. In this comprehensive review Hearn and Parkin make a powerful case for a woman-centered approach to organizational analysis, arguing that gender is a central and inter-related aspect of social and organizational life.

Organizational Culture and the Analysis of Gender: Strengths and Limitations

Analysis of the current concern with the qualitative and symbolic aspects of organizational life suggests that "organizational culture" provides a potentially useful concept for the analysis of gender in that it enables account to be made of societal-organizational inter-relationships. The debate, albeit in a fragmentary fashion, draws our attention to the following crucial factors:

(1) The relationship between societal values and organizational behaviour, as witnessed in the contribution of comparative management approaches in renewing interest in the association between organizational behaviour and cultural milieu (Ouchi 1981; Pascale and Athos 1982). The point is made that people do not leave their cultural perspective at the gates of organizations, they enter with them, and that this has an important bearing upon organizational perspectives.

(2) The importance of powerful actors in the development of value systems. The corporate culture approach, for example, focuses our attention on the role of leaders in the development of organizational life (Allen and Kraft 1982; Peters and Waterman 1982; Bryman 1984; Davis 1984). The aim and general purpose of an organization and their translation and enactment by its leaders will have a determinate effect upon the way things are done, how the organization is experienced by its members and the resulting development of an organization culture (Child 1972; Pettigrew 1979; Schein 1984).

(3) The significance of organization as subjective experience (Martin et al. 1983; Turner 1983; Smircich 1983b). A major contribution to this aspect has come from interpretive accounts and their focus upon the role of "understanding" and "meaning" in the comprehension of any given situation. This focus is on how, through interaction, "a sense of organization" is created and maintained and how common interpretations of situations are achieved so that co-ordinated action is possible. Interpretive accounts of organizational culture are important in drawing our attention to the importance of organizational situations in shaping people's understandings and hence expectations of key aspects of social life.

What the debate fails to do is provide an adequate theory of culture or to locate gender considerations within its concerns. Functionalist (i.e., corporate culture and comparative management) accounts view culture as something that enters the organization by way of its members or as something that is generated within the organization. What is lacking is an adequate synthesis relating organizational with other aspects of social experience in a comprehensive notion of culture. It is a task that interpretive approaches have failed to address. Focusing primarily upon the processes of organizational sense-making these approaches tend to stress the internal "rather than to look to the external, societal, cultural context within which organizations are embedded" (Jelineck et al. 1983: 338). Interpretive accounts fail to locate human ideas in material practice. Dimensions of power, including organizational position, are principally contained within psychological explanations. Largely ignoring questions of the role of "managed understandings" in the prevention of radical change, interpretive approaches unite with functionalist accounts in a focus upon explanations of social harmony (Burrell and Morgan 1979).

The absence of gender concerns from the organizational culture debate leaves a number of important factors out of account, a number of questions unasked. Firstly, social understandings of gender, as with other sets of cultural values and expectations, are not left outside the gates of organizational reality. They very definitely enter. What impact does this have upon the structuring and operation of organizations and how, in turn, does this impact upon gender? Do specific contexts impact differently upon organizations? Do organizations differently "receive" and "mediate" gender understandings? Secondly, given that powerful organizational actors are overwhelmingly males, to what extent do values of masculinity permeate understandings of organizational reality, its purposes and structure? Thirdly, given that understandings of reality are shaped by and within organizations, to what extent do organizational processes maintain and develop a person's gender identity?

A variety of other questions can be posed but the important starting point, revealed by this debate, is that gender discrimination, far from being obvious and overt, is embedded, more-or-less unconsciously, in the processes that make up an organization's culture. In exploring those issues, a feminist materialist approach, in contrast to functionalist and interpretive accounts, provides the methodological sophistication necessary for a conceptualization of culture as a process in which organizations and society, structure and action exist in dialectical relationship.

The Materialist Alternative

Materialist accounts of organizational reality provide the potential for bridging the structure-agency divide. That potential lies in the development and refinement of critical epistemological ("dialectical materialism") and methodological ("historical materialism") tools of analysis (Benson 1977).

The concept of *dialectical materialism* addresses the problem of subject-object divide through an insistence upon the relationship between ideas and material practice. The human condition, for Marx and Engels, consists of essential physiological needs but an absence of a priori factors of cognition. It is through efforts to fulfill those needs that human beings develop ideas. In reproducing themselves materially human beings produce ideas about themselves. But this does not occur in isolation. Material and social conditions have a determinate effect upon the development of ideas. Human beings have the ability to develop and transcend existing ideas of self and of society but that ability is linked in its potential to the material situation and social status of the persons involved.

Through the method of *historical materialism* various materialist accounts have attempted to explain the development of certain ideas and social relations through analysis of their specific socio-economic contexts. Accounts have tended to focus upon material conditions ("forces of production") and class relations ("relations of production") but, as feminist materialists have argued, gender concerns can also be shown to have played a crucial role in the development of knowledge.

In recent years a number of feminists have argued the appropriateness of Marxist methodology for analysis of gender concerns (McDonough and Harrison 1978; Barrett 1980; O'Brien 1981). *The German Ideology* is a useful but relatively unexplored example of how Marxist methodological analysis may be used to further research into feminist concerns. The significance of the work lies not only in its importance as a theory of knowledge but also in its attempt, albeit unevenly, to locate gender alongside class within its analysis. In *The German Ideology* Marx and Engels argue that human understanding was initially limited by primitive means of production, restricting time and energy and the ability to develop more than rudimentary ideas. Within this primitive context those able and willing to exploit physical and psychological advantages played a key role in dominating not only social relations but the way those relations were to be regarded and perceived. The "exploitation" by some of the "surplus labour" of others led to new fetters on human cognition in the form of class relations. Those who came to own the "means of production" were to have a powerful influence upon the way actors' understanding of social reality developed: "The ideas of the ruling class are in every epoch the ruling ideas, i.e., the class which is the ruling material force of society is at the same its ruling intellectual force" (Marx and Engels 1976: 59).

Marx and Engels go on to theorise that ideas also developed in the context of gendered relations. Predating class relations the sexual division of labour in the form of family relations is seen as having developed "spontaneously or 'naturally' by virtue of natural predispositions (e.g., physical strength), needs, accidents, etc, etc" (Marx and Engels 1976: 32-33). In other words, female oppression is viewed as arising out of the ability of males to exploit relative biological strengths (the capacity of men to dominate and protect) and disabilities (female pregnancy). Male dominance over females, established in family groups, is strengthened and solidified as other layers of social organization are built out of such elementary relations:

> The division of labour in which [social] contradictions are implicit, and which in its turn is based on the natural division of labour in the family and the separation of society into individual families opposed to one another, simultaneously implies the distribution, and indeed the unequal distribution, both quantitative and qualitative, of labour and its products, hence property, the nucleus, the first form of which lies in the family, where wife and children are the slaves of the husband. This latent slavery in the family . . . is the first form of property, . . . [and] corresponds perfectly to the definition of modern economists, who call it the power of disposing of the labour-power of others. (Marx and Engels 1976: 46)

Marx and Engels, in this lengthy passage, are clearly suggesting that prior to the development of class divisions there existed sexual divisions based on male dominance. They go on to argue that the elementary stage of the division of labour was but an "extension of the natural division of labour existing in the family" and that the social structure was, therefore, "limited to an extension of the family, patriarchal chieftains, below them the members of the tribe, finally slaves" (Marx and Engels 1976: 33). In other words, the forms of production and organization that developed within a particular social formation came to reflect the earlier development of sexual divisions.

The German Ideology, while contentious in its specifics, provides in outline a useful *method* of analysis that directs our attention to material conditions and the dominance of powerful actors (males/owners) in explanation of the character and development of knowledge. As organizational forms developed they provided an "otherworld" view and reinforcement of existing values and beliefs about the sexual division of labour. As social relations arose out of and around family ties the subordination of women was compounded by a relative inability to play a full part in those societal activities:

> The fact that, in most industrial societies, a good part of a woman's adult life is spent giving birth to and raising children leads to a differentiation of domestic and public spheres of activity that can . . . be shown to shape a number of relevant aspects of human social structure and psychology. (Rosaldo 1974: 23)

Wider social relations and their attendant social attitudes and beliefs became identified as the "cultural" aspects of society, while family relationships became identified as "domestic" factors of human existence:

> The opposition does not determine cultural stereotypes or asymmetries in the evaluations of the sexes, but rather underlies them, to support a very general (and, for women, often demeaning) identification of women with domestic life and of men with public life. (Rosaldo 1974: 23-24)

This results in a situation where men become "the locus of cultural value": "Male, as opposed to female, activities are always recognised as predominantly important, and cultural systems give authority and value to the roles and activities of men" (Rosaldo 1974: 19).

It is a process which finds expression in the development of personality. Drawing upon Chodorow's thesis that family socialization processes prepare and shape the personalities of males and females differently, Rosaldo argues that

> girls are most likely to form ties with female kin who are their seniors; they are integrated vertically, through ties with particular people, into the adult world of work. This contrasts with young boys who, having few responsibilities in late childhood, may create horizontal and often competitive peer groups, which cross-cut domestic units and establish "public" and overarching ties. (1974: 25)

Thus,

> growing up in a family, the young girl probably has more experience of others as individuals than as occupants of formal institutionalized roles; so

> she learns how to pursue her own interests, by appeals to other people, by being nurturent, responsive, and kind. . . . Boys, in contrast, are apt to know manhood as an abstract set of rights and duties, to learn that status brings formal authority, and to act in terms of formal roles. (Rosaldo 1974: 26)

These developments in fundamental gender personality differences have greatly influenced the "public sphere." Over time an historical process of "organizational desexualization" has created an increasingly nonexpressive, rational, emotionally controlled organizational world (Burrell 1984). Sexual expressions have been expelled from organizational life as pressure is placed on people to "privatize" all their impulses. Family ties have been severed from organizations and replaced with bureaucratic, professional structures. Organizational goals and purposes have taken precedence over personal drives. In turn, this expunging of emotionality from organizational life has strengthened the process in which men become associated (in location) with rationality/instrumentality and women with emotionality/expressiveness. Locale and personality become indistinguishable. The development of gendered relationships and personalities have become rooted in a process in which simple biological differences and social interactions are given a certain form or character and are strengthened in a context of economic reproduction (Alexander 1976). Class and gender, although autonomous, have become "overdetermined" (Althusser 1971) in their relationship (Hartmann 1976; McDonough and Harrison 1978). Hence,

> the oppression or subordination of women in contemporary societies is neither simply an offshoot of the development of capitalism, nor to be understood independently of it. The dismantling of sexual divisions would depend . . . on struggles both to transform the social relations of production and to construct radically new relations between women and men. (Bilton et al. 1983: 374)

Feminist Materialism and Organizational Analysis

In applying this (feminist materialist) perspective to an understanding of organizational life the following features are suggested. Firstly, organizational life exists in a dialectical relationship to the broader societal value system, each is shaped and reshaped by the other. Secondly, those occupying key locations within the "relations of production" (i.e., owners of the means of production and their agents) play a dominant role in determining how reality is perceived. This has a crucial impact upon both organizational reality and social life in general. Thirdly, the sexual division of labour, while heavily dominated by a class structured "public" domain of social life, nonetheless retains a significant level of autonomy and, as such, "overdetermines" as well as being "overdetermined" by class. Fourthly, ideas are never simply passively received. Ideas reflect material conditions and those that predominate over them. But material conditions change, they are never always straightforward, they are often contradictory. As a result alternative views of reality arise to challenge existing and dominant views. Ideas change.

Culture is essentially composed of a number of understandings and expectations that assist people in making sense of life. In organizations, no less than other aspects of social life, such understandings have to be learned and they guide people in the appropriate or relevant behaviour, help them to know how things are done, what is expected of them, how to achieve certain things, etc. Indeed, it is the very configuration of such "rules" of behaviour that distinguishes one social or organizational group from another, it is an essential part of their cultural identity. Clegg (1981), although not specifically concerned with organizational culture, provides a useful scheme for the analysis of organizational life by way of a focus upon rules:

> Control in organizations is achieved through what may be termed "rules." These rules are not necessarily formally defined by members of the organization, although they may be. They do not depend on the members' cognizance of them for their analytic utility. "Rules" is meant merely as a term by which one can formulate the structure underlying the apparent surface of organizational life. (Clegg 1981: 545)

The usefulness of the approach is that it is able to deal with the macro and micro aspects of organization simultaneously. At the macro level organizations are located in a dialectical relationship with wider societal concerns (Figure 5.1). Clegg makes it quite clear that organizations exist within/are integrally part of a broad social framework and that within that overall context a variety of rules of behaviour develop which influence and are mediated by organizations in different ways depending upon their character and location within the class structure.

In regard to the micro level, Clegg argues that we are taught, implicitly and explicitly, distinct ways of behaving, with attendant beliefs, values and understandings. In a capitalist society these rules largely control behaviour, confronting people in different ways and, in their different configurations, compose different organizations in different ways.

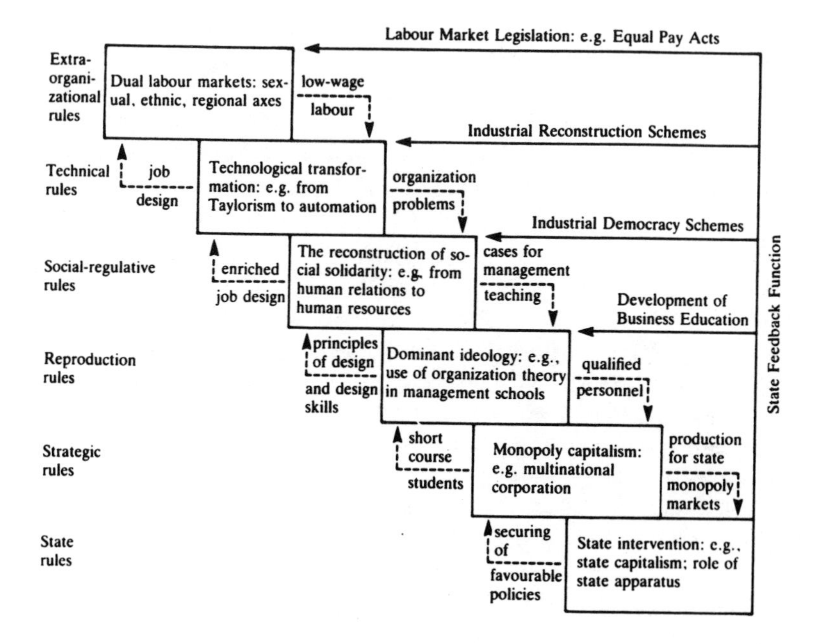

Figure 5.1.

SOURCE: Adapted from Clegg (1981: 553).
NOTE: The figure is a diagonal matrix. The stepped series represents the intersection of types of rules and levels of class structure in the organization. Hatched lines represent the articulation between levels while the solid lines represent the effect of the state.

Clegg's concern to identify the mediation of class through a number of intersecting rules is adaptable, by way of an Althusserian notion of the autonomous yet "overdetermined" relationship of class and gender, to a gender perspective. In this way, it is argued, gender permeates not only extra-organizational rules, as Clegg suggests, but each and every area of rule behaviour.

"Extra-organizational rules" refer to social rules of behaviour which are reflected/reinforced within organizations. They take a number of overt (low pay and authority status) and covert (images of domesticity and sexuality) forms that serve to constrain female opportunity, not only within, but in access and recruitment to, organizations. Male domination of the organizational world, in the form of ownership and control (Bilton et al. 1983), is reinforced and maintained by a cultural system which associates women with "domestic" life—characterising them as "emotional, passionate, and intuitive, yet illogical and fickle," and which associates men with "public" life—characterising them as "rational: analytical and productive but also insensitive and impersonal" (Glennon 1983: 262).

This set of values has played a key part in restricting the entry of women into the labour force (Wolpe 1978); of filtering female entrants into a narrow range of occupations (Barron and Norris 1976) that tend to mirror assumed domestic roles of carers (e.g., nurses), cleaners (e.g., domestics), and food preparers (e.g., canteen assistants); and in attaching low pay and low authority status to the work done by women (Bilton et al. 1983). Notions of female domesticity and sexuality influence the ability of females to enter and prosper within organizations. Dubeck (1979) provides an example of how this operates at the level of organizational culture when it comes to the recruitment and promotion of women to managerial positions. Studying the recruitment of college graduates to industrial management positions in a mid-western manufacturing concern in the U.S., Dubeck observed that the (all male) recruiters, when faced with a male candidate, attempted to ascertain whether the person was "qualified" for the job but were more concerned with "interest in the job" when faced with a female candidate. In this latter case the recruiters' questions and comments centered upon whether the female recruit was "career orientated" and whether she would leave once married. When it came to consideration of qualifications women were judged by much narrower criteria than men. Men not holding a particular degree were made allowances for if it was felt that they would "fit in." That ability to "fit in" was a judgement that recruiters felt less certain about when evaluating females. Dubeck further observed that this recruitment process served to hinder the promotability of successful female candidates. "Leadership experience," for instance, was a factor emphasized in the recruitment of males but not females and, as this quality was perceived as an asset in promotion, its assumed absence in females restricted their ability to move up the organizational hierarchy.

Sexuality is also an important aspect of the cultural milieu of many organizations. It has many facets and can influence entry and expulsion from organizations. "Sexual attractiveness" for instance, is often utilised to influence or stress power within organizations. Certain powerful male organization members may use "attractiveness" as a criteria in the employment of female subordinates and as a symbol of organizational success (Quinn 1977), and sexual harassment as a direct means of emphasizing power over female employees. Nonetheless, sexuality can also be perceived, by managers, as a threat to the organization and often strenuous efforts are made to inhibit the development of "sexual" (Burrell 1984) or "romantic" (Quinn 1977) relationships. Given that a large percentage of romantic affairs involve higher-placed males with lower placed females it is usually the female that is disciplined (Quinn 1977). Regardless of the position occupied by those involved, many organizations are concerned to keep organizational life free of romantic and domestic incursions. Some organizations prohibit liaisons and even marriages between employees. At the British Broadcasting Corporation, for example, the marriage of a leading television presenter to her director invoked "off-screen" tensions within the organization (Leapman 1986). Implicit understandings about a need for separating domestic affairs from organizational life were channelled through expressions about the maintenance of "professional relationships." A BBC rule prohibiting married couples from working together, although not strictly enforced, was used as a way of legitimizing complaints to the director of programmes. Complaints concerning the director centered on his ability to remain objective in his dealings with his wife and in the allocation of resources to her show. As she was a highly successful presenter of one of the organization's top ten programmes he was forced to resign. Complaints concerning the presenter involved the fact that she brought her new baby, and accompanying nanny, into work with her; periodically retiring to breastfeed the child. She came under severe pressure to divorce her domestic life from her working life.

Sexuality is also controlled through language (e.g., "the *girls* in the office," "the dragon lady") and initiation ceremonies (Hearn and Parkin 1987).

"Technical rules" are implicit within production techniques and are often inherently sexist. Assumptions about the nature of men and women have been incorporated into the very design of jobs. Physical strength, aptitudes, danger, and stamina, alongside implicit reference to the "primary domestic responsibility" of women are drawn upon to either exclude women from certain tasks or to undervalue the work that they are involved in:

> It can be seen that the market factors and ideological factors leading to women's segregation in the labour force meet in the systematic undervaluation of "women's work." Qualities such as close concentration, accuracy and manual dexterity which require obvious skill and training in craft

> or technician's jobs are relegated to "natural" and untrained "aptitudes" in women doing women's occupations. (Pollert 1981: 65)

Technical rules, as Pollert (1981) suggests, are often supported by state, reproductive and strategic rules.

"State rules" intervene in the process directly (e.g., legislation prohibiting women from certain types of work [Bilton et al. 1983]) and indirectly (e.g., the "education" of girls into limited occupational expectations [Wolpe 1978]).

"Reproduction rules" are those ideological justifications used to legitimate current practices, i.e., the influence of managerial and organizational theories of control upon work practices. Scientific management, for example, simultaneously stands as a particular form of technical control within an organization and, through its dissemination in schools of management, an ideological legitimation of the practice in general (Braverman 1974). Likewise, the gender bias of much of organizational analysis not only reflects but legitimises existing structures of male dominance. Here we are reminded that organizational practitioners are no less a part of the landscape of organizational culture.

"Strategic rules" refer to organizational control over its environment. This control, as in the case of multinationals or of company-towns, can influence not only the local economy but its particular sexual division of labour. Blauner (1967) and Pollert (1981) illustrate how the strategic importance of a local industry (respectively textiles and tobacco) can influence as well as reflect the kind and character of employment opportunities available. Blauner graphically describes the organic relationship between textile mills and the local community in southern U.S. states:

> Most mills are situated in small towns or villages, where the family and the church are the dominant institutions and where traditional patterns and social relationships that reflect the isolation of both the region and the village community still prevail. (Blauner 1967: 74-75)

As a result integration in the industry tends to be based upon traditional rather than bureaucratic norms. The accent is on "personal relations with management, loyalties of kinship and neighborhood, and a religious sanction on submission to things as they are." (Blauner 1967: 75-76)

The result is a situation where "family and kinship relationships penetrate the work situation" and concentrate women "in non-involving jobs that permit little control or initiative" (Blauner 1967). In such cases local cultural values about "the place of women" can override other concerns about physical stamina. Both Blauner (1967) and Pollert (1981) document how females in the textile mills and tobacco industry are assigned the labour-intensive, often physically exacting, work.

"Social regulative rules" are "hegemonic" forms of control located within the social arrangements of production and organizational processes. They consist of forms of behaviour, expectations, values and rewards that are more-or-less designed to ensure the organizational commitment of employees. The early Human Relations' attempts to develop organizationally approved "solidarity" (e.g., Roethlisberger and Dickson 1939) is one example; current interest in creating organization-sustaining "cultures" or "climates" (e.g., Peters and Waterman 1982) is another example. Often such culture maintenance strategies operate with an inherent understanding of women as peripheral to the organization, with the result that the organization's culture can inhibit female involvement and advancement. A classic example is the corporate culture of the large Japanese companies which gears its benefits to its male employees (Ouchi 1981). European and North American companies are not exempt from this process. Crompton and Jones' (1984) study of British companies found that variations in female inclusion in organizational cultures influenced the level of trade union membership. In "Cohall" they found a relatively high density of trade unionism among the female employees due to an organizational culture in which, despite a lack of promotions, women were accepted as "organizational equals." At "Lifeco," on the other hand, the organizational culture stressed a need to "fit in" with the social as well as the technical "requirements" of the company: failure resulted in a sense of not being accepted or perceived as a "full participant" and hence not being considered for advancement. Given that the "social" consisted primarily of a company sports and social club geared to "male sports" ("football for the younger men, bowls for the older men") female employees were disadvantaged. In this "predominantly male" organizational culture women were not able to fit in, did not feel themselves to be full organization members and hence did not join the available union nor give a full commitment to the company. The barriers preventing females from "fitting in" to the organizational cultures of North American companies have been documented in a number of studies. Dubeck (1979) identifies "informal social networks" and their dominance by men as an important causal factor. Such networks, she argues, function on a basis of trust rooted in assumptions of shared characteristics between key actors. The more unlike those actors an outsider appears the more likely they will remain an outsider. Thus, in a male circle of management a female has an immediate handicap. Male managers tend to regard females as weak and lacking leadership qualities and are less likely to promote them or even send them for professional training (Dubeck 1979). When females do occupy supervisory positions their judgement is less likely to be trusted than that of male supervisors (Rosen and Jerdee 1974) and where women exhibit traits normally positively associated with males they are, nonetheless, regarded negatively and with suspicion (Broverman et al. 1972). Another feature of the informal network that serves to exclude women is language. Riley (1983) argues that the way organizations explain, motivate and legitimise their activities can perpetuate male dominance. She examples "the language of political symbols" which draw upon sporting and military images to engender team spirit.

Contradictions and resistance. As with class, the processes of gender differentiation do not simply operate as a one way street. Women can and do reflect upon their existence, observing contradictions in the way men and women are treated in organizational practices. They can and do resist those contradictions. Resistance has sometimes resulted in legislative changes (e.g., Sex Discrimination Act 1975) that, despite mediation by a number of gendered rule situations, have "worked their way into the cultures of most organizations" (Davis 1984: 9). At work, resistance can take the form of female subcultures, situations which may include collusion with shopfloor sexism, but which can also include female solidarity:

> Sexual oppression at work also has its own dynamic. It provokes resistance—both to patriarchy and to the work discipline often mediated by it. We see escape, bending rules, mucking in, laughs, sexy bravado, biting wit. Defiance is there. What is lacking is shop-floor control and organization. (Pollert 1981: 234-35)

Pollert argues that "the very contradictions in women's experience, the 'double burden' itself, are also the seeds of their strength" (1981: 237), that oppression coupled with exploitation can provide a cutting edge for consciousness and radical action. As with class, these contradictions and forms of resistance are integral parts of the organizational culture in its continual "state of becoming" (Benson 1977).

Conclusion

This paper has argued that gender is a cultural phenomenon, that organizations are a key aspect of a given culture and, hence, that organizational analysis needs to take account of the relationship between gender and organizational life. To this end, the concept of organizational culture, rooted in a feminist materialist approach, is proposed as a useful focus for analysis of gendered organizational experience.

The development of organizations and their cultural arrangements need to be viewed in the broad historical context of the development of ideas and of cultural arrangements per se. Cultural arrangements, of which organizations are an essential segment, are seen as manifestations of a process of ideational development located within a context of definite material conditions. It is a context of dominance (males over females/owners over workers) but also of conflict and contradiction in which class and gender, autonomous but overdetermined, are vital dynamics. Ideas and cultural arrangements confront actors as a series of rules of behaviour; rules that, in their contradictions, may variously be enacted, followed or resisted.

This perspective is developed to an understanding of organizations and gender through a "rule" focus: (1) Organizations are viewed as key "sites" of rule enactment, mediation and resistance and, as such, significant contributors to the maintenance and development of gendered relationships; (2) organizational culture is viewed as being primarily composed of a particular configuration of "rules," enactment and resistance, within which gendered relationships are embedded and manifest; and (3) the gendered character of a specific organizational culture can be understood through analysis of the particular rule aspects (e.g., extraorganizational, strategic, etc.) that compose a certain configuration.

From this overall framework it is argued that organizations be viewed as frameworks of human experience which have key implications for the construction and reproduction of gendered relationships but which, in turn, have implications for the development and existence of the organization itself. Organizational culture as a public sphere of experience raises questions about the value of those experiences. The ubiquitous nature of gender raises questions about the character of organizational culture. The two aspects need to be viewed as inseparable areas of understanding in organizational analysis.

6

A Feminist Perspective on State Bureaucracy[1]

JUDITH GRANT
PETA TANCRED

We want to start this chapter with some rare data that we have recently obtained on a matriarchal state bureaucracy. The data are incomplete but, as an introduction to the development of a feminist perspective on state bureaucracy, they take on particular importance. It is pertinent to note that this matriarchal state bureaucracy is located within a society where fertility has dropped to a dangerously low level. State authorities are wrestling with the consequences of a labor force that is likely to be reduced by one half in each succeeding generation despite widespread

AUTHORS' NOTE: We would like to express our warm appreciation to Deborah Harrison for her rapid, incisive, and very helpful reactions to an initial version of this chapter. In addition, we have benefited enormously from the comments of various colleagues: Caroline Andrew and Katherine Meyer at the Lennoxville conference on "L'Etat contemporain," where the paper was first presented; Arnaud Sales, Carl Cuneo, and Bob Connell, who read various versions of the text; and those who attended seminars in both Canada and Australia where ideas from this chapter were discussed. This chapter was originally published in French (*Sociologie et Sociétés*, 1991.)

encouragement to seniors, who include a significant proportion of women, to continue working.

In this matriarchal state bureaucracy, the main department is the Department of Reproduction (concerned with reproduction on both a daily and a generational basis, as will be discussed further on). The Minister of Reproduction is a woman and the key, higher-level state bureaucrats are all female. The clerical posts of the department are monopolized by males, who play an essential role in record-keeping activities. These records center on the availability of labor power, in both the short and the long term, and include details on general fertility and health problems.

Linked to this key Department of Reproduction are important related departments—the Department of Quality Housing (it is not the housing stock that is problematic but the quality of housing that will facilitate reproduction); the Department of Nutrition (which replaces the former Department of Agriculture, which gave little attention to the necessary nutrients to encourage reproduction and longevity); the Department of Domestic Health (which concentrates on health hazards within the home, long neglected by the former Department of Occupational Health); and, finally, the Department of Science and Reproduction (which is concerned with technological innovations for reproduction on both a daily and a generational basis).

We end with a brief mention of departments that are very low in the internal hierarchy—for example, the Department of Production and the Department of Finance. It should be understood, of course, that much of the production of goods for the reproductive sphere is carried out on a craft or domestic basis and that the state's role is minimal. As to industrial production, both of defense and of consumer commodities, this has been cut back so drastically, because of concern with the dwindling labor force, that these previously significant departments have been "downsized" (to use the latest buzz expression) as the state's main priority turns toward ensuring humanity's continuing existence.

A final mention must go to an extremely low-ranking unit within the bureaucracy—the Advisory Council on Men's Issues. Created as a result of pressure from the men's movement during the past decade and men's increasing concern over their marginality to the reproductive sphere because of technological innovations, the council attempts to respond to men's issues through the co-optation of moderate males, though it is weakened by its attachment to the Department of Production.

While our data on this matriarchal state bureaucracy are sketchy, we are persuaded that our status as female researchers facilitated our research within this very unusual example of a state bureaucratic apparatus, and we feel privileged to be able to inform you of even these minimal details. Quite apart from the rarity of this research, we feel that these few data enable us to outline the character of the dominant bureaucratic state apparatus under capitalism—obviously a patriarchal state bureaucracy,[2] whose characteristics need to be delineated from a feminist perspective.

* * *

Returning to a more concrete situation, in this chapter we are going to argue that existing perspectives for the study of state bureaucracy are gender blind, in the sense that they assume the power of males in positions of significance and ignore the powerless position of females, who are relegated to the more peripheral departments and to marginal positions within departments. Basing our approach on existing discussions of the "unequal structure of representation" (Mahon 1984; Poulantzas 1976), we propose an emphasis on "*dual* structures of unequal representation" to highlight women's reality. In effect, a feminist approach to the bureaucratic apparatus of the state must take into account not only the representation of "women's issues" within a particular unit of the bureaucracy, such representation being easily accommodated within the conceptualization of *one* unequal structure of representation. Instead, this approach must also underline the *second,* implicit structure of representation that permeates the bureaucracy and that places women in relatively powerless positions in terms of departmental locations. This second structure, we will argue, is rooted in women's "adjunct control" positions within the productive and reproductive sectors, positions that facilitate the use of authority without themselves according any authority to the officeholder.

We turn first to feminist comments on the state and state bureaucracy to indicate the way in which women's exclusion has been noted in these theoretical approaches. We then discuss the "dual structures of unequal representation" within the state bureaucracy in some detail, rooting the second structure in a discussion of women's modal position within the productive and reproductive spheres. Finally, we make reference to data on both the federal and the provincial bureaucracies in Canada to illustrate the two structures of unequal representation that permeate the state bureaucracy from women's point of view.

Feminist Comments on the State and State Bureaucracy[3]

Feminism, Catherine MacKinnon (1983: 643) has written, has described the state's treatment of gender differences but has provided no analysis of the state as gender hierarchy. Heather Jon Maroney (1988) has charged that feminist theory has been preoccupied with the development of categories for structural analysis rather than with the development of categories for political analysis. The need for political theory that prioritizes patriarchal relations is all the more immediate as a result of the failure of male-stream theories of the state to consider issues of gender (for example, see Burstyn 1983a, 1983b, for criticisms of Marxism on this point).

What feminist commentators on the state and state bureaucracies do accomplish is to provide an analysis from the standpoint of women. By indicating how the structural relations of gender inequality are inscribed in state institutions, policies, and actions, feminists are correcting the partial, and therefore inaccurate, view of the state put forth in "male-stream" political theories. Nevertheless, there is no single feminist perspective on the state and state bureaucracy. The differing perspectives that make up the range of feminist theory are replicated within this literature; we draw on two pertinent perspectives for this discussion.

From liberalism, feminists derive the argument that the state should be a neutral arbiter in a field of competing interests, but they underline that the state has not shown such neutrality in its treatment of women. In effect, state power has been "captured" by men, and sexist state actions mean that women do not have full rights of citizenship (Franzway et al. 1989; Jaggar 1983). While the liberal awareness of the state's shortcomings has led to much political action and important legislative reforms, this conception of the state is insufficient to account for women's oppression. Instead of placing patriarchy at the center of this analysis, the liberal feminist view contains an implicit sex role theory, which suggests that changing the attitudes and behavior of men and women will lead to the redress of state-sponsored oppression (H. Eisenstein 1985). Zillah Eisenstein (1984) goes on to argue that liberal feminism must move beyond this view if it is to carry out the project of reform that it has put forward and that socialist feminism provides a more strategic analysis of the state and its bureaucracies.

Zillah Eisenstein's writings (1981, 1984) provide the most detailed, although problematic, discussion of the state from a socialist feminist perspective. She begins with a number of points with which few would disagree. The capitalist class, she states, does not "rule" the state or government directly but instead exercises hegemony. To the extent that the capitalist class is hegemonic, the state is a capitalist state. The capitalist class, she continues, is made up of men and is therefore able to represent both the class and the "sexual class" interests of these men. In this way, the state institutionalizes patriarchal and class hegemony. A large part of the mystificatory role of the state is in this seeming identification of male interests and bourgeois interests (Eisenstein 1984).

While we would reject Eisenstein's contention that men and women form distinct "classes," we note the insight that the state represents, reproduces, and conceals both class power and male power (see also Burstyn 1983b on this point). This point is fundamental to a socialist feminist perspective on the state.

In an extension of this argument, Franzway et al. (1989) have argued that the state is involved with the overall patterning of gender relations or the gender order. They argue that the connections between the state and the gender order are fourfold: (a) in the basic constitution of the realm of the state, (b) in the composition of the controllers of the state apparatus, (c) in the staffing of the state machinery and its internal organization, and (d) in what the state does, who it affects, and how. These connections may be investigated by considering the female and feminist presence in state bureaucracies.

Alternatively, the gendered nature of bureaucracy may be discussed in terms of how masculinity is embedded within it. Hester Eisenstein has cited a range of mechanisms within state bureaucracies—recruitment practices, job definitions, and complaint procedures—that institutionalize unequal access to power. She argues that reform is not merely a matter of changing the personnel at the top but involves the reordering of institutional arrangements that intersect with the construction of masculinity and femininity (Eisenstein 1985).

Patriarchal interests also may be embedded impersonally in the hierarchy of units and functions within the state bureaucracy. Significant here are the gendered division of labor throughout the bureaucratic apparatus, the gendered process of selection, and the construction of career paths that shape the gender politics of the bureaucracy. For example, state bureaucracies have constituted gender politics such that the masculine bureaucratic elite cannot function without a feminized support staff. This and other gender hierarchies are historically constituted and are the objects of social struggle.

In line with these approaches, we argue that the exclusion of women from powerful positions in the state bureaucracy and the marginality of women's issues have not been solely a matter of the lack of women representatives within the state. The state bureaucratic apparatus itself has a gendered nature. While the state sustains patriarchal relations, state structures are themselves patriarchal in form (see Franzway et al. 1989).

Thus feminist comments on the state and its bureaucratic apparatus underline the limitations inherent in a purely class approach. Rather than seeing the exclusion of women as a by-product of class society, such exclusion should be put at the center of an analysis of the patriarchal state and its bureaucracies. At the same time, omnipotence should not be attributed to the state, nor should the masculinity embedded within it be assumed to be inevitable. Feminism has begun to challenge the state's constitution of the gender order.

In the ensuing discussion, we recognize that we are modifying certain male-stream definitions of accepted terms. In particular, we collapse the traditional division between the public and private spheres and envisage work as taking place in both sectors. In addition, we refer at times to these two spheres as the *productive* and *reproductive* sectors to delineate the nature of the main tasks that take place within them.[4] We would like to clarify that we use the term *reproductive* to refer not only to biological or generational reproduction but also to the reproduction of labor power on a daily basis. The term's wider referent is used increasingly in the feminist literature and summarizes the nature of the main tasks in the private sphere in a concise and useful manner. Finally, the term *representation* has no pluralistic connotations in our usage. Instead, we follow and elaborate on a tradition whereby divisions rooted in the productive and reproductive spheres are hierarchically and unequally represented within the bureaucracy of the state.

Dual Structures of Unequal Representation[5]

One of the most valuable approaches to an understanding of the state bureaucratic apparatus has been provided by Poulantzas (1976) and Mahon (1977, 1984), who argue persuasively that the state bureaucracy, in terms of power differentials, represents a deliberate hierarchy, in class terms, that ensures a particular pattern of hegemonic class domination (Mahon 1984: 38). Mahon illustrates her argument by discussing the relative power of the Departments of Finance and Labour such that the representation of specific productive forces is hierarchically reflected within the bureaucracy of the state. She goes on to outline the mediating role of the state between and among these various hierarchically arranged units, such that a "contradictory unity" is effected and hegemonic class domination is assured. She also emphasizes that this form of representation performs two roles, that is, "representation of the specific interests of their [the units'] respective groups in the negotiation process and regulation—the attempt to 'persuade' and/or coerce their group into accepting the compromise" (Mahon 1977: 183). But the state cannot simply accede to the demands of particular forces:

> The maintenance of hegemony requires that at least part of the interests of the subordinate classes and of nonhegemonic fractions of capital can continue to be realized. The state cannot afford to ignore dissident forces persistently, nor can it rely solely on repression. . . . It can be the 'instrument' of neither the leading fraction . . . nor dissident forces. (Mahon 1984: 38)

Neither Poulantzas nor Mahon specifically mentions gender within this discussion of "dissident forces." It is fairly easy to extend their argument, however, to the unequal representation of gendered divisions within the bureaucratic state apparatus. This, in fact, has been done by Findlay (1987: 31), who discusses a developing structure of representation that incorporates "women's interests" into the policymaking process. Her investigation illustrates the need to consider the state as an organizer not only of bourgeois hegemony but of patriarchal hegemony as well. Findlay describes the organization of the representation of women's interests within the state as a process shaped by years of demands and responses, reflecting struggles within the women's movement and within the state, and between the movement and the state. This process, she argues, is marked on the one hand by the resistance of a state preoccupied by the potential interests of the "dominant groups" that are reflected in the state as well as by men's "patriarchal perceptions" of the relevance of women's interests to the political process. On the other hand, there is the recognition of politicians and senior bureaucrats that the state must be seen to act in the interests of all. As a result, "The process of organization evolved in a contradictory way, alternating between resistance and response as the state mediated between and among various political interests" (Findlay 1987: 33).

Findlay's analysis is useful in translating into gender terms the uneven structure of representation argument, and she goes on to comment upon the isolated and vulnerable position of "Status of Women Canada" within the federal bureaucratic structures. She also raises, though does not deal with, the divisions within the women's movement; instead, she states that, by 1980, "the representation of women's interests was well established in the structure of the federal state" (Findlay 1987: 47). This is a curious feature of her argument for she simultaneously recognizes the fractions within the women's movement in ideological terms but assumes, together with the state, that these varying hues of ideological opinion can be represented within the bureaucratic apparatus through one isolated structure. In effect, this rather mechanical application of the unequal structure of representation argument can treat women as one potentially "dissident force," among many others, whose due representation was resisted but who finally succeeded in achieving a suitable channel for their concerns through pressure generated by the women's movement.

We wish to argue that this perspective on the bureaucratic structure of representation takes a very narrow view both of the forms of representation that are possible and of the diversity of interests that characterizes the female half of the population. Findlay shares with Mahon and Poulantzas a tendency to pass over the representation of male interests that is built into the bureaucratic apparatus generally. For example, it is possible for Mahon to argue that departments or branches represent the interests of particular forces within society when she can take for granted that, with respect to any of these so-called forces, male interests will be included. This is a clear example of the feminist argument that the patriarchal nature of the state is masked by the implicit structuring of male interests within bourgeois interests. This, however, is obviously not the case for women, and the representation of "women's issues" cannot take for granted that women's other interests are served within alternative sectors or branches. Where it counts, women's interests are highly likely to be excluded or absent (as will be discussed in a later section).

This is what is meant by *dual structures of unequal representation*. In one unequal structure, women as a potentially dissident force are represented within special units of the state bureaucracy, including advisory councils and units with particular responsibility for women that are to be found throughout the bureaucracy. In a second unequal structure, women's varied participation in the productive and reproductive sectors is represented in the gendered hierarchy of each and every department and branch. The interdependence of the structures is assumed, and their specific configuration would be a matter for empirical investigation. The unequal structure of women's representation is ensured in two ways: first, through the relatively powerless position of the units that allegedly represent "women's issues" and, second, through the relatively powerless positions of women who serve in the other branches and departments of the state.

Adjunct Control in the Productive and Reproductive Sectors[6]

To grasp the nature of women's participation throughout the bureaucracy of the state, we must have some understanding of their role in the productive and reproductive sectors, that is, of their part in the various forces that will be reflected within the state bureaucracy. Fortunately, feminist writings during the past decade and a half have devoted considerable attention to the nature of women's work. Much of this writing is descriptive and statistical, but it has been useful in pointing out that just under *half* of contemporary women (Peitchinis 1989: Table 2.3), in Canada at least, work exclusively in the private sphere. Their colleagues in the public sector (who also participate, of course, in the private) are largely concentrated in clerical, sales, and service occupations (one third of all women). Accordingly, the private sector plus these three leading female occupations would include nearly 80% of all Canadian women.

The descriptive data have been useful in facilitating attempts to conceptualize women's work experience. Within this literature, the work of Glenn and Feldberg (1979) has been particularly helpful. They argue that women, during the past 70 years of their gradual entry to the ranks of paid labor, have moved into those jobs that have expanded most rapidly under advanced capitalism. Recent trends, they argue, include

(a) the growth and differentiation of organizations of production; and
(b) the extension of market production to certain services and goods that were previously produced within the home, including educational and health services as well as the production of food and clothing.

These two trends, they suggest, have given rise to contradictions: "On the one hand, capitalist control has been gradually extended to diverse areas; on the other, control and coordination over production processes and the labor force as a whole has become more problematic" (Glenn and Feldberg 1979: 3).

"Disjunctures," or antagonistic divisions, have arisen both within the productive system and between the organization of production and consumption. Because of opposing interests and scarce resources, these divisions are accentuated and serve to threaten capitalist control (Glenn and Feldberg 1979: 4).

The authors are interested in an occupational approach to women's work, and they go on to discuss the *content* of such work. From an organizational perspective, however, it is clear that women's work facilitates organizational control in these new circumstances. In effect, twentieth-century developments have vastly increased the distance between employer and worker, producer and consumer. It is *between* these groups that women's main contribution to the public sector is located in organizational terms.

For example, the vast army of *clerical workers* has been necessary to ensure the employer's control, both over the employee and over the profit realized in the production task. In effect, employers would be unable to maintain control over the enterprise without the detailed information collected and categorized by clerical workers, which covers not only the specificities of each employee's contribution but also the overall image of the production rate and of the costs involved. This form of control is exerted through *the categorization of information.*

Second, the extension of products to be purchased on the market has necessitated an army of *sales workers* who not only act on behalf of management in delivering the product to the consumer but also control the behavior of the latter group, ensuring that appropriate behavior is maintained and the relevant price extracted. In effect, consumers could behave very inappropriately, such that their behavior could become destructive of all capitalist purposes, were it not for the interface provided by the sales workers and their controlling presence and soothing demeanor in times of dispute. This form of control takes place through *socialization of the group-in-contact.*

Finally, the *service workers* personally deliver services to clients and, in so doing, once again ensure that this group behaves appropriately. As in the case of the sales workers, the demeanor of the service workers is very important in encouraging appropriate reactions and, in practice, they instruct their clients not only on how much to pay but also on how to pay and how to behave in general. Once again, they control through *socialization of the group-in-contact.*

In effect, these three groups of workers—clerical, sales, and service—occupy the newly developed spaces between producer and consumer, employer and worker, providing adjunct control over the vast masses with whom the late capitalist firm must deal; taken together, as noted above, these three groups constitute nearly two thirds of the contemporary female paid labor force or one third of all Canadian women.

It should be noted that, while these female workers are in direct contact with the worker, consumer or client, they have limited personal authority. They *participate* in the authority of management and are often identified with management for that reason. But they have limited say in the determination of policies or in the nature of the product to be delivered. Participation in the authority of others is seductive, however. It follows that these have been some of the hardest groups to unionize; the management identification that comes with the job must be transformed into an opposition to management with respect to their own working conditions before this can be accomplished. Thus the *adjunct control* positions, as the term suggests, carry with them an essential ambivalence concerning management or labor identification.

Turning to the reproductive work (the exclusive occupation of about 50% of Canadian women), the feminist literature is less helpful in conceptualizing the modal contribution that women make through this work. There are suggested categorizations concerning the nature of domestic labor. For example, Armstrong and Armstrong ([1978] 1984) put forward the categories of housework, reproduction and child care, tension management, and sexual relations; Luxton (1980) formulates the four categories of housework, mother work, "making ends meet," and catering to spouse. There are also some early discussions of the parallels between women's work in the public and private spheres (though the implicit causality is usually from the private to the public, rather than vice versa). But none of these discussions enables us to conceptualize the core activity within the domestic sphere, except to underline that the tasks are enormously varied.

Perhaps more helpful is the discussion by Dorothy Smith and others (Wilson 1977; McIntosh 1978; Barrett and McIntosh 1982) of the family as a "service organization to the productive enterprise" (Smith 1977: 22), that is, the area where the capitalist worker is nourished and refreshed from the workplace (reproduction on a "daily" basis) and where new members of the work force are created and socialized (reproduction on a "generational" basis). From this perspective, women's labor in the private sphere can be envisaged as maintaining labor force reproduction or, more specifically, constituting adjunct control over the replenishment of labor power. Once again, the women concerned do not have authority to take far-reaching decisions, for example, as to what types of qualifications are required for specific occupations or even what exact labor force positions will be occupied by close family members. While women appear to be accorded some control over generational reproduction, this is "shared" with their male partners and channeled by the state's intervention in policy terms. As Smith (1977: 37) says: "Nothing is left to women, but the execution of an order whose definition is not hers." Nevertheless, without their constant labor—cleaning, nourishing, managing tension, and reproducing—the replenishment of the labor force would not take place. In this instance, adjunct control takes the form of *renewal of the labor force* without which the capitalist firm could not continue to operate.

Thus it is women's modal role in both the productive and the reproductive sectors that is reflected within the bureaucracy of the state. In effect, women are included within an "adjunct control" force that is represented—and regulated—through its presence within state arenas. Because of this, we would expect to see women in those state positions, branches, and departments where the various forms of adjunct control are most evident. In empirical terms, they would be associated with units where control over a large work force or client group proves difficult, where information categorization is required for control, or where issues of labor force renewal are at the forefront. In none of these situations would women predominate in positions of authority or decision making; rather, they would assist in ensuring control over the work force and over the client group, which is necessary for capitalist society to continue.

Representing "Women's Issues," Representing Women

This final section can only illustrate the analytical principles outlined, for details of the dual structures of unequal representation for women remain to be uncovered. Instances of the representation of "women's issues," however, can be cited at both the federal and the provincial levels.

For example, the Canadian Advisory Council on the Status of Women was established in 1973. This federal structure representing "women's issues" was controversial from the outset. At a conference of Women for Political Action in Toronto in June 1973, the Advisory Council was called "a political manoeuvre to get us off their [the government's] backs" and "another way for the Government to pass the buck" (Campbell 1973: 664). In a direct illustration of the regulative role of this form of representation, it was contended that more "radical" appointees had been given shorter terms, and it was noted that the recommendation that the council report to parliament had been rejected.

Advisory councils on women's issues were established at provincial and territorial levels throughout the 1970s and 1980s. These bodies are often at the mercy of poor funding and of varying degrees of concern with women's issues on the part of the responsible governments. While the Federal Advisory Council is able to hire a full-time president and a research staff, provincial councils are of various sizes; presidents may work on a part-time basis for low pay; and appointees receive only a small honorarium. Research may be done by government directorates, nested in the bureaucracies and staffed by bureaucrats who have even less independence than the members of the women's councils.

The appointment of women's council members is made through Order-in-Council. It is widely perceived as affected by patronage. This criticism has been made by Lynn McDonald, former president of the National Action Committee on the Status of Women and former NDP member of Parliament. McDonald charges that the councils "very much show the politics of the party in power, and the people are not chosen to make waves" (Rhodes 1984: 177).

Criticisms of advisory councils also come from within. Members indicate their concerns with insufficient budgets. Ann Bell, head of Newfoundland's advisory council from 1980 to 1989, has stated:

> Women should be questioning their governments on why they set up councils that are doomed to failure. See how many other boards you can find that are appointed with a pittance, with people expected to do all the work on weekends—and with all the other groups out there, some of them with government grants too, dumping on them. There's no doubt that some advisory councils have been set up to fail. (Rhodes 1984: 180)

Advisory councils have been high profile and controversial government-sponsored agencies, but the representation of "women's issues" within the state bureaucracy in Canada predates these agencies. For example, the Women's Bureau of the Federal Department of Labour (now Labour Canada) was established in 1954, after a long period of lobbying. Sharleen Bannon (1975: 629) notes that the Women's Bureau was established long before the demands of second-wave feminism and that it was founded "on the premise that society can make full use of its human resources only when women exercise fully their rights and responsibilities in all areas." One can note that "all areas" for women are apparently limited to those areas that the state wishes to regulate.

For it is noticeable that, in the variety of bureaus representing "women's issues" that have developed over time within the Canadian state bureaucracy, the overriding concern is with the management of women's productive roles, for the vast majority of bureaus are concerned with labor issues,[7] either national or international. The only exception would be the Office of the Senior Advisor on the Status of Women in Health and Welfare Canada, though one might well argue that women's health needs to be managed for both their productive and their reproductive roles. As might be expected, all these bureaus are nested in low-status departments.

As to the representation of women rather than of "women's issues," Kathleen Archibald's (1970) study of gender relations in the Canadian public service remains the most exhaustive. Archibald states that, although the Government of Canada adopted the principle of equal pay for equal work from the outset, women were always promoted more slowly than men and were consequently constrained in their progress within the service. Reports of the early Civil Service Commission stated explicitly that women were not considered suitable for, or capable of, work at responsible levels in the civil service.

The commission was particularly concerned with limiting the number of women in the civil service. In 1918, the commission was given explicit authority to limit competitions on the basis of sex, age, health habits, residence, and moral character. In 1921, restrictions were placed on the employment of married women. These restrictions were lifted during World War II but were tightened in 1947 and not revoked until 1955. It was only in 1967 that it became forbidden to discriminate on the basis of sex.

Archibald concludes that differences in capability, experience, and work interests do not fully explain the lower levels and salaries of women in the Canadian public service. She suggests that the remaining difference in occupational success is a result of restricted opportunities for women. Nicole Morgan's (1988) recent study of women in the Canadian Federal Public Service from 1908 to 1987 puts the point even more strongly, arguing that patriarchal relations at work largely account for women's inequality in the bureaucracy. She states:

> If one wishes to understand the situation of women in the public service, one must stop trying to explain the phenomenon in terms of what women lack to be equal to men, and try instead to understand how men have resisted the idea of sharing their territory and their privileges. (Morgan 1988: 1)

The net result of the limitations placed on women's employment and promotion throughout the service is that, while women account for a significant proportion of federal state employees in Canada, they are very unevenly distributed across occupational categories. In 1987 (Morgan 1988), women made up 42.4% of permanent employees in the public service yet constituted only 8.7% of the executive category and 13.2% of the senior management category while composing 82.8% of the administrative support category. In terms of salary, 83.9% of women earned less than $35,000 compared with 54.7% of men.

Data on departmental distribution in a suitable format are more difficult to obtain. According to successive Public Service Commission reports, however, significant proportions of women are concentrated in Health and Welfare and Employment and Immigration while the lowest proportions are to be found in Transport and Public Works, suggesting differing adjunct control requirements in these contrasting departments.

In general, then, while the necessary detailed research remains to be undertaken, we would argue that women's modal locations within the productive and reproductive spheres are reflected in their occupational location within the state bureaucracy, their relatively powerless status vis-à-vis men, and their concentration where adjunct control activities are of paramount importance.

Is State Bureaucracy Patriarchal?

Because we started this chapter with the imagined construct of a matriarchal state bureaucracy, we return, in this conclusion, to the question of whether the state bureaucracy, under capitalism, is patriarchal. It is certainly true that we have no evidence of an ideological commitment to male values, or even subjective opinions on the importance they are accorded. Nevertheless, we have structural evidence that strongly suggests a coherent pattern of the subordination of women to male interests and priorities. For example, we have underlined the isolation of the representation of "women's issues," whether through so-called advisory councils or through the departmental bureaus ostensibly representing women's interests. We have cited evidence of their powerless positions within the state bureaucracy, but we would like to highlight the bizarre conception according to which the interests of one half of the population can be accorded due importance through underfunded councils or so-called advisers who are scattered throughout the bureaucratic structure. The need for these weak structures to incorporate women's issues within state concerns bears witness to women's quasi exclusion from the dominant departments and branches of the state. Second, the evidence of women's low-level positions within bureaucratic structures takes various forms but bears witness to the powerless and labor-intensive adjunct control location, both within the state as well as within the productive and reproductive sectors. The underrepresentation of women in the senior ranks and decision-making posts of the state hardly can be compensated through the weak, isolated structures already mentioned.

Finally, we are arguing that, to view the state bureaucracy from women's point of view, women must be dignified by the recognition that they do not merely constitute yet another potentially dissident force but a massive societal category whose importance must be grasped through placing gender at the center of any understanding of state structures. To apprehend their representation through one set of weak structures charged with "women's issues" is to ignore their generally limited presence, in very constraining positions, throughout the bureaucracy of the state. To view the state as a "gender hierarchy," one must expand the perspective of the representation of "women's issues" within the state and recognize the implicit gender inequality that permeates the hierarchy of the state. In addition, one must "demystify" gender representation within the state bureaucracy by collapsing the public/private dichotomy and by highlighting the representation of all women, not only those who labor within the productive sector.

Notes

1. This alphabetical listing of authors has no significance in terms of "first" and "second" authors. We collaborated on some sections and wrote others independently; we are joint and equal authors of the chapter.

2. In using this phraseology, we do not intend to suggest that only state bureaucracies under capitalism are patriarchal. On the contrary, patriarchy underlies and penetrates a wide range of economic structures; the terminology merely suggests that we are concerned, in this chapter, with state bureaucracies under capitalism.

3. Some of the material in this section is discussed more fully in Grant (in preparation).

4. In underlining that we are designating the main tasks, we recognize that certain tasks of production are still carried out within the home and that this proportion might well increase with the shift of computerized tasks to the household. We also recognize that a number of "reproductive" tasks have moved out to the public sphere, as will be discussed in a succeeding section of this chapter.

5. As one commentator has pointed out, the predominant maleness of the existing argument implies certain assumptions that we may not have chosen in building a feminist framework rooted in experience. We recognize this disadvantage, and that similar criticisms have been leveled at the very use of male-stream language, which, in and of itself, makes certain nonfeminist assumptions. As will be seen, however, we unravel certain hidden assumptions within the framework as one means of propelling the argument forward, and we would argue that this can be a fruitful approach for feminist theorizing.

6. A parallel argument will be found in Tancred-Sheriff (1989), although this latter version discusses only the productive sector and emphasizes the way in which sexuality forms part of the control system.

7. Recent examples would be the Office of Equal Opportunities for Women in the Public Service Commission, the Human Resources Division in the Treasury Board, the Women's Employment Division and Affirmative Action Division in Employment and Immigration Canada, the Women's Programme and Native Women's Programme in the Secretary of State's office, and a Senior Adviser on the Integration of Women in Development in the Canadian International Development Agency. In addition, "Integration Mechanisms" devoted to women's concerns exist in all federal government departments, though we suspect that they constitute linking mechanisms for the state rather than any powerful avenue for the expression of women's interests (Canadian Advisory Council on the Status of Women 1983).

PART III

From Theory to Application: Explorations in Feminist Organizational Analysis

Alongside the development of feminist organizational analysis, there have been a number of feminist studies focused upon the impact of organizations upon women. These studies have examined such things as opportunity structure (Kanter 1977a), sexual harassment (Gutek 1985), recruitment processes (Dubeck 1979), the impact of management practice upon female self-image (Sheppard and Fothergill 1984), female resistance and work culture (Pollert 1981), sexist procedures for merit awards (Burton 1987), the impact of male-dominated organization upon communication style (Mills and Chiaramonte forthcoming), employment equity policies (Tancred 1988), and many more. In this section, we have included a selection of studies that exemplify a feminist approach to a particular aspect of gendered organizational reality.

In the field of empirical research into sexuality and the workplace, the work of Barbara Gutek has been to the fore (Gutek 1985, 1989; Cohen and Gutek 1985; Gutek and Dunwoody-Miller 1986; Gutek et al. 1983; Gutek and Nakamura 1982; Konrad and Gutek 1986). In the first chapter of this part (Chapter 7), Gutek and Cohen set out to reveal the various ways that sexual behavior influences and is influenced by paid-work organizations. Sex role spillover—"the carryover of gender-based roles into the workplace"—is exacerbated, they argue, by having a highly skewed ratio of the sexes at work. The sex roles associated with the majority sex become incorporated into the work roles. Thus, in male-dominated job activity, rationality and aggressiveness are stressed while, in female-dominated jobs, nurturing and passivity are stressed. Exploring the impact of organizational settings on sexual behavior, Gutek and Cohen contend that the workplace, more often than not, is sex segregated, and this contributes to "sex role spillover," in which women are assumed only to be capable of a limited range of (relatively low-paid) tasks. This in turn draws attention to and stresses gender at work, one of the effects of which is to encourage the phenomenon of "organizational attractiveness"—with women being seen by men as sex objects.

In "Women Managers' Perceptions of Gender and Organizational Life" (Chapter 8), Deborah Sheppard attempts to "get inside" the perceptions of female professionals. It is an important piece of research that draws together some of the strands that we have seen introduced throughout the book. In particular, it extends aspects of Kanter's work by exploring how women managers and professionals can feel isolated from other women in the same organization. Rooted in a concern with the experiences of women's lives, Sheppard exposes a reality in which female managers constantly struggle to mesh their experiences as women with those of the male-oriented business world. Sheppard has continued to explore the experiential world of female image making in a number of studies (Sheppard 1988, 1989; Hearn et al. 1989).

In Chapter 9, Susan Porter Benson provides us with a much needed analysis of the work culture of women. Through a historical analysis of saleswomen in U.S. department stores, Benson challenges us to rethink the nature of workplace relations—in particular, to rethink our definitions of *skill*—to find new ways to conceptualize work that are not bound by traditional male-oriented notions of skill; second, to be alert to the fact that a "linear degradation of work was not the inevitable fate of the woman worker"; and, finally, to investigate the ways that women's work culture has acted to limit management's freedom of action. Benson's subsequent contributions to these tasks culminated in her book on *Counter Cultures* (1986).

Clare Burton's work (Chapter 10) is interesting not only in what it has to say about sexist procedures for merit awards but in the fact that it is an example of developing Australian feminist interest in the question of gender and organizations.[1] Burton's work is very much akin to that of

Kanter and of Sheppard in that it sets out to explore gender bias *within* the context of organizational realities. In this case, she investigates the ways in which male bias is embedded within various organizational arrangements and as a result negatively affects the promotability of females in the Australian public service.

Between them, the four chapters in this part are important starting points for the development of our understanding of gender at work and, in the process, they raise a number of interesting methodological questions about sexuality, women's self-image, organizational practices, and the cultures and the subcultures of organizations.

Note

1. Australian feminists have, of course, been at the forefront in challenging sexist thought in a number of fields, beginning with Germaine Greer in 1970.

7

Sex Ratios, Sex Role Spillover, and Sex at Work: A Comparison of Men's and Women's Experiences[1]

BARBARA A. GUTEK
AARON GROFF COHEN

Sex role spillover is the carryover into the workplace of gender-based roles that are usually irrelevant or inappropriate to the work setting (Nieva and Gutek 1981: 60). Sex role spillover means that being a woman or a man has implications for the work one does which are not inherent in the job itself. It exists for several reasons (Gutek and Dunwoody-Miller 1986): (1) sex is the most salient social characteristic; it is noticed immediately; (2) people learn their gender roles

AUTHORS' NOTE: This chapter originally appeared in Barbara A. Gutek and Aaron Groff Cohen (1987) "Sex Ratios, Sex Role Spillover, and Sex at Work: A Comparison of Men's and Women's Experiences," *Human Relations* 40(2):97-115; reprinted by permission of Plenum Press Journals.

early in life and they remain powerful influences in nearly all domains of life, whereas work roles are more specific and are learned relatively late in life; and (3) both men and women are usually comfortable interacting with the opposite sex in ways which are congruent with these gender roles, even when this conflicts with optimal work-role behavior. For these reasons, people frequently interact according to gender role at work, i.e., sex role spillover occurs.

Gutek and Morasch (1982) contend that sex role spillover is a central contributor to social-sexual behaviors at work. This article will briefly review and also extend the work of Gutek and Morasch in regard to women's experiences of sexual behavior at work, examine the same issues from the perspective of working men, and compare the experiences of women and men.

Sex Ratios and Sex Role Spillover

Although gender roles interfere with work roles in all work situations, sex role spillover is exacerbated by skewed sex ratios. Several researchers and theoreticians (Fairhurst and Snavely 1983a, 1983b; Gutek, Larwood, and Stromberg 1986; Kanter 1977a, 1977b; Konrad and Gutek 1986; Reskin 1984; Taylor et al. 1978) have argued that sex ratios, the relative proportion of women and men, are important in determining many social and organizational dynamics of the work environment. This work is usually imprecise about specifying sex ratios; e.g., studying the ratio of male to female billing clerks at ABC Company is different from studying the ratio of male to female social workers in the U.S. Our research involved three different sex-ratios: (1) the work-role set is the extent to which the sexes interact in their day-to-day work environment, (2) the sex ratio of the job is the degree of integration of the workers' specific job category within the organization in which they work, and (3) furthest removed from daily experience is the sex ratio of the occupational category, the relative percentage of men and women across the nation who were in the same occupation as assessed by the United States Bureau of Census in 1970.

Sex role spillover is facilitated when these sex-ratios, the ratio of the work-role set, job, and occupation, are highly skewed in one direction or the other. When this happens, the work role takes on many aspects of the sex role of the majority sex. Male-dominated jobs are often seen as encompassing the traits of activity, rationality, and aggressiveness, while female-dominated jobs are frequently associated with nurturance and passivity (Deaux 1985).

Because the work role takes on aspects of the majority sex, the minority sex may encounter difficulties, although the experiences of minority women and men are likely to be quite different. The negative effects of being the minority sex are well documented in the case of women in male-dominated jobs (Kanter 1977a, 1977b; Laws 1975; Northcraft and Martin 1982; Taylor et al. 1978). These women are seen as women rather than as job holders by their male co-workers. Their sex is noticed (Bem 1981; Grady 1977; Kessler and McKenna 1978; Laws 1979), and it becomes difficult for men to ignore the fact that they are women because they are visible deviates from the norm. An analogous argument can be made regarding men in female-dominated jobs; they are especially visible when they are in the minority.

Sex role spillover can also cause problems for the majority sex at work. In their case, the sex role and work role become fused together as the job itself takes on aspects of the sex role. Thus, men's jobs are viewed as involving rationality, activity, assertiveness, and power. Since men are in a dominant status and power position in our culture, and since the male traits of activity, rationality, and aggressiveness are valued in organizations, this rarely creates problems for traditionally employed men. In the case of "women's jobs," however, the entire job comes to be perceived as embodying stereotypically female traits when women constitute the majority of workers. Since the traits associated with the stereotype of women are not particularly valued in the work world, female-dominated jobs may be devalued. In a pair of experimental studies, Touhey (1947a, 1947b) has shown that the entrance of women into stereotypically male jobs lowers the prestige of the jobs while the entrance of men into women's occupations raises prestige, although subsequent studies have been unable to replicate this finding (Crino et al. 1983; Suchner 1979; White et al. 1981). Research showing that women's jobs receive lower pay and have poorer advancement opportunities than men's jobs (Madden 1985; Oppenheimer 1968, 1973; Treiman and Hartmann 1981) is consistent with the point of view that women's work is devalued.

In sum, sex role spillover builds upon but is different from a theory of group proportions. A theory of group proportions postulates that majority-minority ratios determine intergroup dynamics and the experience of tokenism. The numerically rare man should be subject to the same token dynamics as a woman who is the sole woman in a group of men. The sex role spillover perspective suggests that sex ratios have important effects. Because the gender roles of men and women are very different and have different status and power characteristics in the workplace, however, each sex experiences the effects of sex role spillover in different ways. The token man will not have the same experiences as the token woman because the gender roles are different (see also Fairhurst and Snavely 1983a).

In the discussion of theory and the supporting data that follow, we have subdivided types of employment into three major classes: nontraditional, integrated, and traditional. Nontraditional work is defined as having more opposite sex people in both the job and occupation. It is nontraditional in that it is rare for people of these respondents' sex to be holding these jobs. Integrated work refers to employment where both sexes have approximately equal numbers in the job and occupation. Traditional jobs have more people of the same sex than the opposite sex in the job and occupation. Since traditional jobs are quite common and since the work-role set is the most immediate sex ratio in most workers' everyday experiences, we have subdivided traditional work into two further categories; jobs with more same-sex people in the work-role set, and those with work-role sets where one's own sex is not in the majority. In both instances, we are talking about traditionally female and male jobs. In some instances, these jobs entail a great deal of contact with the other sex (as in the case of most female secretaries or some male managers), whereas other traditional jobs (such as female telephone operators or longshoremen) involve no contact with the other sex. It is our contention that these very different types of work are also quite different in the way sex roles spill over into the work roles with consequent differences in their inhabitants' work environments and interpersonal experiences at work.

Sex Role Spillover and Sex at Work

Sex role spillover can be manifest in many ways, such as when a woman is expected to make coffee for a group of colleagues or a man is expected to pay for a business lunch with female colleagues. Here, we are interested in sexual behavior at work, so it is the sexual aspects of gender roles that are most relevant. The extent to which the sexual aspects of gender roles spill over or interfere with the work role is likely to influence the number and kind of men's and women's sexual experiences at work.

Impact of Sex Role Spillover on Women

Sex role spillover predicts that women in traditional employment with a strongly male work-role set as well as women in nontraditional types of employment will experience more spillover of the sex object aspect of female sex roles than other women. The nontraditional women will be deviants who are noticeably different from the men in traditional male jobs. They will experience the negative ramifications of sex role spillover in the form of sexual overtures and sexual harassment directed at them (see Gutek and Morasch 1982). On the other hand, the traditionally employed women, those in female-dominated occupations and jobs, will experience spillover in the form of having their sex role and work role merged together. The sex object aspect of the female sex role is emphasized by members of the work-role set when most of them are men. The traditional women who work a great deal with men (such as cocktail waitresses) are likely to be targets of sexual overtures and advances because it is expected in the job. Another group of traditional women, those who work in female-dominated work-role sets, are not likely to feel the interpersonal impact of the spillover because they work only with other women and have minimal contact with men at work. The sexual aspect of the female sex role is irrelevant in an environment with no men. Women in integrated work environments are not likely to experience sex role spillover because their work is not associated with either stereotypically male or female traits.

Impact of Sex Role Spillover on Men

The analysis of sex role spillover in women's jobs rests heavily on the assumption that men tend to emphasize the sexual aspects of the female sex role in their interactions with women at work. Sexuality appears to be a central aspect of the male sex role, although it is rarely acknowledged in measures of male stereotypes or masculinity (Doyle 1983: 197-204; Gutek and Dunwoody-Miller 1986). Their focus on rationality, activity, and work orientation (Bem 1974; Constantinople 1973; Deaux 1985) draws attention away from the fact that sexual overtures and conquests are part of the male sex role. This male sexuality becomes incorporated into male-dominated work environments through the process of sex role spillover. In the case of nontraditional jobs for women, men see women as women first, workers second, and while they might respond to women in many different stereotypically feminine ways, e.g., as their mother or daughter, they prefer to respond to women as potential sexual partners when they fit that image (Benet 1972; Gutek et al. 1983). In the case of traditional jobs for women, the job becomes "feminized." When the work-role set is male dominated, the sexual aspects of the female sex role are emphasized in the job over other aspects of the female sex role such as nurturance or cooperation.

A man is likely to be noticeable in female-dominated work just as a woman is noticeable in male-dominated work. It is not clear, however, how the gender salience will manifest itself and if it will manifest itself in a way that contributes to sexual behavior at work (Brewer and Kramer 1985).

Trying to make a case that women prefer to emphasize the sexual aspects of the male sex role is much more difficult than arguing that men emphasize female sexuality. It is not at all clear that women prefer to relate to men at work in a sexual manner over other types of interaction. In fact, the evidence suggests that they do not (Gutek 1985: chap. 6). One study (Gutek et al. 1983) showed that women view sexual interaction as less appropriate at work than do men. Thus, to argue that men in nontraditional jobs (female-dominated occupations and jobs) have the same problems as women in nontraditional jobs is not very convincing. In fact, since women report that they personally prefer to leave sexuality out of the workplace (Gutek 1985: chap. 6), men in nontraditional jobs may report less sexuality at work than other men with comparable levels of contact with women. All of this may remain speculation; it is questionable whether many men will be in nontraditional jobs as we have defined them.

Men in traditional work (male-dominated occupation and job) where the work-role set is strongly female are an interesting case. We assume that, in the case of traditionally employed women with male-dominated work-role sets, men are in a position to emphasize whichever aspects of the female sex role they want because many of the men are probably supervisors or peers. When traditionally employed men have female-dominated work-role sets, however, it is not clear that women will be able to emphasize whichever aspects of the male sex role they want. It is unlikely that most of the women are supervisors or peers, particularly if the man's occupation and job are male dominated. It is much more likely that the man is the supervisor of the many women.

If the sexual aggressor aspect of the male sex role is a salient aspect of men's behavior at work, it is likely to assert itself in this very situation. In a male-dominated occupation and job, the work itself should reflect the male sex role, and part of that male sex role is being a sex-seeker or sexual aggressor (Gutek, Cohen, and Konrad 1986; Gutek and Dunwoody-Miller 1986; Hearn 1985b). If, in fact, the male sex role contains elements of sexual assertiveness, then traditionally male work should exhibit spillover of these aspects of the male sex role too. In that case, discussing sexual matters or comparing sexual experiences may be relatively common in male-dominated work environments. If that is the case, when men interact frequently with women in these jobs, they may use the workplace as an opportunity to approach women in a sexual manner. Another possibility is that if sexuality is emphasized, men will interpret their encounters with women as sexual overtures by women, whether or not a sexual overture was intended (see Abbey 1982). Yet another possibility is that if sexuality is heightened in these environments, women will respond to the organizational ambience and make more overtures toward men than they would in other settings. In any event, it seems likely that men will perceive more sexuality in what is for them traditional rather than nontraditional work.

Method

Participants

The data reported here came from a telephone survey of 827 female and 405 male working adults in Los Angeles County in the summer of 1980 (Gutek 1981, 1985). Random digit dialing was used to obtain a representative sample, with women oversampled. Interviews were conducted in English and Spanish. Five subsamples of the female survey respondents were identified:

1. Nontraditional: Male majority in occupation and job.
2. Traditional 1: Female majority in occupation and job but not in work-role set.
3. Traditional 2: Female majority in occupation, job, and work-role set.
4. Integrated: Integrated occupation, job, and a work-role set which is not dominated by women.
5. The total sample of female workers.

Note that women in the nontraditional, traditional 1, and integrated subsamples all have a lot of contact with men.

Comparable to the female survey respondents, five subsamples of the male respondents were identified:

1. Nontraditional: Female majority in occupation and job.
2. Traditional 1: Male majority in occupation and job but not in work-role set.
3. Traditional 2: Male majority in occupation, job, and work-role set.
4. Integrated: Integrated occupation, job, and a work-role set which is not dominated by men.
5. The total sample of male workers.

Comparable to the female subsamples, nontraditional, traditional 1, and integrated men all have a lot of contact with women.

On the survey, occupation was assessed through the open-ended question "What kind of work do you do?" and coded using the three-digit occupational codes of the United States Bureau of Census. The sex ratio of the occupation was the percentage of women in that occupational category as assessed by the U.S. Bureau of Census in 1970. An occupation was considered to be male dominated if it was 0%-35% female, 36%-65% female was defined as integrated, and 66%-100% female was female dominated. Sex ratio of the job was measured by the survey question "Thinking about your job classification at work, are there more men, more women, or about an equal number of each?" the responses "more men," "equal number," and "more women" defined male-dominated, integrated, and female-dominated jobs, respectively. The sex ratio of the work-role set was measured by the question "How much time does your job require that you work with men [for female respondents] or women [for male respondents]." A response of "none" indicated a same sex work-role set and "a great deal" indicated an opposite sex work-role set. (Those who answered "some" were not included in the differential analysis of work-role sets.)

Analysis Strategy

These data are used to discover whether the sex role spillover perspective can be a useful explanatory tool in regard to sexuality at work in general and also to particular social-sexual behaviors. Since the data were collected to describe social-sexual behavior at work, not to test specific *a priori* hypotheses regarding sex role spillover, they will be used only in a descriptive sense, without reference to inferential statistics. Because our hypotheses were developed after the survey was completed, our measures of the sex ratios of the work-role set and to a lesser extent of the job are somewhat crude. This is another reason why we will only present descriptive statistics.

Our primary method of analysis is to compare the relative frequency of responses of women and men in the various work categories pertaining to their experiences at work and to note the general patterns that emerge.

The dependent measures fall into two categories: actual social-sexual behaviors directed at the respondents by person(s) of the opposite sex in the course of their current job, and a broad range of questions which measure the sexual ambience at work, questions assessing topics such as the incidence of sexual joking at work and the importance of physical attractiveness to the job. Thus, we consider sexuality at work at two levels; the experience of behaviors directed personally toward the respondent, and the generalized sexualization of the work environment (see Gutek, Cohen, and Conrad 1986).

Results

Eighty-nine women surveyed (10.8% of the sample) were in nontraditional, male-dominated occupations and jobs such as architect, manager, history professor, advertising agent, upholsterer, furnace smelter, and sheriff. Fifty-five percent of these women said they were in supervisory positions and 81% said they had a supervisor. On the other hand, only nine men (2.2% of the sample of men) were in nontraditional, female-dominated occupations and jobs. Among the nine were a registered nurse, a cashier, a waiter, and an elementary school teacher. Six of the nine men reported that they were in supervisory positions.

The data show clearly that nontraditionally employed women experience more of almost all kinds of social-sexual behaviors than any other group of women, as is predicted by the sex role spillover theory (see Table 7.1). They also report that sexual harassment is a problem at work more frequently than the other groups. Thus their visibility as a sexual minority makes nontraditional women the object of social-sexual attention from men.

Since only nine of the 405 men were in nontraditional jobs as they were defined here, female-dominated occupation and female-dominated job, their reports are not meaningful because of the small sample size. They do suggest, contrary to expectations, that the men might experience some of the less severe social-sexual behaviors (see Table 7.1). This is probably the result of simply working in an environment with a great deal of women. Receiving complimentary comments, looks, and gestures is part of the everyday informal male-female interchange, which is rare in a

Table 7.1. Direct Experiences of Social-Sexual Behaviors

Experienced on Current Job	*Nontraditional*	*Traditional 1*	*Traditional 2*	*Integrated*	*Total Sample*
Sample Size					
Women	89	100	33	46	827
Men	9	53	56	8	405
	%	%	%	%	%
Complimentary Comment					
Women	74.2	57.6	28.1	67.4	50.1
Men	66.7	52.8	32.1	50.0	46.0
Complimentary Looks, Gestures					
Women	66.3	63.0	45.5	54.3	51.6
Men	55.6	56.6	37.0	25.0	47.3
Insulting Comments					
Women	20.2	12.1	3.0	15.2	12.2
Men	33.3	13.2	7.3	37.5	12.6
Insulting Looks, Gestures					
Women	13.5	16.0	0.0	11.1	9.1
Men	11.1	13.7	10.7	37.5	12.3
Sexual Touching					
Women	31.5	18.0	3.0	21.7	15.3
Men	33.3	25.0	7.1	57.1	20.9
Required Dating					
Women	6.7	2.0	0.0	0.0	2.8
Men	0.0	0.0	1.8	12.5	2.7
Required Sex					
Women	4.5	4.0	0.0	2.2	1.8
Men	0.0	0.0	1.8	0.0	1.0

predominantly male work environment. As was predicted, however, none of the men said that physical attractiveness was more important than having a good personality, none said physical attractiveness was an important aspect of the job, and none said that swearing occurred frequently; thus, the work environment does not appear to be sexualized (see Table 7.2).

One hundred women (12.1% of the sample) were in what we have defined as traditional 1 work, female-dominated occupation and job but an integrated or male-dominated work-role set. Frequently occurring jobs in this category included registered nurse, bookkeeper, cashier, receptionist, secretary, waitress, airline stewardess, and hairdresser. Forty percent of the women in this group said they were supervisors and 92% said they had a direct supervisor. In contrast, only 33 women were in traditional 2 work (female-dominated occupation, job, and work-role set), indicating that very few women work in mostly female work environments. Only 21% of the women in this group reported that they were in supervisory positions, but 88% said that they had a supervisor. Among the women in this group were a bank teller, a key punch operator, a legal secretary, a telephone operator, a nursing aide, several preschool teachers, and several elementary school teachers. Because traditional 1 women are not deviating from social stereotypes of women, they are less likely to experience sex role spillover in the form of personally directed acts. Instead, they experience spillover because their job requires them to be sex objects to some degree. Thus, physical attractiveness is seen as a very important part of the job to a greater extent than in the other job categories and also a greater percentage of women in these jobs dress to be physically attractive (see Table 7.2). It is not just physical attractiveness which is a part of these jobs but female attractiveness in particular. Forty percent of these women reported that a physically attractive woman would more likely to be hired for their job, whereas, only 1% reported that a physically attractive man would have the advantage. (The remaining 59% said it makes no difference.)

The women in traditional 2 jobs have very different experiences from the other female respondents. Unlike the other three groups of women considered in this study (nontraditional, traditional 1, and integrated), which involved women who were in male-dominated or integrated work-role sets, these women do not come into contact with very many men at work. As we hypothesized, women who work predominantly with women report substantially fewer social-sexual incidents than any of the other groups of women shown in Table 7.1, including the sample as a whole. None of the 33 women, for example, reported experiencing insulting sexual looks or gestures, dating as a requirement of the job, or sexual

Table 7.2. Sexual Ambience at Work

	Nontraditional	*Traditional 1*	*Traditional 2*	*Integrated*	*Total Sample*
Sample Size					
Women	89	100	33	46	827
Men	9	53	56	8	405
	%	%	%	%	%
Sexual Harassment Is a Major Problem at Work					
Women	9.0	5.1	3.0	0.0	2.8
Men	0.0	0.0	5.5	0.0	1.2
My Physical Attractiveness Is Very Important in How [the Opposite Sex] Treat Me at Work					
Women	21.6	18.0	6.3	23.3	16.0
Men	11.1	15.4	8.0	0.0	6.4
Physical Attractiveness Is More Important Than a Good Personality in Treatment by [the Opposite Sex]					
Women	14.8	10.1	3.2	11.1	9.9
Men	0.0	5.8	5.8	0.0	4.3
Physical Attractiveness Is an Important Part of Job					
Women	18.0	23.2	15.2	10.9	18.4
Men	0.0	15.1	7.1	12.5	11.1

continued

Table 7.2. Continued

	Nontraditional	*Traditional 1*	*Traditional 2*	*Integrated*	*Total Sample*
Attractive [Same Sex] Likely to Be Hired on This Job Over Attractive [Opposite Sex]					
Women	12.4	40.0	33.3	15.7	21.9
Men	22.2	13.2	16.4	0.0	15.3
Most Women Here Dress to Be Physically Attractive					
Women	31.5	40.0	33.3	23.9	31.7
Men	22.2	13.2	16.4	0.0	15.3
Most Men Here Dress to Be Physically Attractive					
Women	9.1	18.8	15.6	13.0	15.1
Men	11.1	18.9	25.9	0.0	18.5
Frequent Sexual Talk and Joking					
Women	28.4	35.4	6.3	21.7	24.2
Men	33.3	34.0	35.7	25.0	30.7
Frequent Swearing at Work					
Women	20.5	13.0	3.1	17.4	13.9
Men	0.0	34.6	30.9	12.5	25.6
Organization Accepts Dating Among Employees					
Women	51.2	58.3	52.2	69.2	61.1
Men	62.5	63.0	69.8	62.5	63.3

activity as a requirement of the job. Whereas 18% of the women in traditional work with a highly male work-role set reported being sexually touched, only 3% of women in traditional work with female work-role sets reported being sexually touched by a man. The percentages of women who received comments, looks, and gestures that were meant to be complimentary were also substantially lower. It is clear that much of the reason why traditional 2 women experience fewer social-sexual encounters at work rests in their lesser work contact with men.

The work environment of traditional 2 women as opposed to traditional 1 women is also substantially different. Only 6.3% of the traditional 2 women reported that physical attractiveness is very important in how men treat them at work, and only 3.2% of the women reported that physical attractiveness is more important on the job in terms of treatment by men than having a good personality. This is, of course, a natural consequence of being in a work environment devoid of men. Compared to the women doing traditional 1 work, these women were less likely to say that women dress to be attractive (21.2% vs. 35%). They also report substantially less swearing and obscene language (3.1% vs. 13%). Only 6.3% women with female work-role sets reported that sexual comments and jokes occur frequently in contrast to 35.4% of women who work with men a great deal of the time. In summary, on all of the measures shown in Table 7.1, the scores of this group of women were lowest, indicating the lowest levels of social-sexual experiences and the least sexualized work environments.

Fifty-three men (13.1% of the sample of men) were in male-dominated occupations and jobs yet not in male-dominated work-role sets (traditional 1). Among the men in this group were several managers, a purchasing agent, several engineering technicians, a telephone installer, an office machines mechanic, and a bus driver. Sixty-two percent of the men in this group said they were in supervisory positions; 76% said they had supervisors themselves. The comparison group of traditional 2 employees, male-dominated occupation, job, and work-role set, contained 56 men. Most of these men were in blue-collar jobs, including plumber, roofer, photo-engraver, truck driver, construction laborer, fireman, janitor, warehouseman, longshoreman, gardener, and welder. Only 7% of the 56 were in professional or managerial jobs.

One of the main conclusions from our analysis of male jobs is that very few men work in integrated or female-dominated jobs. Thus, the only meaningful comparisons between men involve those who work in traditional jobs and have male work-role sets and the men who work in traditional jobs but have female-dominated or integrated work-role sets.

The men who work in male-dominated occupations, jobs, and work-role sets (traditional 2) interact with fewer women than the men who work in male-dominated occupations and jobs but female-dominated or integrated work-role sets (traditional 1), and their answers reflect the difference in contact with women. Almost 53% of the men in work-role sets with a great deal of women (traditional 1) reported receiving complimentary comments, 56.5% reported receiving complimentary sexual looks and gestures, and 25% said they were sexually touched by a woman at work. These figures are fairly similar to the reports of women in traditional work with male-dominated work-role sets (traditional 1). The percentages of men in exclusively male work-role sets (traditional 2) who report these social-sexual behaviors are smaller by about 20% from the men who work a great deal with women (traditional 1; see Table 7.1).

An interesting contrast exists between the men and women who report they spend no work time with the opposite sex (traditional 2). The reports of social-sexual activities by men with male work-role sets tend to be higher than reports by women with female work-role sets (see Table 7.1). For men, reports of sexual activity do not seem to be as closely tied to contact with women the way women's reports seem to be tied to contact with men.

Table 7.2 shows that the work ambience of men in the two classes of traditional work is very similar. This is in sharp contrast to the reports of women. For example, 34.6% of the men in the traditional 1 group reported that swearing is common at work and 30.9% of the men in the traditional 2 group reported that swearing and obscene language are common. Of the men in traditional 1 jobs, 34% said the sexual talk and discussion is common in comparison to 25.7% of the men in the traditional 2 group where there is little contact with women.

We contended that traditionally employed women who have work-role sets with a strong male presence would work in a sexualized work environment. This assumes that men are in a position to shape the work environment to emphasize whichever aspects of the female sex role that they please. In general, the data supported both the contention and the assumption. The fact that women in traditional work with female work-role sets worked in different, nonsexualized environments suggested that men preferred and were able to emphasize the sexual aspect of the female sex role when they numerically dominated the work environment. The fact that traditionally male work environments, as reported by the men, appear to be somewhat sexualized, suggests that a sexualized work environment, in particular one characterized by obscene language and sexual conversation, may be an aspect of the male sex role that is emphasized by men rather than by women and takes place whether or not women are present.

There were 46 women and only eight men in integrated jobs that correspond to the definition of integrated work used here, integrated occupation and job, and a work-role set which is integrated or dominated by the opposite sex. Among the women in this group were a social worker, a designer, an editor, a painter/sculptor, and several cashiers and postal clerks. Of these women, 45% said they were supervisors and 96% said they had a direct supervisor. The eight men in integrated jobs included two college professors, two real estate agents, and a postal clerk.

No women in integrated jobs reported that sexual harassment is a problem at work. They also were least likely to claim that physical attractiveness is an important part of their job. Thus, women in these jobs are not experiencing the negative fallout of sex role spillover.

The reports of the men in integrated jobs, like those of men in non-traditional jobs, lack usefulness because only 2% of the men are in such work situations. Those eight individuals report sexual overtures (see Table 7.1) but appear to work in nonsexualized environments (see Table 7.2).

One final interesting difference in the reports of men and women concerns their responses to the question about the organization's stance toward dating among employees (see Table 7.2). Across categories, women are less likely than men to report that their organization accepts dating among employees. For example, 51.2% of the women working in nontraditional jobs said that their organization accepts dating in contrast to 69.8% of the men who work in traditional work with male-dominated work-role sets. These reports should be similar since they are about male-dominated occupations, jobs, and work-role sets. These differences may reflect less on organizational policy and more on men's and women's perceptions of their own potential gains and losses from dating a co-worker, supervisor, or subordinate.

Discussion

In this paper, we have tried to increase our understanding of sexual behavior at work with the concepts of sex role spillover and sex ratios. We argued that skewed sex ratios at work facilitate sex role spillover which often results in a sexualized work environment and increased sexual overtures at work. Sex role spillover, the carryover into the workplace of gender-based expectations about behavior, is a mechanism that can be empirically studied as an underlying factor contributing to sexual overtures and harassment.

When members of one sex are the majority in an occupation, aspects of the sex role for that sex spill over into the work role for that occupation, especially if the majority gender also occupies the high status positions in the work-role set. The sex role spillover is of two types; its effects depend upon whether the person is a majority or minority member. The first type of sex role spillover is that which happens to the person of the gender in the minority. For such a person, there is an incongruence between sex role and work role, because the sex role of the gender in the majority has spilled over to the work role of the occupation. The person of the numerically subordinate gender is essentially a "role deviate" and it is this deviating aspect, gender, that is visible. Hence, a nontraditionally employed woman is a woman "in a man's job." She is perceived and treated differently. Because her gender is salient to herself as well as to others, she perceives this differential treatment to be discriminatory in general and harassment when the context is sexual. She is aware that the differential treatment she receives is due to the fact that she is a woman.

Men are rarely in this position because so few are in nontraditional work. The position of the nontraditionally employed person may be sufficiently uncomfortable that both sexes prefer to avoid the situation. Women are motivated to persist in the face of the discomfort because many of the jobs involved are high in status and/or financial remuneration. Studies of changes of the sex composition of occupations in the United States show that female-dominated occupations have become more sex-segregated in recent years and that male-dominated white-collar and professional occupations have become less sex-segregated (Beller 1984, 1985). There is little that men stand to gain by putting up with being role deviates in "women's work." Jacobs (1983) showed that men who go into female-dominated jobs tend also to re-enter male-dominated work. Female-dominated jobs are not becoming less segregated (Beller 1984, 1985).

If the first type of sex role spillover is to the person in the job, the second type of sex role spillover is to the job itself. Most other people holding the same job are treated similarly. In the case of women, this sets up a condition under which they generally will be unaware of sexual harassment. If overtures, propositions, and even threats happen to other workers in the same job, they are viewed as part of the job and therefore acceptable (or at least expectable) for those jobs. The sexuality aspect of the female sex role spills over to the work role in traditional jobs with predominantly male work-role sets because men apparently prefer to emphasize the sex object aspect of the female sex role. The traditionally employed man with a work-role set in which women are significantly represented also experiences a variety of social-sexual behaviors. Men who are in traditional work with work-role sets with many women, however, do not face the same kind of problems that women do because women do not focus on male sexuality the way men choose to focus on female sexuality. Thus, the traditionally employed man who has a strongly female work-role set is not expected to be physically attractive and dress to be attractive to women. Women in comparable positions are expected to be attractive and dress to be attractive.

Women in integrated work are less likely to have the problems of either traditional 1 or nontraditional women because there is less sex role spillover experienced in those jobs. Their work is not associated with either male or female traits and neither the male nor the female sex role is emphasized. In this study, very few men (about 2%) were in sex-integrated work.

An alternate, more parsimonious hypothesis to the complex spillover perspective is that sheer contact with the opposite sex is related to social-sexual behavior and harassment. Kanter (1977a, 1977b) contended that proportion alone leads to predictable effects. For both sexes, the simple presence of the other sex seems to be related to experiencing social-sexual behavior. Yet, by itself, simple proportion cannot explain the differences between traditionally employed men and women or the differences among integrated, traditional, and nontraditional women where contact with men is generally comparable. Thus, our analyses support the general utility of the spillover framework in understanding social-sexual behavior in the workplace, and can serve as a guide to future research.

Note

1. An earlier version of parts of this manuscript appeared in Chapter 8 of *Sex and the Workplace: The Impact of Sexual Behavior and Harassment on Women, Men, and Organizations,* by Barbara A. Gutek. The authors would like to thank Bruce Morasch for his previous contributions to these analyses. This research was in part assisted by support from the National Institute of Mental Health Grant USPHS-MH-32606-01.

8

Women Managers' Perceptions of Gender and Organizational Life

DEBORAH SHEPPARD

This chapter discusses the ways in which women in management positions see themselves as women and as organizational members, based on interviews with women managers in Canadian organizations (discussed below) and earlier qualitative research involving dual-career couples (Sheppard 1981) and gender and organizational culture (Sheppard 1989). These studies raise both theoretical and methodological questions related to the investigation of women's subjective accounts of their own experiences. The chapter also examines substantive aspects of organizational life. In in-depth interviews, women managers were asked to describe the intersection of two statuses—gender and organizational—through the following questions:

AUTHOR'S NOTE: This research was supported by Grant 482-83-1012 of the Social Sciences and Humanities Research Council of Canada. Parts of this chapter were based on an earlier paper, "Image and Self-Image of Women in Organizations" by D. Sheppard and P. Fothergill, Canadian Research Institute for the Advancement of Women Annual Conference, Montreal 1984.

- How do they experience organizational life?
- How do they see themselves as organizational decision makers?
- How do they define the issues and problems with which they are confronted?

Invisibility of Gender Difference: Theoretical Implications

The reality of gender differences and the content of gender experience tend to remain invisible or taken for granted in situations where one gender moves into areas traditionally designated as the territory of the other. Explicitly, in a male-dominated organizational world, the expectation is that women's experiences can be adequately understood through the filter of the dominant gender culture, and thus the reality of gender is not addressed. An alternative view is not to see organizations as gender neutral or without gender but to understand them as social constructions derived in part from the gender-based experiences of social actors. Literature of the past 20 years has demonstrated the gendered basis of interpretations of organizational experience as well as of social domains such as morality and power (see Chodorow 1971; Miller 1976; Kanter 1977a; Gilligan 1982). These differences, however, have had to be recovered from invisibility within a male-defined social science. The "different voice" to which Gilligan refers in the title of her book has been silenced under an assumed unity of gender experience. The conceptual categories of these (male) theorists, derived from their own taken-for-granted interpretation of the social world, did not allow for the different interpretations of women and men or else distinguished such interpretations or experiences in an evaluative manner. For example, the work of Broverman et al. (1972) has demonstrated that the characteristics perceived as necessary for mature adulthood are seen as healthy when identified as masculine and unhealthy when identified as feminine by mental health practitioners.

Another conceptual device that has served to keep women's experiences either invisible or differentially evaluated when compared with men's has been the analytic distinction between "work" and "family" as two apparently distinct social spheres. The Parsonian dichotomy of instrumentalism/work and affectivity/family has been a most influential construct in shaping research agendas and ensuing theoretical explanations of behavior found in each sphere. The prevailing approach to intrafamily behavior and structure, to organizational behavior, and to the interrelationship between family and work has generally been characterized by an empirically oriented world view, in which the world exists a priori and is knowable through objective observation. Such an approach obscures understanding of how work and family are experienced, perceived, and formulated by women and men and how such perceptions may vary with gender. It also "reif[ies] the social organization of industrial capitalism" (Laslett and Brenner 1989: 399). Such reification makes existing structural arrangements and underlying assumptions appear to be unquestionable. This in turn makes the development of a critical perspective on gender and other power relationships problematic.

This analytic separation between family and work mitigates seeing and understanding how each gender experiences the linkages and interaction between the private-family and public-work domains. The tasks done within families continue to be largely the responsibility of women, whether or not the women work outside the home. Women's and men's work and family roles are characterized by what Pleck (1977) has called "asymmetrical permeable boundaries." Thus, while men are expected to use family time to continue to meet their work responsibilities, women are required to adjust their involvement in paid work to meet responsibilities at home (Sheppard 1988). As the number of women working for wages steadily continues to grow, the organizational demands made on both genders become more similar. The gender asymmetry, however, continues in terms of answering family demands. This imbalance would be expected to affect women's and men's experience of work differently.

Invisibility of Gender Difference: Methodological Implications

The methodological implications of the Parsonian assumptions of gender symmetry between empirically bounded worlds of work and family were revealed in earlier research, in which an investigation was made of family decision making in 25 dual-career couples (Sheppard 1981). This investigation of perceptions of family decision making as part of an ongoing marital reality led to the recognition of the importance of *awareness* of reflection and action as a crucial concept. The findings strongly suggested that the assumption of a concrete, quantifiable marital power structure, implemented as decision making and measured by Likert-type scales, was largely an artifact of the measuring instrument. Respondents' own accounts of decisions painted a picture of a process that is for the most part unseen.

The role of gender as a factor in awareness of decisions emerged in some unexpected ways. Most people in this study were unaware of making family decisions. Women and men differed, however, in their perception of many aspects of family decisions. For example, women were more likely than men to perceive themselves as unaware. Women were less likely than men to formulate their behavior in terms of decision making. Nonetheless, women appeared to be more sensitive to the nuances of decisions than men.

Moving beyond the example of family decision making, these findings impel us to ask: To what extent are people cognizant of their own part in creating their social world? Women and men inhabit what appears to be the same family world and yet have different experiences of that world and formulate those experiences differently. In the case of the respondents in the decision-making study, they also inhabit the same type of work world: the world of the organization. Would they experience the same or other differences in this other social context?

The family decision-making study reveals how conventional quantitative methods lead to a discounting or ignoring of the processual, interpretive aspects of action. The continued use of these methods reflects and reinforces the assumption of the dualism of expressivism and instrumentalism through an emphasis on objectivity and the separation of observation and analysis from values (Glennon 1983). An alternative, ethnographic approach casts the researcher in the position of learner. To do ethnography is to learn about the social world from the standpoint of the actor in the situation. Much of women's experiences appear to have a "hidden" quality when treated with prevailing approaches. For example, the notion of "decision" as used in much of the organizational literature does not connote interaction or relationship, but the decision-making study suggests that "decision" as understood by women has a stronger relational component than for men, even within the personalized context of the family. The notion of "decision" was more embedded in a particular context for women, and they were generally less likely than men to respond to the concept as meaningful when considering it in an abstracted way. An "empathic ethnographic" approach (Smircich 1983a) allows for the emergence of meanings created and sustained by all social actors. The concept of "women's standpoint" used by Smith (1987) and others (e.g., Harding and Hintikka 1983) raises the centrality of women's self-expression and the centrality of the problems in the encounter between researcher and subject. The need to talk and listen from that standpoint is an essential task of feminist research (Devault 1990).

Women's Self-Perception and Organizational Life

This research explores the different ways in which women managers and professionals formulate their experience of organizational life and the types of questions that are useful in eliciting such formulations. As the goal of this study was the elucidation of themes, not hypothesis testing, a purposive sample with a relatively small number of respondents was used. For this purpose, sample selection is based on the detailed exploration of individuals who can articulate particular experiences rather than on typifying or representing a larger group (Stewart 1990: 266). Using a "snowball" sampling method, in-depth interviews were conducted with 15 women who are managers and professionals in 10 large public and private organizations in Canada. This discussion focuses on three questions in particular.

The first research item examined the question: "Do women and men have different organizational lives, in your experience?" All the respondents said there were differences, with two respondents saying that individual differences were at times more important than gender differences.

An essential difference is the perception that men's gender and organizational roles are coterminous, while women often experience the contradiction of being both "feminine" and "businesslike." This contradiction in statuses has produced a range of responses that can be termed *strategies of gender management* through which women try to stay "feminine enough" so as not to challenge prevailing sex role conventions and "businesslike enough" so as to be seen as credible organizational members; that is, being "too feminine" means being seen as "unbusinesslike" (Sheppard 1989). These strategies may be more or less consciously derived, with different attributions of responsibility for needing such behavior. Thus some women assume without overt questioning that it is their responsibility to conform to existing gendered norms, while (fewer) others may have a more explicitly political explanation that cites male domination. Most women express a desire to "blend in," to soften the rigidity with which they believe they are perceived by their male peers.

Kanter (1977a) referred to the paradoxical situation of "tokens." On one hand, they are *invisible* as individuals because their particular characteristics are subsumed by unchallenged stereotypical assumptions (e.g., "women have trouble handling authority"; "women do better handling personnel issues than technical aspects of the job"). On the other hand, tokens are highly *visible* as members of a category because their small number makes them stand out against a background of other organizational actors of a different social group (e.g., gender or race). This high visibility may bring both positive attention and unwanted notoriety. Kanter's use of tokenism suggests that numerical distribution per se, rather than specific social characteristics such as gender or race, can be used to understand and ameliorate organizational inequities.

The gender neutrality of this theory has been called into question, however, suggesting that men tokens do not experience the negative consequences described above in the same way as do women tokens. Ott's (1989) study of male nurses and female police officers suggested that low-status majorities (i.e., women) defer to high-status minorities (i.e., men), while high-status majorities resist low-status minorities. Zimmer (1988) concluded that, for males, the disadvantages of tokenism are minimal and may become advantages, while, for women tokens, the disadvantages may actually increase with growing representation. Overall, the experience of the "feminine-businesslike" contradiction and the ensuing strategizing were seen by women as gender specific: Men did not need to expend anxiety and energy on this issue, as their gender "fit" their organizational status.

A number of other related themes emerge concerning the differences managerial women perceive between their own experiences in organizations and those of their male peers. *Isolation* is cited by most respondents in a variety of contexts. The lack of support from male colleagues, the need for a network of women managers, and a fear of being identified with the other women who are in clerical positions and of lower organizational status are recurrent themes. Women can't take for granted with whom they can associate, as they perceive the political consequences that may devolve from even the most casual or informal contacts. The salience of traditional sex roles makes certain social contexts beyond the reach of women, such as taverns, strip joints, private clubs, or sporting events, where men socialize but also carry on organization-related discussions. Women are thus excluded from such discussions and relationships.

Managerial and professional women continue to experience a *double standard* of treatment in relation to other managers (both peers and senior level), staff, and clients. Women cite examples concerning differential treatment regarding travel opportunities, promotions and transfers, and working late or overtime, whereby they are bypassed, ignored, or discounted as serious candidates. This double standard may be rationalized through explanations that are protected from real scrutiny. For example, in a study of North American women in positions in Asia, Adler (1987) examined North American companies' continuing reluctance to send women managers to international positions despite examples of successful individual women in such postings. This double standard has been justified by widely held beliefs about women managers being culturally incompatible in such settings, the implication being that this was a pragmatic rather than a discriminatory rationale. Women, however, found that managers in host countries considered foreign status more important than gender. It was the women's home companies that considered gender to be more salient.

The double standard is also felt with regard to explicitly sexual behavior. Sexual *harassment* has been recognized by researchers as a form of social control in the workplace. But it is important to understand the general pervasiveness of sexuality as a feature of organizational life and the relationship of sexuality to the maintenance of the existing patriarchal power structure (Hearn et al. 1989). Sexuality is often used to punish women who are seen to violate gender or organizational norms. That which constitutes such a violation, however, is subject to constant change, over which women have little or no control. Thus women are subject to having their sexual identity unpredictably override their organizational identity as a means of protecting the status quo (Sheppard 1989: 154).

A number of examples were cited by respondents that suggest managerial and professional women in male-dominated environments are vulnerable to having their organizational status overridden by their sexual identity. It is not clear how frequently such instances occur, as sexual innuendoes are often emotionally charged and their interpretation or disclosure is not necessarily forthcoming from respondents. One woman described several incidents where informality and alcohol led to a "Dr. Jekyll and Mr. Hyde" transformation of men with whom she worked. One involved an executive with whom she had enjoyed friendly and helpful relations; at night on a business trip that included a number of managers, the executive "banged on my hotel room door for two hours." Another incident involved an industry social function where a considerable amount of alcohol had been consumed by many of the men present (this respondent was the only woman manager attending). A relatively new male manager made a loud and crude remark about the size of the respondent's breasts. She said that her colleagues appeared disconcerted, but their response was directed toward her response rather than toward the man who had made the remark.

In addition to questions of overt sexuality, a double standard in relation to aging and to pregnancy was mentioned. Others mentioned problems in being seen as "inexperienced" rather than "up and coming" because of their age; some talked about the need to stay looking youthful, while men's gray hair was a sign of experience and wisdom. Double standards related to body language and speech were also cited.

Interaction between women and men reflects differences in organizational experience. Women are singled out and their visibility heightened through verbal strategies of boundary maintenance, so clearly identified by Kanter (1977a). Many women mentioned swearing as a way of establishing normative rules and of challenging women to confront or accept the status quo. Humor is often used in a testing way. One woman commented: "Men build themselves up by using putdowns." Another woman mentioned that she is addressed in meetings so as to heighten her marginal status: "Gentlemen . . . (pause) and lady." Another woman described how men who are uncomfortable dealing with her interpret her business manner as aggressive and tell her, "Why don't you smile?" Behavior that is overly solicitous or patronizing carries a message of trivialization; for example, one woman described a fellow manager's questions about making travel arrangements, or consoling remarks after she had her ideas rejected in a meeting, as well meaning but offensive and out of place, suggesting that she was either helpless or subject to hurt feelings. Several women describe a strategy of assertiveness whereby they deliberately take the initiative in interaction.

This strategy has in common with other strategies mentioned earlier the fact that they are exactly that: *strategies*. Whether they attempt to modify speech and appearance or to be more assertive, these women talk of a self-consciousness concerning self-presentation as organizational members that they do not perceive men as sharing. Men are sometimes seen as behaving differently with women than with men; a personnel manager described how men have used a much more personal manner with her in private, to the point of crying, but maintain a different demeanor in public with other men present. She described the pressure to behave in a "macho" way by saying that, for men, it was like having a "football club at work," with the ensuing peer pressure toward conformity along sex role lines.

Approach to career and work is another differentiating theme. A common statement was that women need to work harder than men for the same recognition and that career moves are interpreted differently for women than for men. Respondents frequently described men as being more aware of building a career and of having a long-term view of their organizational involvement. Several women said that they felt women tend to be too specialized and too person oriented, and that these characteristics keep women from being able to be upwardly mobile. One woman said that women tend to develop expertise in a particular area and are fearful of trying to expand their function, especially in a male environment, whereas she described men as seeing themselves as generalists who "always have the answer." While these women generally feel that opportunities are opening up for women in organizational careers, and feel that they are proof of this, there is also a perception that, at senior levels, mobility for women is blocked. The senior management is frequently described as the "old guard" who don't understand women who work. The younger men with working wives who are seen by some managerial women as more sympathetic to women's situation have not yet moved up in the hierarchy, and it remains to be seen how these men will continue to regard claims of gender equity as competition for upper-echelon positions increases.

The perception that women need to work harder than men reflects a double standard held by other organizational members but is due also to an attitude of greater consciousness or anxiety about getting the work done. This perception also leads to a dilemma: Women may be held to a higher standard of performance yet may be negatively labeled as "ratebusters" (Sheppard 1989: 155). The isolation of women managers means that they have more difficulty in learning the informal rules of organizational functioning (and possibly the formal ones as well). Not knowing the discretionary limits means that there is less flexibility possible with anxiety resulting from not knowing how much room for manoeuvering is available. One woman described how, on being transferred to a new city, she got her house organized during lunch hours and after work, while a male manager of comparable rank took three days off work when he was transferred. She described her behavior as "overcompensating" for not knowing the rules and felt that her neophyte status spilled over into gender status: "When you're not familiar [with the rules], you follow the straight and narrow. If you happen to be a woman, you're seen as less flexible, but it's because you don't know the rules."

Women's Self-Perception and Decision Making

The second research item focused on the question: "Do you think women and men make decisions in the same way, or differently?" Of the 15 women, 12 identified differences. Some of the answers were qualified; either respondents felt that, because there were so few women managers, they hadn't been able to observe systematic differences, or else they felt that personality differences outweighed gender differences.

Women were generally described as "more humanistic" and "person oriented" as opposed to being primarily "cost oriented" when making decisions. Their style was often seen as being service oriented, having a greater concern with maintaining good relations rather than with hard negotiating, and characterized by a greater use of persuasion and appeasement. Women's decisions were seen as being more emotional, less calculated, and more personalized. It was suggested by one respondent that women are more concerned than men with how a decision will be perceived by others because they have a higher profile. A somewhat different perception, but one that also emphasizes the personal aspect of decisions, sees women as tending to be motivated more by job satisfaction issues than by the political dimensions of decisions. (This lack of political awareness will be discussed below in reference to the third question posed to the respondents.)

There were some variations in the perception of how quickly or decisively women act. More respondents said that women tend to take longer with decisions, that they are more thoughtful; some related this to the fact that women may be less confident in their organizational role and are reluctant to make "hard economic decisions" because they are less willing than men to run the risk of making a mistake. Several respondents believe that women need to be better prepared, that they are more meticulous and tend to study a decision longer.

Quick, "gut-level" decision making is attributed to both women and men but is perceived as being evaluated differently for each gender. Thus men who use this style are seen as decisive and prepared to take some risks. It is behavior seen as both gender and context appropriate. One woman said that men's gender status and length of organizational tenure give them enough credibility that, even if they have limited experience, they don't have to prepare and don't have to suffer the consequences. She said that, for a woman, the same behavior is seen differently: "I can't talk off the top," and in the past she had "been shot down for being dogmatic."

Others said that women tend to make decisions more quickly, are more spontaneous, and use gut feelings more. This view of "women's intuition" suggested that, while culturally associated with women, their gender status detracted from the credibility of this approach in an organizational setting. One comment on this style connected its use by women to a need or desire to impress men; this respondent said that many men are impressed with "big grandstand statements" and that some women may feel pressured to appear to perform in this manner. As suggested above, women who use this style may be viewed more negatively, as dogmatic or unprepared, when compared with men who make decisions in this same way. Because of the implicit value placed on the gut-level style when associated with men, however, women who use a more deliberate or slower-paced decision style may be seen as tending to vacillate or hedge on their decisions, with their conclusions not being stated decisively, using tentative language such as "I think" or "I hope."

These women managers perceive their male peers' decision making in terms that emphasize an involvement with the process of decision making rather than with substantive decision areas. It was not ability to make decisions that was cited; the style and approach of men were seen as producing apparent differences. Men are characterized as being more likely than women to make organizational decisions based on personal career paths. Men are described as more calculating, more direct, and more politically aware in decisions. In the words of one respondent, "I don't take into account the political implications, whereas men are influenced by this. They check upward, checking with the boss to see if there are any other factors they should be aware of."

Men are seen as less consultative and as being less open to persuasion than women. Personal and social factors, which are seen as different than organizational politics, are described as figuring less in men's decisions than in women's. One woman manager who heads a very large department in a public agency dominated by male technical professionals said that the men in her department tend to consider personal factors as peripheral; she described them as "straight line thinkers."

Men are perceived as having a more individualistic approach to decisions; one woman described this as "a need for men to put their personal stamp on decisions." This style is identified by respondents with men's earlier experiences in boys' schools, universities, and sports clubs. Respondents saw men as having had the chance to develop a buddy system and to learn how to make decisions in that context, which also prepared individuals to compete for star status. This earlier learning is believed to give men greater comfort than women have with the decision process. As a result, women perceive men as needing to prepare less for organizational decisions but as not experiencing negative consequences from this. One woman said, "Men don't go through a process of analyzing. They go through a gut level and 25 years of experience." The competitive aspect of male peer group culture is reflected in what several women described as men's greater interest in the negotiating or political process than in the substantive or business aspect of decisions. Men are also seen to have greater access to bargaining resources, including such "bait" as tickets to sports events. The presence of other men is seen as affecting men's decision style; the respondent who talked about the tendency of some men to make "grandstand statements" described this behavior as "chest pounding" carried out for the benefit of a male audience and said these men tended to behave less aggressively or assertively in private. The very language is seen as different; men are described as being more forceful and decisive in their speech. One manager stated, "We don't speak the same language. We give different interpretations to things like anger."

Women's Self-Perception and Organizational Concerns

The third research item dealt with women's evaluation of their experience of organizational life: "If you were studying the experience of women managers, what kind of question would you want to ask? Could you try to answer that question now?" Derived from the work of Bougon (1981: 178), this technique reveals the "cognitive maps" of actors, that is, "the enacted self and enacted environment of a social actor, as well as the pattern of their relationship." Responses to this question suggest a sense of organizational life as it is experienced and interpreted and also suggest substantive areas for further research investigation. Eight basic themes emerged. (Respondents generated varying numbers of questions, often covering several theme areas.) The key underlying experience basic to all these themes involved a sense of *isolation,* as discussed above. These respondents express a great need to know about the experiences of other women in their situation. The ambiguity and general lack of informal information and reference points can be attributed directly to the marginal, token status of these women. They may not know how to proceed or what to say in various circumstances but, unlike male organizational "learners," they do not have a reference group whose direct advice or example is available. This lack of a frame of reference contributes to a pervasive sense of anxiety concerning possible future developments with unknown consequences, such as career mobility, interactive effects of work and family demands, and so on.

Questions of *power and organizational politics* were raised explicitly and also emerged as subthemes in the context of other questions. Respondents wanted to ask questions such these: "Who are your strongest allies, women or men?" "How do women get into positions of power?" "Where does power come from?" "How much in control do people feel with their work lives?" "How do women and men handle organizational politics?"

A related theme emerged involving *strategies for organizational survival and change*. Most of these strategies involved the need to overcome the negative effects of isolation. Women were concerned with forming networks with other women or with establishing positive relationships with male colleagues. Learning how men managed and how men thought and behaved was seen as a politically based strategy. Education for young women in math, science, and business; good guidance programs; and on-the-job training were seen as contributing to a sense of ability and efficacy and thus helping to overcome the feelings of marginality and uncertainty. While several women saw increased assertiveness as necessary, others counseled against confrontation and advised using humor, developing a sense of perspective and a "comfort factor." The high visibility likely to result from assertiveness was seen as counterproductive. In assessing men's reaction to such a strategy, one manager said, "Men don't forget or forgive." Credibility and acceptance are seen as being achieved through blending in, which helps reduce the sense of isolation.

The theme of *victimization and double standards* expressed fears of exploitation. Women were seen as needing to work harder than men and to appear more serious and responsible about their jobs while not always receiving the recognition, salary, or title that were warranted. Questions were raised about promotion opportunities. Several women described having a "smaller margin for error" in making decisions, being challenged on issues about which male colleagues assume they are ignorant, and having their arguments trivialized. A number of respondents gave specific examples of harassment and discrimination.

Perception by others was expressed through questions concerning how the respondents were seen by male peers and superiors, male and female subordinates, aspiring women in the organization, and family members and friends. One woman, for whom personal recognition is important, said that her boss regards this as immature and feels that "recognition of a good manager is being ignored." This led her to pose the question: "Are you seen as too concerned with people's response to you and is this more likely if you're a woman?"

A connected theme involves *other women's experiences and relations with other women.* Questions were asked about relations between women managers and other women within the organization, between women in different organizations, between women bosses and subordinates, between successful and unsuccessful women. This theme reflects the underlying problem of isolation; the lack of an established and accessible reference group creates a vacuum of experience for these women, who express a strong need to compare their own situations and reactions with those of other women.

The theme of *self-perception* involved questions concerning feelings of success and inadequacy, of how demanding women are of themselves and how they feel about politics and competition.

Expectations concerning work, salary, promotion, and career development emerged in questions that were generally comparative, wherein women expressed a need to know how much money other women managers earned or to know how their own salaries compared with the male managers in their organization. One woman described how she had backed off from an offer of promotion because she didn't feel ready; she felt that a man wouldn't have reacted in this way. Reasons for having selected a nontraditional occupation and the need for measuring women's progress in the business world were other questions that were asked. Again, these concerns reflect the feelings of uncertainty stemming from a position of perceived isolation and powerlessness. Women appear to have difficulty knowing how to compare their own work experiences directly with others', lacking an obvious reference group. It therefore becomes problematic to judge whether one is actually succeeding at work in terms of reward and career mobility.

Questions concerning *competing demands of work and family* were generally raised in anticipation of future problems, usually the prospect of maternity. Women were concerned about how the men with whom they worked would feel about their taking maternity leave. They worried that they would be seen as less committed or serious about work. Concern was also expressed about pressures to work extra hours, nights, and weekends and the implications of these pressures for family life. One woman feels pressure from her personal relationships about her work life ("My husband's friends wonder why he married a career woman; [my friends] think I'm screwed up because I'm seen as giving things up for my career") and anticipates pressure about the morality of "leaving kids in day care." These women's responses suggested that they feel they are breaking new ground in dealing with the combination of work and family pressures. They don't have a clear sense of what solutions or strategies to follow, or even what the particular problems may be. The men with whom they work are not seen as having to deal with these problems, and there aren't enough women in their work environments to serve as examples or sources of advice.

Conclusions and Implications

These research findings suggest that the organizational experiences of women managers and professionals are to be likely characterized by deep tensions and ambivalence. Despite their own sense of entitlement or competence, women may find themselves subject to what Barbara Gutek and her colleagues have called "sex role spillover"—the carrying over of expectations based on gender into the organizational context that are inappropriate to work (Nieva and Gutek 1981). In their attempts to minimize this spillover, women can be seen to have developed a variety of strategies for keeping organizational and gender statuses from being seen by others as in conflict. The *content* of these norms may change somewhat over time, but the perceived conflict between the two continues to be a problem for women. This means that it is problematic to keep track of the line distinguishing the statuses, because it changes as the content of the statuses changes. It is also problematic because women do not know predictably when the men for and with whom they work will ascribe more importance to what they perceive as women's family obligations over their work responsibilities. Regardless of how carefully women may plan for pregnancy, for example, so as to minimize loss of time from work, or if they have decided to not have children, they may find that assumptions of absence and withdrawal from work are made without verification. Thus the asymmetrical character of women's and men's work-family boundaries, discussed at the start of this chapter, is carried over from the family to the work world as well, with assumptions of separation for men and of permeability for women.

For women, the balancing act involves maintaining a view of their organizational position that acknowledges the factors outside their control but that still gives them a sense, or illusion, of efficacy and power over their own situations. This balance is precarious. All these women, including the ones who are confident of their organizational situation, walk the high wire.

These findings provide an essential balance to the very partial picture of women's work experience provided by statistics of labor force participation, numbers of women in management positions, and so on. Much of the prevailing literature has presented a falsely optimistic picture of the future, suggesting that gender discrimination and imbalance can be remedied through different socialization processes or intraorganizational restructuring (Blum and Smith 1988). The embeddedness of sexism in social structures beyond a particular organization continues to profoundly shape the reality of the individual workplace. This is borne out not only in the analyses of macro-level data (Blum and Smith 1988) but also in the perceptions of individual women as described here. What are the implications for women's lives when they begin to enter the male culture of the organization in other than stereotypical female roles, not only at management levels but at all organizational strata? The proliferation of popular magazines aimed at working women attests to the isolation and sense of marginality expressed by so many respondents. These findings suggest that such women have a strong and urgent need to know about each other's experiences and that these experiences reflect a continuing fundamental inequity in the reality of women's work lives.

9

"The Clerking Sisterhood": Rationalization and the Work Culture of Saleswomen in American Department Stores, 1890-1960[1]

SUSAN PORTER BENSON

The work of recent historians has made it clear that work culture is an important key to understanding the lives of past generations of workers. By work culture I mean the ideology and practice with which workers stake out a relatively autonomous sphere of action on the job, a realm of informal, customary values and rules which mediates the formal authority structure of the workplace and distances workers from its impact. David Montgomery and Harry Braverman (Montgomery 1976; Braverman 1974), in particular, have shown us the power and importance of the work culture that united

AUTHOR'S NOTE: This chapter originally appeared in Susan Porter Benson (1978) "The 'Clerking Sisterhood': Rationalization and the Work Culture of Saleswomen in American Department Stores, 1890-1960," *Radical America* 12:41-55; reprinted by permission of *Radical America.*

conception and execution in the hands of skilled male workers in the nineteenth century. The tales they tell, however, are those of decline, despite Montgomery's vivid evocation of workers' struggles to preserve their traditional control over production. In the end, the effect of scientific management on these workers was decisive: skill was undermined, the work degraded, the control of the informal work group over the work process and the social relations of the workplace inexorably eroded.

The history of women's paid labor and of the work culture growing out of it is somewhat different. My research on the work of saleswomen in American department stores from 1890 to 1960 suggests that, at least in this major women's occupation, the effect of changes in management practice over the twentieth century was, ironically, to increase the level of workers' skill and thus inadvertently to permit the development of a powerful and enduring work culture. There are critical differences between women's work and the men's craft work which is the central concern of Montgomery and Braverman. First, for most women in the paid labor force at the turn of the century, work was so poorly paid and so brutally demanding of mind and body that it would be difficult to conceive of its further degradation. This is as true of women's white collar work as of women's factory work; women were never career clerks like Bartleby the Scrivener or fledgling entrepreneurs like R.H. Macy, but entered office and sales work only as they were becoming proletarianized. In the case of women's occupation, therefore, the story is not one of unrelieved degradation of the work process. Second, the study of women's work shows that craft skill was not the only basis of an effective work culture. The informal work group which throve among saleswomen was grounded in the social relations of the selling floor. It was, in fact, exactly because new management practices in the department store industry altered these social relations only minimally that they failed to undermine the position of the informal work group and the strong influence of work culture over worker behavior.

As defined by the Census Bureau, a department store must sell a wide assortment of home furnishings as well as clothing and related items, but for my purposes this definition is too narrow. I include in the category "department store" those stores which saw themselves as part of the department store industry and which behaved like true department stores in their internal organization and policies. My arguments would therefore apply to specialty stores which carried only apparel, such as Filene's in Boston, as well as to chains such as Sears, Roebuck, which are outgrowths of mail order houses. Even by the Census Bureau's limited definition, however, the department store has had since 1929, when figures were first compiled, a larger share of total retail sales than any other detailed classification except grocery stores, auto dealers, and gasoline dealers.

Department stores have historically been major employers of women; since 1900, the job of saleswoman has ranked among the top ten women's occupations. The proportion of women in the department store workforce seems to have stayed fairly stable at around two-thirds since the early twentieth century. Most of these women have been in selling positions, with clerks making up from just under half to ninety per cent of the total store force, depending upon the level of extra services provided by the store. The experience of the non-selling workers had far more in common with production workers in manufacturing industries than with clerks, and so I have omitted it here. Saleswomen have not only been important numerically, but have played a central economic role as well. As Braverman notes, a key aspect of management is marketing, or the production of customers (Braverman 1974: 265-66); in this process, salespeople are basic production workers, and the only ones who have close and frequent contact with the customers.

Work culture is constrained but not determined by management practices: the two are constantly in struggle and cannot be understood separately. I focus below on some large continuities in the department store industry's development, minimizing short-term changes and fluctuations in order to suggest an overall conceptual framework. Probably the single most important factor in understanding large-scale retailing both as an industry and as an employer is the split consciousness of retail managers. On the one hand, they have been businessmen pure and simple, seeking to maximize profits by reducing costs. On the other, they have thought of themselves as purveyors of a service, managers of social institutions which sold not just merchandise but also style, respectability, and urbanity—things not strictly accountable in dollar terms, but which were of course expected to pay off in a general way.

In the early twentieth century, department store managers improved their physical plant, ameliorated basic working conditions, and centralized control in much the same way as the factory managers described by Daniel Nelson in his admirable book *Managers and Workers* (Nelson 1975). What he calls "the new factory system" appeared in the factory between 1880 and 1920, and about a decade later in the large store. The department store management strategies which emerged during these years would be elaborated and spread more widely in the next thirty years, but not fundamentally changed.

First of all, department stores grew impressively. By 1898, for example, Macy's had 3,000 employees, making it comparable in size to such manufacturing giants as the Merrimack cotton mills in Lowell, the Waltham Watch Company, and Carnegie Steel's J. Edgar Thompson Plant, as well as larger than the towns in which sixty per cent of Americans then lived. Although most stores were far smaller, the change in scale from the early nineteenth century's typical small, highly specialized shop to the department store was enormous. Retailers preceded factory managers in coping with the problems of scale; as early as 1905, for instance, department stores had widely adopted a functional structure which major manufacturing firms were only beginning to adopt by the 1920s (Chandler 1962). This four-part functional organization consisting of merchandise, service or store management, publicity, and control or accounting divisions was the rule in department stores until after World War II.

Selling work in the turn-of-the-century department store had much in common with both sweated and machine-tending modes of manufacturing. Elements of the sweatshop in the department store included squalid surroundings, minimal sanitary facilities, unlimited hours, and mandatory unpaid overtime. From another point of view, clerks in most large stores were taught to regard their counters as machines to be tended but not controlled; they were expected to wait passively for customers, politely give them what they asked for, and send the merchandise to the wrapper and the payment to the cashier. Their work was defined negatively; they should not violate store rules or commit blunders of etiquette.

Department store sales work changed not just as part of a general change in business climate and in accepted managerial wisdom, but also as a response to two problems specific to department stores. First was the bad publicity given to department store working conditions by the Consumers' Leagues after 1890. Department stores were peculiarly vulnerable to public observation of their labor policies. The contrast between the work lives of their employees and the atmosphere of gentility and even luxury which they tried to convey to their customers was telling indeed. Worst of all, the reformers came from the same upper income strata as the stores' most valued customers. As one magazine writer put it, "The public resents the worn out, famished type of clerk and its feelings are hurt by seeing women faint behind the counter." (O'Hagan 1900: 535)

The second factor was the lagging productivity of the distribution sector of the economy compared to the production sector. While the output per person-hour in production increased two and a half times between 1899 and 1929, output per person-hour in distribution increased only one and a half times in the same period. Within a given store, the figures were sometimes even more discouraging to managers: for example, at Macy's the average yearly sales per employee doubled between 1870 and 1938, while the average weekly salary quadrupled.

Department store managers met the challenge of public relations and productivity with the full range of measures used by their counterparts in manufacturing, but with somewhat different results. Nelson has classified the elements of the new factory system into "three interrelated dynamics—the technological, the managerial, and the personnel;" of these, the technological was by far the least important in the department store. Basic urban technology such as electric lighting, elevators, and improved ventilation helped to make the store a cleaner and more pleasant work place, but did not affect the sales transaction. Well-designed display cases and clothes racks, when substituted for the old practice of storing goods in huge piles, made it easier for the salesperson to show goods to the customer, but left the social interaction of the sale unchanged.

The managerial dynamic in the department store took much the same form as it did in the factory. After the depression of the early 1920s, the merchandise division, traditionally the foremost among the store's four divisions, found its territory invaded and colonized by other divisions, in large policy matters as well as in day-to-day operations. The controller, armed with sophisticated new accounting procedures, exerted a degree of financial surveillance over the merchandise division which had earlier been impossible. Second, with the development of advertising and the consumption economy of the twenties, retailers redefined their economic role: it was now "to act as purchasing agent for the consumer, rather than as sales agent for the manufacturer" (Judelle 1960: 14). In this new atmosphere, the merchandising division's traditional close relationships with manufacturers and wholesalers took a back seat to the judgment of the publicity division and its prophet, the fashion stylist. Third, this new active type of selling demanded salespeople who were more carefully selected and trained, functions which were assigned to newly created personnel departments.

From the perspective of the individual selling departments, these changes meant the diminution of the power of the buyers and floor-walkers, whose jobs changed in much the same way as that of the factory foreman. Buyers had traditionally been prima donnas, running the departments with intuition and high-handedness; the new buyer was hedged in on all sides by financial, style, and personnel requirements imposed by the other three dimensions. Similarly the new floorwalker was no longer the suave host to the customer and the tyrannical disciplinarian of the sales force; at best, his job was downgraded, and at worst his tasks were split up among lesser employees. The new effect of these changes in the authority structure of the selling floor was to limit broad discretion on the part of the salesperson's immediate supervisors; authority moved up the hierarchy.

Finally, the personnel dynamic led to the gradual centralization and standardization of hiring, training, and employee service functions under the aegis of a single department. Beginning around 1890, department stores undertook extensive employee welfare activities frequently outdoing factories in providing lavish dining, recreation, and health facilities to elaborate social programs, and even vacation retreats. By the twenties, the welfare departments were being transformed into personnel departments which took over the old program and combined them with the newest techniques of employee recruiting, testing, and training.

These innovations, whether technological, managerial, or personnel, failed to change fundamentally the basic tasks of the salesperson, as they did the work of most factory employees. In 1960 as in 1910, sales work was made up of the same combination of waiting on customers and attending to stock. In fact, while most manufacturers wanted to dilute skills and to produce a new category of "semi-skilled" workers, retailers strove to upgrade an unskilled workforce into a skilled one. They sought to inculcate not the skill of the nineteenth-century machinist, or of the hand craftsman, but rather a new twentieth-century form of skill: skill in complex social interaction, skill in manipulating people rather than objects, a skill which would be taught by management rather than one that grew out of the workers' own grasp of the work process. An insistence on the centrality of selling skill is the dominant theme of retail management literature from the time of World War I to 1960.

The emphasis on selling skill grew partly out of retailers' ideal of service to the public, and partly out of the resistance of retailing to standardization and control in two major ways. First was the fluctuation of volume in the store's work place; the flow of customers varied from department to department, season to season, day to day, hour to hour. Equally unpredictable were customers as individuals: their wants, moods, and personalities varied in infinite combinations and made each transaction a unique situation. Management's best efforts to standardize conditions on the selling floor availed little, and it remained a highly unpredictable and largely uncontrollable environment in which the salesperson was expected to make the most of every opportunity to sell.

Department store managers resisted the alternatives to skilled selling which other branches of retailing devised; they were never wholly satisfied with allowing customers to be pre-sold by advertising or to sell themselves in self-service departments. These methods were part of the department store arsenal of selling tactics, but only preliminary steps in a strategy of skilled selling. On the one hand, person selling (as it came to be called) differentiated department stores from their crasser competitors, giving customers a reason to shop at Gimbel's rather than at J.C. Penney's; on the other hand, the department store's high proportion of fixed costs for such expensive services as parcel delivery meant that the payoff for sales efforts to boost the size of each transaction was high. In one department, for example, an 80% increase in the size of a sales transaction meant a 600% increase in the net profit.

Everything, then, converged on selling skill; the nature of the work, the managers' image of themselves, and the financial structure of the business. It was, however, difficult to define and transmit this skill. Was selling an art? A science? Was it inborn? Learned? Managers' definition of it varied as much as condition of the selling floor, in large part because of the contradictions surrounding the work of selling in store life.

The first contradiction in fostering selling skill was the contrast of bosses' high verbal valuation of sales work with their own avoidance of the selling floor and the low social status of the work. The retail literature constantly urged executives to spend more time on the selling floor, teaching by example and proving that management regarded selling with respect, yet department store managers were notorious for fleeing to their offices. Their behavior reflected not only their own sense of store hierarchy but also the generally bad image of sales work. Most saleswomen could console themselves only with their marginal prestige as white-collar workers and some minimal reflected prestige from their association with wealthy customers and luxurious goods, for the physical strains, psychological demands, hours, and pay of their work did not compare very favorably with factory and clerical work. Moreover, sales work had a number of similarities with domestic service, an increasingly unpopular occupation. John Wanamaker's classic statement that the customer was always right subjected generations of saleswomen to the idea of unquestioning obedience to customers' whims. Dress codes set uniform-like limits on what saleswomen might wear. And, finally, saleswomen found distasteful the personal services, such as helping customers try on clothes, which they had to perform.

The second major contradiction in skilled selling was between store managers' belief that they should and must teach it to their workers, and their actual unwillingness or inability to do so. When training became a formal store activity with the establishment of Filene's training department in 1902, it was negative, remedial, and mechanical, focusing on eliminating error in paperwork and procedure. Conceptions of training subsequently broadened to include sales techniques, merchandise and fashion information, and general education, but the 1942 lament of a saleswoman was sadly true. "The average salesperson does not respect her job because management too often doesn't seem to care as long as her book [sales tally] is passable and she doesn't make too many errors in her transactions" ("A Saleswoman Speaks to Management" 1942: 18).

The problem was that selling skill was learned not in the store classroom but rather in experience with merchandise and customers on the selling floor. Managers recognized this, and a Macy's program to collect and codify salespeople's "selling secrets" into a booklet entitled "20,000 Years in Macy's" was typical of their efforts to take over shop-floor knowledge. It should be emphasized that training difficulties were not due to resistance by salespeople; one survey showed them eager for substantive training (in merchandise training and techniques of selling and display) but uninterested in classes on trivia such as personal grooming. Sometimes, salespeople did balk at training, but small wonder when they were required to chant in unison "Personal service means showing interest" when an instructor held up a cutout of "a cheerful smile" ("How Bloomingdale's Trains" 1964: 24-25).

The final contradiction in the upgrading of selling grew out of the fact that any but the most perfunctory sales transaction depended for its success on rapport between people of different classes. In most large department stores, the counter was a social as well as physical barrier. On the selling side were women of the working classes; middle class women with a choice shunned the low status and difficult conditions of store work. On the buying side were women of the middle and upper classes; as late as 1950, the department store clientele included twice as high a proportion of upper income people as the population as a whole. One observer sympathetically reported on the resulting tensions:

> "It seems," a salesgirl said to me, "as though all the women who have servants they dare not speak to, or a husband who abuses them, take special delight in asserting their independence when they come to buy from us girls, who must say 'Yes ma'am' and 'Thank you' in the sweetest possible way."

> Often, within the hearing of sales people, a woman will make to the friend accompanying her some such remark as this: "I wouldn't buy that if I were you; only the shop girls are wearing them."
>
> It is common for customers to show, at least by their manner, that they consider the sales people beneath them. (Leffingwell 1922: 150)

Managers persistently tried to ease this conflict by giving their employees a veneer of bourgeois culture; most of their efforts were absurd and superficial, such as requiring saleswomen to memorize a few French words and the names of chic Parisian streets, but a few spoke hopefully of remaking saleswomen's "inner consciousness" with "a cultural background which would enable [them] to talk easily, informedly, about the qualities of [their] merchandise . . . in such a way as to express its esthetic values as well as its use values" ("Expose Employees to Knowledge" 1938: 35). Such programs generally backfired; saleswomen bungled (often, I suspect, intentionally) the minutiae, snubbed and therefore offended customers if they took the training too seriously, and for the most part simply continued to judge their customers' needs and means by their own class values.

The Development of a Work Culture

While managers, caught in these contradictions, were unable to control skilled selling behavior, the saleswomen themselves were developing a strong work culture and durable informal work groups. Conditions on the selling floor encouraged worker autonomy. Saleswomen spent only a small part of their time—some estimated as little as one-third—with customers and so had many opportunities to socialize with one another, enhanced by their relative freedom to move about their departments. Moreover, it was difficult to supervise a salesclerk closely. A supervisor who meddled during a sale risked annoying both clerk and customer and thus sabotaging the sale. The saleswomen's duties while not actually serving customers were often indistinguishable from the activities of the informal work group; a gathering of clerks might be discussing new stock, but then again they might simply be gossiping, and the lines between the two were never clear. Finally, unlike production workers who could only play production off against the bosses, saleswomen could play a complex three-way game, manipulating managers, customers, and merchandise to their own advantage.

Despite wide variations in time, place, and type of store, the basic features of the work culture of selling are clear. Sources discussing highly diverse situations from very different points of view reveal quite similar practices and standards. I do not mean to suggest that all saleswomen everywhere shared an identical work culture, but rather that the situation on the selling floor evoked analogous reactions among workers in different departments. What I am outlining is the range of variation of the work group's rules and tactics; every department devised its own individual subculture within the parameters of the work culture of selling in general.

The foundation of the informal work group was some degree of departmental solidarity. Departments were not only the administrative and accounting units of the store, but were social units as well. The selling departments of a large store were far more independent from one another than the production department of factories, and were unlinked by any sequential processes. Moreover, personnel managers staffed departments selectively: young, attractive women were hired for the first-floor departments, glamourous women to sell high-fashion clothing, heavy women to fit their half-size sisters. There was an unofficial hierarchy of departments in the store, and solidarity frequently developed around a given department's place in it. The custodians of the fine linens regarded their stock, and therefore themselves, as a cut above the rest of the store in elegance; the women in one chaotic bargain basement refused transfers to upstairs departments because they preferred the liveliness and bustle of the basement. The physical and functional differences between departments, therefore, became social barriers as well, contributing to the power of the informal work group by emphasizing the uniqueness of the department.

Social interaction on the selling floor was friendly and supportive. The tendency of saleswomen to "huddle" or "congregate" on the floor was the aspect of their behavior most frequently remarked by managers and customers alike. Bosses constantly complained of high spirits and boisterous sociability in the departments, and did their unsuccessful best to stamp out loud laughing, talking, singing, and horseplay. Saleswomen in the more solitary departments shared stockwork and paperwork even when it was assigned to individuals, and reinforced day-to-day contact with parties, both on the job and after hours. They integrated the rituals of women's culture into their work culture; showers and parties to commemorate engagements, marriages, and births (women in Boston stores who left to be married were sent off with a shower of confetti) are reported in employee newspapers by the score. Not all departments were this close, this intensely friendly, but it is significant that even when managers note that a department is quarrelsome and divided, they almost always marvel that it still unites in self-defense against outside threats.

The practices of the informal work group continually reinforced departmental solidarity. Work culture provided, first of all, an initiation process whereby new members were received, taught the ropes, and kept in line until they showed themselves willing to go along with the group. The initiation was not always a friendly one; new, part-time, and temporary clerks complained long and loud about mistreatment by regulars. Second, work culture supplied a common language with which saleswomen could discuss their world. Clerks had terms for types of selling behavior as well as for varieties of customers. A "crepe-hanger," for instance, was a salesperson who ruined a sale by talking a customer out of something she had resolved to buy; a saleswoman who called "Oh, Henrietta," while waiting on a customer was alerting her co-workers to the fact that the customer was a "hen," or a difficult type. Third, work culture imposed sanctions on those who violated the group rules: penalties included messing up a transgressor's assigned section of stock, bumping into an offender or banging her shins with drawers, public ridicule and humiliation, and complete ostracism, which sometimes drove people to leave the department. If the informal work group demanded loyalty, it repaid it with protection: it insulated the individual worker from the demands of bosses and customers alike.

Saleswomen had an ingenious variety of tactics for manipulating managers, customers, and merchandise to their own advantage. The first element, management, was well aware that saleswomen's highjinks were not just a way to blow off steam, but were evidence of an underlying unity. Bosses understood that the selling floor was the turf of the clerks, that it had its own elaborate rules and social system which were distinct from and often in conflict with the store's formal structure. They tried sporadically to suppress the more disruptive outbursts of the informal work group but in general they treated it with a wary respect and at least partially yielded control of the floor to it. They relied on the "clerking sisterhood" to maintain good order and high morale; they cautioned new workers to tread lightly until they learned the customs of the department; they even tried to co-opt and institutionalize the informal initiation process by designating one saleswoman an official sponsor of new clerks. Saleswomen were astute observers of their superiors, punishing the bad and rewarding the good. A boss who gave offense received the cold shoulder or petty harassment in return; the ultimate penalty was to embarrass a buyer or floor manager in front of his or her superiors. A boss deemed worthy of respect could count on the saleswomen's backing when it counted, particularly against upper management.

Management directives frequently emerged from the crucible of work culture in quite altered form. Saleswomen reorganized cumbersome paperwork routines to fit their own convenience, and sometimes completely thwarted their purposes: in one department, they effectively short-circuited a management scheme for subtracting returned purchases from individuals' sales totals. Clerks refused to take on extra duties which would eat into their "spare time," and when they felt threatened by new practices, such as self-service, they fought back by doing sloppy or eccentric stock work on the new displays. Concerted action could bend rules quite sharply: the eight women in one especially well-unified women's shoe department unilaterally lengthened the lunch hour from 45 minutes to a full hour and compounded the insult by wearing huge hoop earrings forbidden by the store's dress code. A helpless management acquiesced. The informal work group also covered up for a certain amount of theft of merchandise and materials; managers warned one another worriedly that a department infected with the virus of thievery was a serious threat indeed.

The most important and effective way in which work culture worked against the interests of the bosses, however, was in restricting output and limiting intradepartmental competition. Each department had a concept of the total sales that constituted a good day's work. Saleswomen used various tactics to keep their "books" (sales tallies) within acceptable limits: running unusually low books would imperil a worker's status with management just as extraordinarily high books would put her in the bad graces of her peers. Individual clerks would avoid customers late in the day when their books were running high, or call other clerks to help them. Saleswomen managed to approximate the informal quota with impressive regularity, ironing out the fluctuations in customers' buying habits in ways the managers never dreamed of. They adjusted the number of transactions they completed to compensate for the size of the purchases; if they made a few large sales early in the day, they might then retire to do stockwork. During the slow summer season or during inclement weather, they were more aggressive with the smaller volume of customers; at peak seasons, they ignored customers who might put them over their quota.

Department store managers attacked the workers' stint with a bewildering variety of commission, commission-plus-salary, and quota-bonus payment schemes beginning in the years just before World War I, but monetary incentives to break worker solidarity were no more effective with saleswomen than with skilled craftsmen. The definitive industry study of these plans concluded, not surprisingly, that no pay scheme could increase sales output, but that sales levels were linked to the overall atmosphere of the workplace. Bosses reported similar failure with competitive devices such as sales contests, even when they offered cash prizes, although they occasionally reported successes with group, as opposed to individual, incentive schemes. As universally as managers complained about restriction of output, nowhere did a boss testify to the successful elimination of the practice, even in the most insecure days of the depression.

The strongest epithet in the saleswoman vocabulary—"grabber"—applied to those unwary clerks who ran excessively high books. The grabber seized on customers out of turn, sometimes two and three at a time; she shirked stockwork and paperwork; she gave the department a bad name for offensive overselling. The fear of grabbing accounts in large part for the rigors of the departmental initiation process. Ignorant of the amount of the informal quota, and perhaps even of its very existence, outsiders—new, part-time, or temporary clerks—required stern socialization. In some departments, newcomers were effectively prohibited from making any sales at all for the first few days; part-time and temporary clerks were exiled to the dullest corners of the department. The retaliatory power of the informal work group was amply demonstrated in one children's wear department when the management made the mistake of firing a popular though unproductive saleswoman and immediately replacing her with a new employee. The new clerk, experienced in the ways of saleswomen's work culture and sensible of the hazards of her position, tried eagerly to learn how the department defined a "good book," but her co-workers kept the information from her and thus excluded her from the work group.

Customers were the most strainful and least constant factors in saleswomen's work lives, barraging them with a kaleidoscopic succession of demands, moods, and quirks and constantly coming in for special treatment by the informal work group. While management ingenuously maintained the fiction that all customers could expect equal service, saleswomen picked and chose among their customers and served them with widely varying degrees of interest and efficiency. As one clerk, clearly near the end of her rope, put it, "All customers are crackpots!"; her co-worker, more relaxed and still wary, grimly affirmed, "I like a counter between me and the customer" (Lombard 1941: 348, 355). The customer was not an unambiguous enemy, for under the right conditions she might become the saleswomen's ally against management, but she was always a potential threat.

A theme that appears in management literature almost as frequently as "huddling" is that saleswomen, even those on commission, used a variety of tactics to avoid waiting on customers. Methods ranged from the subtle (pretending not to notice customers while engaged in stockwork or in conversations with fellow workers) to the blatant (disappearing on sudden errands) to the outright rude (explicit refusals to show merchandise). The work culture allocated customers among saleswomen in ways that included rough rotation as well as reserving certain types of customers for certain clerks; to violate this order was to risk being labelled a grabber. But there was a larger message to management and to the public in this behavior: the saleswoman was taking her clients on her terms and not theirs; while they might have a superior class position, she had the upper hand through her control of merchandise. Hence, two important subthemes in management's laments about clerks' indifference to customers: first, they displayed goods reluctantly and usually only on direct request; second, they often addressed customers with unbecoming familiarity—the term that made bosses especially apoplectic was "dearie."

A customer whose only sin was to appear in the department when saleswomen were not prepared to greet her met with indifference, but far worse awaited the customer who committed a more active offense against the "clerking sisterhood." If a customer appeared to a saleswoman's practiced eye to be a looker, she might be harassed or treated rudely; if she asked for something that was out of stock, she might be told scathingly that no one wanted those anymore; if she was too slow in making up her mind, she might find a number of clerks ganging up on her to force a choice. Saleswomen discussed the worst customers loudly within earshot of other customers, an unsubtle warning to those who might dare to cross them.

Customers could be allies, however. A saleswoman who took a liking to a customer and sincerely tried to please her might be genuinely upset if she failed. In order to smooth rough transactions, saleswomen had a number of tactics with which they could secure the good will of the customer, often causing store management extra trouble and expense in the process. Clerks could suggest the delivery of small parcels to close a sale quickly, or suggest that a tediously undecided customer send home a selection of merchandise to reflect on at leisure. Dry goods clerks generously over-measured yardage while their pleased customers looked on. To quiet customers' doubts, saleswomen would make wild guarantees or outrightly misrepresent merchandise; they also encouraged customers to place costly special orders instead of trying to talk them into something in stock.

Saleswomen often built up clienteles of frequent customers, keeping files of their addresses and purchases with their employer's encouragement. On the one hand, close clerk-customer relations could encourage extra purchases, but on the other saleswomen gave their clientele special treatment that was contrary to managers' interests—for example, they withheld items from display until markdowns could be taken on them, and then alerted favorite customers. Moreover, it was not uncommon for saleswomen to concentrate so exclusively on "their" customers that they completely ignored new or unknown customers.

Just as saleswomen would not wait on all customers equally, so they would not sell all goods with equal energy. Saleswomen developed legendary instinct for good sellers; as one retailer put it, they could "spot a lemon quicker than a Mediterranean fruit fly" (quoted in Eerkes 1934: 78). It was an unwritten rule that buyers should heed their judgments, a rule which saleswomen enforced ruthlessly. In one toy department saleswomen refused to sell stuffed toys that they had pronounced too low in quality, labelling them "drug-store Easter bunnies" (Farquhar 1933: 14). Frequently, saleswomen took a real proprietary interest in their merchandise, occupying themselves with stockwork and displays to the practical exclusion of selling. They eagerly showed fresh and interesting goods, consigning older or worn items to bottom drawers where they awaited profit-eating markdowns. Managers were sometimes able to introduce new items only with great difficulty. Domestics saleswomen were so impressed with the virtues of all-wool and Irish linen goods that they strongly resisted the introduction of synthetic fibers after World War II; buyers reported that clerks undid the advertising efforts of stores and manufacturers with their "silent scorn" for the new materials ("Training for Better Sales" 1953: 28).

Investigators who were dismayed at this lack of interest with which saleswomen presented goods and the noncommittal or even inaccurate answers which they gave to questions were even more appalled when they discovered that these same saleswomen were extremely knowledgeable about their wares. One notable silent saleswoman, for example, was so intrigued to know more about her stock that she eavesdropped on a manufacturer's representative. There was no doubt that the training in merchandise information was conveying the message to the clerk; the problem was in convincing her to pass it on to the customer. In general, clerks persisted in selling what they themselves preferred, if they made special efforts to sell anything at all. A woman who tried to buy service-weight stockings from a clerk enamored with sheer silk hose would be treated insultingly; a customer contemplating a purchase, such as expensive silverware, which a saleswoman considered extravagant would be strongly discouraged.

Saleswomen not only policed the merchandise offered by the department, but also keenly observed the selling skill displayed by co-workers. A sociologist doing field work in a women's dress department observed the saleswomen "Playing Customer." They watched in total absorption as two among them acted out a sale, re-creating familiar types from both sides of the counter. The skits were social glue, shared rituals in which the saleswomen reemphasized their group solidarity against the perennial threat of the customer. They also constituted an oral tradition, passing along and elaborating the wisdom learned on the selling floor. Finally, they reinforced the department pecking order by the ways in which different members were caricatured. Other departments had other forms of selling drama; frequently, saleswomen would demonstrate their selling skills to their co-workers by lavishing attention on "lookers" on slow days.

This recognition of selling skill suggests that the informal work group could tolerate a certain limited amount of amiable competition as long as it did not threaten the relationship of the whole group to managers and customers. Clerks could compete over favored customers, preferred selling locations, or rights to certain kinds of merchandise. Sometimes, these competitive aspects could erupt into outright conflict; more often, however, it appears that the relative flexibility of the selling floor allowed individuals to stake out special roles which were then tacitly recognized by the group. Hierarchies of age, experience, ethnicity, and skills played some part in assigning these roles, but there was ample room for simple personal inclination. In one department, the turf was elaborately allocated by the informal work group, despite bosses' persistent efforts to change the arrangement; the group functioned peacefully because everyone knew her place and kept to it. The clerking sisterhood was not invariably one big happy family, although it often was; but whatever the internal discord, it was clearly saleswomen's work culture and not managers' conceptions of selling skill which determined their conduct.

Conclusion

The outline of the development of the work of American department store saleswomen from 1890 to 1960 suggests some factors which we should bear in mind in studying the history of women's work. We must, first of all, rethink our definitions of skill. Whether in the store, office, or factory, most women's work has been regarded as unskilled, but we should find new ways to conceptualize work which reflect its real nature and are not bound by traditional male-oriented notions of skill. Second, we should be alert to the fact that a linear degradation of work was not the invariable fate of the woman worker. It is critical to understand the impact of the whole process of rationalization: the limits of the application of scientific management, its differential effects on men and women, and the importance of other types of management reform, particularly personnel work and human relations. In many occupations, the impact of a more wholesome work environment may have been greater than that of Taylorism, and in some occupations managers actually sought, at least for a time, to upgrade employees' skills. Finally we must investigate the ways in which work culture and the informal work group limited management's freedom of action and provided a measure of workplace autonomy for workers. The work culture of women workers is particularly ill-understood, but sales work provides an example of an enduring work group in the face of rapid turnover, a high incidence of part-time and temporary work, and women's supposed primary identification with home and family rather than with paid work. The prospects for the future are mixed; innovations in data processing and the pressure of discount store competition may well have undermined the conditions favoring the work culture of saleswomen, and increasing numbers of workers are seeking the formal protections of a union in addition to those of the informal work group, but the practices which I have described here are hardly a thing of the past.[2]

Notes

1. The phrase "the clerking sisterhood" comes from Zelie Leigh (1926: 205).

2. I wish to thank Edward Benson, Ann Bookman, Roslyn Feldberg, Maurine Greenwald, Barbara Melosh, and Susan Reverby for helpful and supportive criticisms on earlier versions of this paper.

Because of space limitations, I have only annotated direct quotations and sources that do not apply to department stores below. The sources I have used for this paper fall into five categories:

a. Management literature: *System* and its successor, *Business Week*; the *Bulletin* (later titled *Stores*) and other publications of the National Retail Dry Goods Association, the major department store trade association; the *Dry Goods Economist,* later the *Department Store Economist*; the *Journal of Retailing*; and a variety of retailing handbooks and training manuals. This material is useful principally in learning about managers' ideas and practices, but it is also possible to deduce a great deal about workers' behavior from management's complaints about them.

b. Store histories: although all are management-oriented, and some nothing more than long advertisements, they provide some useful information. The best are LaDame (1930); Ralph M. Hower (1943); Henry Givens Baker (1953); Robert W. Twyman (1954).

c. Master's theses written by students in retailing at Simmons College and the University of Pittsburgh: Most of these take the form of case studies, based on the student's field work in a selling department; they are especially revealing because of the students' position as present worker and future manager. Rich sources of anecdote.

d. The single most valuable source I used was a human relations study of the children's wear department at Macy's, Lombard (1955), and the thesis on which it is based, Lombard (1941). Lombard is an extremely astute observer, and, more important, he has great respect for the people whose work lives he studied.

e. Articles from the popular press, social investigators' reports about department stores, novels, films: I have used these here only for background, but they are rich sources indeed for the study of the cultural aspects of consumption.

10

Merit and Gender: Organizations and the Mobilization of Masculine Bias

CLARE BURTON

The contribution of organisational processes to women's subordinate status in the labour market needs particular emphasis. It has been too easy for critics of Equal Employment Opportunity (EEO) programs to refer to women's child-care responsibilities, or to their prior-to-work socialisation, or the choices they have made in education and employment when attempting to explain their lack of career advancement or lower rates of pay.

There is a further reason for concentrating on organisational processes. EEO plans are developed in acknowledgement that it is within work organisations that inequalities may be initiated or reinforced, through rules and practices that directly or indirectly discriminate against women.

AUTHOR'S NOTE: This chapter originally appeared in C. Burton (1987) "Merit and Gender: Organizations and the Mobilization of Masculine Bias," *Australian Journal of Social Issues* 22(2):424-35; reprinted by permission of the Australian Council of Social Service.

Yet EEO initiatives tend, in practice, to concentrate on strategies which might lead to a redistribution of women among existing job categories without questioning the distribution of tasks among jobs, or the relationships among jobs in different occupational categories. Neither do they promote close investigation of daily practices which use gender as the basis for decision making.

We need to explore organisational arrangements by going beyond the assumption that a neutral administrative logic prevails or can be forged, and ask, to what extent do gender relationships inform the application of rules, hiring decisions, initial assignment practices, training and development decisions, promotional matters, performance evaluation, salary offers and conditions of work?

It would appear, and illustrations are provided in this paper to support this view, that ideas about masculinity and femininity are embedded in organisational arrangements and that the opportunity to accumulate "merit" and the attribution of "merit" are structured along gender lines. If we accept that merit, defined as job-related qualities of individuals, is reproduced and/or changed by organisational activity, then we must look closely at how this affects different categories of workers. It may be that perceptions of gender-based competencies and inclinations affect assignment and other practices and therefore the distribution of women and men among different types of opportunity structures within work organisations. It may be too, that as EEO programs successfully eliminate discriminatory rules, discriminatory practices based on interpretations of such rules produce similar effects but go relatively unnoticed at an official level.

We need to emphasise the social nature of the gender relationships to which we refer. It is not possible to speak of the fortunes of individual women without reference to the structure of relationships between men and women in our society. Women, historically speaking, have not been as active nor as successful as men in pursuing their work related interests and neither have they had the same opportunities to do so collectively, through trade unions or professional associations. Whether it be "coercive or cultural," it is unlikely that women "will exploit the opportunities for bargaining presented by their working environments as intensively as do their . . . male counterparts" (Ryan 1981: 17). If organisational practices have been built up historically with men's typical life patterns as their foundation—including men's reliance, generally speaking, on domestic support—through a "mobilisation of masculine bias," then reference to women in organisations is a reference to a general condition at the work place, despite variations in women's experiences there. That is why we need to cast our investigative net to the structural arrangements which, if left intact, will continue to operate to the disadvantage of women in paid employment and which will be activated to re-create women's subordinate status.

A central question, if one is going to counter the ideology of individual choices in job and career decisions, is whether women are in positions within organisations because they choose to be there, or because there are allocative processes occurring which lead them to be appointed to or remain in positions where advancement opportunities are not readily available. This is clearly not a cut and dried matter, but I choose to emphasise the allocative processes because the evidence suggests their impact is more significant than much of the writings on the subject would allow. Certainly different answers to this question underlie the arguments for and against affirmative action programs.

The concept of choice informs liberal political thought and neo-classical economic thought, and both are dominant modes of explanation of individuals' public activity. They inform the arguments of those who believe that affirmative actions are a new form of injustice, a form of positive discrimination. Those arguing in the tradition of liberal democratic thought find the concern with "abstract groups and their purported rights" violates that "essence of liberalism [which] has always been concerned with the welfare, rights and responsibilities of *individuals qua individuals*" (Hawkesworth 1984: 340, citing Nisbet 1977: 52). On the other hand, proponents of affirmative action implicitly or explicitly question the adequacy of these theoretical formulations for explaining the distribution, indeed the generation of economic and other rewards in our society. They suggest that if individual members of a group are disadvantaged as a result of their group membership, then the structuring of opportunities in education and employment are neither neutral nor fair (Hawkesworth 1984: 343). Redress and positive measures, then, need to be addressed to the group and to relationships between groups.

An exploration of the different conceptions of individuality underlying the opposing points of view gives a clearer picture of what is being contested. Hawkesworth's discussion is particularly useful for our purposes here. She contrasts what she calls an atomistic conception of individuality with a socialised conception. The former "asserts the primacy of choice and effort as determinants of individuals' success," the latter emphasises the impact of cultural norms and group practices upon the development of individual identity (1984: 346, 336). She argues that the atomistic conception "overlooks the extent to which the individual's impressions, desires, sensations and aspirations are socially constructed, founded upon a host of intersubjective understandings, incorporated into language, culture and tradition" (1984: 345). Those who base their propositions on the atomistic view are in effect asserting that organisational processes or labour market processes deal even-handedly with each individual party to the employment situation (Ryan 1981: 4). Orthodox economic theory is based on the atomistic conception of individuality. The human capital school, for instance, characterises

> an individual's productivity as almost entirely under that individual's control. He or she is born with certain capacities, develops them through training or education, "chooses to invest" in himself or herself, and then presents the prospective employer with these capacities for appraisal and reward (Bergmann and Darity 1980: 156).

The socialised conception—that individuality is a product of historical processes, of racial, sexual or cultural experiences (Hawkesworth 1984: 336)—can be extended into organisational life. We can go beyond conventional explanations of an individual woman's employment opportunities and look at perceptions of her at the work place which are consistent with wider social evaluations of women's work and which affect her initial job assignment and subsequent advancement.

But the socialised conception of individuality gives us another leverage point. It indicates that identity is in constant construction through social practices, including those at the work place (Game and Pringle 1983: 16). The atomistic view gives a static picture of identity, and omits work organisations as a ground on which it develops. Furthermore, identity in the atomistic view is neither masculine nor feminine, but sexually undifferentiated (Pateman 1983: 10), whereas in the socialised view, masculinity and femininity are integral dimensions of the continuing process of individual identity formation.

The following examples of organisational processes provide evidence to challenge the atomistic conception of individuality on which opposition to affirmative action is firmly based and which "influences [one's] very capacity to perceive the existence of discrimination" (Hawkesworth 1984: 336).

Initial Job Assignment

Initial job assignment discrimination achieves its importance through the ways it feeds into other forms of discrimination, including wage discrimination (Newman 1982; Rosenbaum 1980, 1985).

A study was conducted into a New South Wales government department to establish whether patterns of job assignment and subsequent advancement emerged within a cohort of base level clerical recruits, all of whom came in under an identical entry standard. Areas with flat career structures "attracted" more women; at the next level females were spread over fewer streams (despite an overall majority in numbers) and there were fewer female promotions above the second level (MR 1982). At base grade level or during the year following, when decisions allocating people to areas of work are made, most recruits are not aware of the career implications or advancement opportunities in different clerical specialisations. The allocator may well know that a particular area is a "dead end" and this study suggests that women are more likely to be streamed in those directions. The women end up receiving what Rosenbaum calls a "custodial socialisation" (1979: 237) rather than a challenging one, affecting self assessment and other's assessment of capacity for advancement.

If we look further up, and ask why women are not entering higher grades, we need to look back at initial assignment and early decisions about streaming. If caution is exercised in allocating women to challenging positions, the problems are reinforced further up the hierarchy. The evidence suggests that initial assignment to challenging positions is more significant for subsequent advancement than later events, that "assessments in an employee's first few years have profound and enduring effects on later career outcomes" (Rosenbaum 1979: 223; see also Berlew and Hall 1966; Veiga 1983). To the extent that choice is exercised, it is governed in large part by the ways the situation is structured by the allocation process, ways informed by sex of the recruit, but consisting of processes which the atomistic conception of individuality does not provide for.

Training, Development and Study Leave

We can distinguish training which enhances people's current job performance from that which is preparation for promotion. Indeed, this distinction may well be formalised in an organisation's procedures. But there remain areas where the distinction is blurred. Supervisors then interpret the circumstances according to their own views.

An investigation was carried out in a Commonwealth government department of supervisors' comments on application forms filled in by candidates for the Study Assistance Scheme. The investigation explored the reasons given by supervisors for approving the applications for study leave of women and men in jobs which had no opportunities for advancement built into them (routine) and jobs from which people normally advanced to positions higher in the hierarchy (non-routine). The focus of the study was on whether the supervisor approved the application for short-term benefits only (that is, for improving current performance) or for long-term and more general benefits (that is, for career development). For men in non-routine jobs, 100 percent of supervisors' comments focused on long term benefits; for women in non-routine jobs, 60 percent; the supervisors of men in routine jobs focused on long-term career benefits in 91 percent of the cases, and for women in 56 percent of the cases (Major 1985). Approval for study assistance, then, was given to more men in routine jobs on the basis of career development than to women in positions which allow for some advancement. Sex of the applicant was a more salient characteristic than organisational position.

This example indicates that the situation is not simply that people in routine jobs are assumed not to be capable of moving out of them: men and women are dealt with differently, whether they be in routine or non-routine jobs (see Kanter 1980). Expectations of them are different. We have already noted the importance of expectations as determinants of behaviour and aspirations. There is no possibility of reconciling these practices with the atomistic formulation of individuality which denies the force of social cues (Rosenbaum 1979: 225), of others' expectations, and of the limitations others impose on one's career prospects.

"Trying Helps Men, Hurts Women"

This example relates to perceptions of ability or competence. Effort—individuals' efforts to improve themselves—is significant for productivity and therefore advancement and wages, in orthodox economic thinking. However, we can criticise the gender blindness of this framework by referring to research results which indicate that the perception of effort, and the interpretation of it, are different when viewed in men and women, with subsequent effects on reward structures.

Sex stereotyping has been shown to affect the evaluation of people's performance on tasks and the attribution of causes of good and poor performance. Men and women tend to rate men's work more highly than women's and men's performance on tasks more highly than women's identical performance (Nieva and Gutek 1980; O'Leary and Hansen 1982; Ruble et al. 1984; Shepela and Viviano 1984). When the participants in experimental studies are asked to give explanations for successful performance on the part of men and women, they tend to rate the female as more motivated and less able than the male. In other words, good female performance is perceived as due to effort, and good male performance as due to ability:

> The process of evaluation includes not only the judgement of the worth of the performance being evaluated but also the attribution of causality for that performance. Causal attributions are important because they determine whether specific performances are seen as accidental occurrences or as likely to be consistently repeatable in the future. (Nieva and Gutek 1980: 269)

If, for instance, successful performance is attributed to ability, then one would suppose that the level of performance might be repeated for some time to come. This is relevant to decisions about advancement (Ruble et al. 1984: 351). If, on the other hand, the performance is due to effort, then this could be regarded as a temporary or situationally determined event, leading to no firm conclusion about future performance. O'Leary and Hansen conclude from their review of a range of research findings that "trying helps men, hurts women": effort is "perceived as diagnostic of men's ability, and compensatory of women's lack thereof" (1982: 117).

Job Design and the Politics of Skill

Many jobs have been designed on a gender base. By this is not meant simply that we can describe typical men's jobs and typical women's jobs, or that we can identify features of jobs that might make them more appropriate for one sex or the other. While we do need to investigate how some have been designed in such a way that being a man or being a woman is viewed as fundamental to their performance, we have to understand that as a reflection of gender *relationships*. Cockburn, for example, in reference to the design of work in some typically masculine trades, comments that

> units of work . . . are political in their design . . . the appropriation of bodily effectivity on the one hand and the design of machinery and processes on the other have often converged in such a way as to constitute men as capable and women as inadequate. (1981: 51)

Secretarial and "boss" jobs are probably the clearest expressions of work that developed and is structured into organisations using gender relationships as their basis. Characteristics regarded as typically feminine—notably, dependence and lack of ambition for oneself—are the complement of the masculine characteristics of the incumbent boss, to whom the secretary is attached. The perception of the job incumbent—the female secretary—informs the job definition. The definition of the main components of the job stress the relationships of it to another job. This definition is used for the evaluation of performance in it: the job is selectively perceived as a "circumscribed helping role" (Schrank and Riley 1976: 94), performance is assessed in terms of effectiveness in assisting a higher ranking incumbent. What is not assessed, because it is perceived as unimportant, are the skills which actually equip the incumbent to assume a higher ranking job herself.

The skills valued, then, are the skills in looking after the interests of another job incumbent. This has wide-reaching effects on the opportunities offered to secretaries:

> Many female jobs "tied" to higher ranked male jobs would probably provide superb training experience for upward mobility. It is a commonplace observation that many women, especially secretaries, actually perform many of the tasks that constitute the associated male job. Such women are brought into decision-making and they exercise control over the male incumbent's subordinates. If one were to construct a training job that would allow the trainee to see and participate in the work of a higher ranking office, the design in many respects might resemble the secretarial job. (Schrank and Riley 1976: 93-94)

The determination of the relative worth of jobs, then, currently reflects a masculine bias and undermines the training and experience that much of women's work involves. Many examples can be presented of this. A general condition for this situation is the combination of three factors: the higher value placed on masculine work; the fact that even when women's skills have been acquired through training and experience they have been explained partly in terms of "natural" ability; and the lack of recognition of the informal training ground that the domestic sphere provides for many of the skills for which women are employed (see Burton 1985: 126). For example, the job evaluator for the United States Government Printing Office

> awarded no points to female bindery workers for training or experience in hand sewing "because the sewing was of the variety that most women know how to perform" thereby undervaluing the female compared to the male bookbinder jobs. (Ferraro 1984: 1170)

The male counterpart was paid more for doing the same job because he had to acquire the skills. However, the masculine equivalent of "natural" ability is highly rewarded at the work place, as witnessed by the remuneration paid for many jobs demanding physical effort.

We can extend this view even further by taking account of the fluidity of the category of skill or merit. Definitions of what is meritorious can undergo change depending on the power of particular groups to define it. Phillips and Taylor remark that skill is a direct correlate of the sex and power of those defining it, an ideological category rather than an objective economic fact (1980: 79). Kessler and associates suggest that "women pursuing expertise may find it being redefined as they reach for it" (1985: 46). This partly results from the process already referred to: women's successful performance is less likely to be attributed to ability than men's successful performance. We have, too, to take into account the likelihood that if jobs can be filled by women, they will come to be perceived as less difficult.

The Exercise of Authority

The examples of allocations to and remuneration for positions where the exercise of authority is important, illustrate a range of practices which together contribute to the unequal fortunes of women and men within work organisations. The cultural association of masculinity and authority (Caplow 1954: 238-41) is reproduced through the decisions made by managers and supervisors who are concerned, for productivity reasons, not to disturb this "natural" relationship. Arguments are put forward about women's incapacity to perform in supervisory positions, not because of a lack of competence, but because of the effect it would have on groups of workers, and therefore on productivity levels.

> If one person is assigned to supervise a group of employees, the supervisor will be more effective in expediting production if the supervisor has no personal characteristics that make it difficult for some of the assigned subordinates to give respect and to submit to direction. (Bergmann and Darity 1980: 157)

In other words, the "taste for discrimination" can be justified in productivity terms. Here productivity is acknowledged to be a function of a group's relationships and not simply a function of individual effort. This example reinforces the argument I began with: the relationships between motivation, aspiration, effort and opportunity are not located within an individual but are a function of relationships between individuals. The chances of a person to acquire and demonstrate "merit" are heavily dependent on the content and quality of the social relations of the work place.

This example, too, needs to be put into the social context as a whole, where the exercise of authority is highly regarded and rewarded. Level of remuneration is a concrete and visible symbol of authority (Rosenbaum 1980: 2; see also Greenwood 1984), and of the hierarchy within organisations. Indeed, the association of high salary with authority legitimates the hierarchy. The allocation of women to "complex staff positions that involve significant discretion" and of men to positions "involving considerable supervisory authority and control of major assets" (Sigelman et al. 1982: 668)—the latter defined as being of greater value to the organisation—simultaneously legitimates the relative status positions of men and women and their income differential.

Conclusion

Current practices do not wholly rest on individual merit or competence but on a range of perceptions, evaluations and decisions already based on a set of arrangements and understandings which provide women with less access to opportunities than men. Analyses of the distribution of opportunities as determined by daily practices could be carried out through the setting up of careful monitoring devices directed at practices which research such as that detailed above brings to light. These might add to our understanding of the ways in which people are favoured because they are *perceived* to be more capable, or more deserving, of advancement, on other than job competency grounds.

The illustrations provided above highlight the ways in which social processes enter organisations through perceptual and cognitive maps which emphasise gender as one of the more significant guideposts for interpreting organisational behaviour. They serve as a warning to those who seek to teach women simply to "fit in" to existing organisational arrangements. These are not experienced by men and women in the same way. Behaviours important for men's success are not directly transferable to women because identical behaviour is not perceived or treated in the same way. Success is not defined in sex-neutral terms.

The implementation of EEO programs tends to concentrate on the distribution of opportunities in organisations, opportunities for certain jobs, promotion, financial rewards, training and development, and mobility. It tends, too, to concentrate on who has what job, and what women must learn to compete effectively for existing jobs. This concentration is at the expense of a critical examination of the current shape of the opportunity structures within organisations and the activities which tend to reproduce it.

The attempt to dismantle indirectly discriminatory rules as if they are a relic from the past, as if their elimination will effectively eliminate the problem of discrimination, is to deny that their presence has continued to structure the interests and perceptions of current organisational participants. The attempt to remove them will generate a new field of protective activity, in the practical application of the now non-discriminatory rules. The mobilisation of masculine bias does not disappear with the elimination of discriminatory rules. It is to practices that we must turn our attention, as well. When we refer to equitable organisational arrangements, we are not restricting our view to the "narrow, distributive concerns of equity" (Pateman 1981: 36) which address who has what job, nor to the formal rules governing the allocation process, but to the exercise of power at the work place, how jobs are organised and practised and the fundamental preconditions for the development of alternative arrangements.

EEO programs have the potential to take account of the bases of inequality which are not captured by the atomistic conception of individuality. The concept of "disparate impact" embodied in EEO programs shifts the emphasis from the process of distribution of employment opportunity and the role individual choice plays in that distribution, to the processes whereby opportunities are generated, structured and allocated in ways which perpetuate the dominance of masculine values and priorities.

EEO practitioners are in a position to work towards shifting the ground rules so that it is harder to mobilise a masculine bias in a wide range of decision making processes, and easier for EEO advocates to apply in practice the principles they believe to be fair. A case in point is some guidelines for selection processes developed recently by a small working party set up by the Australian Public Service Board. The recommendations arising out of the working party's deliberations included one which attempted to get a grip on an apparent paradox of EEO practice: the more attempts were made to eliminate subjectivity from decision making, the more rigid became the criteria on which decisions were made, thus excluding from consideration valuable options, or in this case, applicants with relevant qualities or experiences not considered when the criteria were set up. The working party recommended that, rather than determining *a priori* the qualities and experiences relevant to performance in the job, the selection criteria could be framed in relation to job outcomes, and applicants asked to demonstrate the suitability of their qualifications and experiences for performance directed to those outcomes. In this way, experiences in apparently dissimilar contexts could be brought to the attention of the selectors, and experiences previously regarded as "unsuitable" would not be ruled out of consideration.

This is an example of how a formal rule change can affect the likelihood of particular outcomes, and minimise the possibility of particular biases systematically being applied in decision making processes. The research findings dealt with above provide examples of areas where formal rule changes might also affect potential outcomes in particular ways, giving EEO advocates a greater likelihood of achieving their aims. Further research of this kind, of course, needs to be carried out to inform strategy development.

An organisational focus on how gender operates as a central structuring principle at the work place draws attention to the dynamics of the relationships among job holders and thus captures a dimension of the position of women workers not highlighted by the more conventional industry and occupational analyses of gender at work. The understanding of discrimination and inequality within work organisations might be furthered through an exploration of the historically structured linkages between perceptions and evaluations of individual "merit" on the one hand and gender relationships on the other.

P A R T IV

Contemporary Voices

As the end of the 1980s approached, feminist organizational analysis had established a critical presence within organizational and management science[1]—moving from critique, through a series of theoretical developments, to a range of empirical studies. It had reached the, perhaps inevitable, point where it was time to take stock and to reappraise developments. Numerous articles and conference papers began to appear that challenged feminists to rethink the direction and foci of organizational analysis. In particular, the neglect of race and ethnicity came into question alongside a more general questioning of the "modernist" character of organizational research.[2] From 1988 on, issues of race/ethnicity and feminist poststructuralism have formed central areas of debate at successive organizational and management forums;[3] contributions have been disquieting[4] not only in challenging "traditional," male-stream thinking but in forcing a rethinking among feminist theorists about the nature of organizational theorizing and research. In this part, we present exemplars of both developments—four papers that fundamentally challenge the way we have, until now, come to conceptualize the nature of feminist organizational analysis.

The first contribution to this part is perhaps the most disquieting in that it questions the very possibility of organizational theory and research. Marta Calás's paper (Chapter 11) focuses on the problematics of representing nontraditional populations when developing organization theory and research. Beginning with a critique of existing organizational research, Calás is particularly concerned to expose the ways in which doing and "writing management research and theory is, in itself, the problematic activity," activity that excludes certain forms of talking, writing, and questioning. Through analysis of—"universalistic," "comparative," and "relativistic"—organizational research on Hispanic women, she reveals how issues of "time," "race," and "voice" are colonized and represented from the point of view of the Western researcher. This type of research, as a result, "constructs a more generic ethnic gendered subject whose only possible mode of existence depends on its mimetic characteristics, on its potential similarity to a 'normal cultural subject.' " Calás goes on to argue for a poststructuralist ethnographic approach as an alternative strategy for the study of race/ethnicity and gender in organizations. Yet, even here, we are left with the disquieting "suspicion" that "you cannot do management research and theory which address issues about other cultural groups anymore."

Poststructuralist analysis—exemplified in Calás's analysis of ethnicity—began to attract the attention of feminist organizational analysts in the early part of the 1980s (see Ferguson 1984) and is evident in the work of Gibson Burrell (Chapter 4, this volume). But interest in poststructuralism percolated slowly through much of the remainder of the decade and has only recently attracted wider attention (Acker 1990; Martin 1990b; Mumby and Putnam 1990; Calás and Smircich 1991). A work that played an important role in encouraging feminist poststructuralist analysis was a 1989 Academy of Management conference paper by Marta Calás and Linda Smircich. Winner of the Dorothy Harlow Best Paper Award at the conference, the impact of the paper can be witnessed in the numerous citations that it has already received in the short period following its presentation. It is included here as Chapter 12.

"Using the 'F' Word" is challenging on a number of levels. Beginning with a critical review of the women in management literature, the paper questions the ultimate value of challenging organizational barriers to women's entry while leaving unquestioned the "genderedness" of organizational management practices and conditions. The paper goes on to pose alternative feminist perspectives of "women's voice/women's experience" and "postfeminism." Analysis of organizations from the perspective of women's experiences, Calás and Smircich argue, helps to call attention to the gendered nature of standards in the production of knowledge—exposing the ways in which organizational science has come to reflect male experience and male realities. Postfeminism, on the other hand, "question[s] the very stability of such cultural categories as gender, race, and class and cast[s] doubts on the idea of validation of knowledge by experience." In a complex, yet highly readable discussion, Calás and Smircich go on to argue that, while "poststructuralist feminism stands in a problematic relationship with the women's voices position," both perspectives are a necessary part of a revised feminist organizational analysis. The women's voice approach allows us to understand the gendered nature of organizational science through a questioning of the categories of understanding, while postfeminism helps us to notice how categories of gender per se function as limits in our discourses and institutions.

Issues of race and ethnicity—like those of gender—have generally been missing from the foci and concerns of organizational research and theorizing. In the first chapter (Calás, Chapter 11) in this part, we see how the study of race and ethnicity is problematic. In the third chapter (Chapter 13), Bell and Nkomo set out to lay the groundwork for research into the relationship between gender, race/ethnicity, class, and organization.

Since the mid-1980s, the work of Stella Nkomo and Ella Bell has been in the forefront in taking up the issue of women of color within organizational research (Nkomo 1988; Cox and Nkomo 1990; Bell et al. 1992). In 1989, they were recipients (along with Dr. Toni Denton) of a substantial Rockefeller Foundation grant to study the "Life Journeys of Women Managers in Corporations," and the following year they received additional support from the Ford Foundation. Their research project is unique in that, while it includes study on white female managers, it has as a central concern a focus upon women of color in management. In a chapter written especially for this book (Chapter 13), Bell and Nkomo lay the theoretical and methodological groundwork for the study of women managers in the United States (see also Bell 1990; Bell et al. 1992). They argue for a "life journey framework" of analysis that "takes into account women's lives from a holistic perspective." It is an argument for a holistic approach to understanding women's organizational realities that includes the "core identity elements of (a) gender, (b) race, (c) ethnicity and (d) class" and that captures "both the internal (intrapsychic) factors and the external conditions."

In a summary chapter, Joan Acker provides both a useful overview of developments within feminist organizational analysis and a thought-provoking poststructuralist strategy for developing a theory of gendered organizations. It is a strategy that begins with an inventory of gendered processes that Acker locates in four analytically distinct aspects of the same reality: (a) the production of gender divisions; (b) the creation of symbols, images, and forms of consciousness; (c) the multitude of interactions that occur between individuals; and (d) the gendered social constructions of reality that form in the minds of individuals. Acker, exploring the implications of analyses of gendered processes, goes on to argue for short-term strategies aimed at transforming parts of large organizations from the inside while aiming at a long-term strategy for a fundamental reorganization of production and reproduction with new ways of organizing complex human activities. Written especially as an "end piece" to the book, Joan Acker's chapter should be read more as a summary than a conclusion, more as a beginning to a new series of feminist theorizing than as a closure to debate.

Notes

1. In the Canadian Sociology and Anthropological Association (CSAA), for example, "Critical Approaches to Organization" sessions have been focusing on feminist work since 1987. Within the Administrative Sciences Association of Canada (ASAC), the establishment, in 1988, of a women-in-management section has served as a focus for feminist work on management and organizations. Likewise, the British Academy of Management (BAM) has featured sessions on gender and organization and women-in-management from the 1989 annual meeting on. In the United States, the women-in-management section of the Academy of Management is one of the largest, most dynamic sections and serves—despite its name—as a broad forum for feminist organizational and management analysis. It played a central role in the organization of preconference workshops and themes at the 1991 Annual Meeting in Miami.

2. See, for example, Wallis (1989), Bell (1989a, 1990), Acker (1990), Calás and Smircich (1991), Townley (1991), Mighty (1991), Morouney (1991), and Cianni and Romberger (1991).

3. In 1991, for example, poststructuralism and race/ethnicity were prominent areas of discussion in the women-in-management sections of the U.S. and British Academies of Management and at the ASAC and the CSAA in Canada.

4. The term *disquieting* in this context should be taken not as a negative expression of anxiety but as a contribution to the process of disturbing organizational silences; the process of dis/quieting existing organizational texts.

11

An/Other Silent Voice? Representing "Hispanic Woman" in Organizational Texts

MARTA B. CALÁS

> The relationship between "Woman"—a cultural and ideological composite Other constructed through diverse representational discourses (scientific, literary, juridical, linguistic, cinematic, etc.)—and "women"—real material subjects of their collective histories—is one of the central questions the practice of feminist scholarship seeks to address. This connection between women as historical subjects and the re-presentation of Woman produced by hegemonic discourses is not a relation of direct identity, or a relation of correspondence or simple implication. It is an arbitrary relation set up by particular cultures . . . [which] . . . discursively colonize the material and historical heterogeneities of the lives of women in the third world, thereby producing/re-presenting a composite, singular "third world woman"—an image which . . . nevertheless carries with it the authorizing signature of Western humanist discourse. (Mohanty 1991: 53)

AUTHOR'S NOTE: An earlier version of this chapter was presented at the symposium "Research on Race Effects: What Have We Learned and Where Do We Go From Here?" Taylor Cox, Jr., Chair, Academy of Management Annual Meeting, August 1989.

As the preceeding epigraph suggests, this chapter focuses on the problematics of *representing* nontraditional populations—nonwhite, nonmale, and located in specific relationships with dominant populations—when developing organization theory and research. The particular focus of my analysis, in this case, is the possible representation of Hispanic women in organizational scholarship in the United States.

This last sentence requires further clarification. If I were to follow from my title, the chapter would end right here. In general, ethnic research and theory is very sparse in the organizational literature (Cox and Nkomo 1987) and particularly so regarding Hispanic populations. It is even more rare to find organizational texts addressing, explicitly, Hispanic women as their subjects of interest. I suspect, however, that Hispanic women, among others, will become prime candidates for the attention of organizational researchers in the years to come. As general demographics and certain organizational conditions in the United States make the discourses of "diversity," and its "management," part and parcel of contemporary organizational research, more attention is likely to be given to the particulars of "the diverse." By the same token (no pun intended), if historical trends in the development of organizational research are an indication of what to expect, it is also likely that Hispanic women—and other diverse populations—will become homogenized within dominant organizational discourses as much as "women in management" were for several years (Calás and Jacques 1988).

But this need not be so. Recently, critiques from feminist theories pertaining to the "women in management" discursive domains have called attention to the representational difficulties posed by dominant modes of organizational research and theorizing, as they obscure and limit the "voices" of the studied population (e.g., Smircich 1985b; Calás and Smircich 1989b, 1991; Jacobson and Jacques 1989; Martin 1990c). Thus the current intersections of feminist theories with the "women in management" literature might be considered a different path to follow within organizational discourse when theorizing "the diverse."

Yet, this may be a too optimistic interpretation. Well-known feminist theories, even when standing in a subordinated position to dominant patriarchal discourses, have often stood in a privileged position in regard to the "marginal." Said differently, feminist theorizing has been criticized for representing only the "voices" of white, Western, middle- and upper-class women and silencing the interests, issues, and conditions of women outside such ethnic/racial, cultural, and social realms (e.g., Hooks 1981; Moraga and Anzaldúa 1983; Collins 1989; Hurtado 1989). Feminist analyses, in the Western mode, may be a necessary but not a sufficient step toward representations of "the different" in the discourses of knowledge.

Thus, of necessity, the project that I undertake in this chapter is twofold. First, inspired by a more general critique of Western epistemology, both feminist and nonfeminist (e.g., Flax 1987; Foucault 1972, 1973), I deconstruct elements of dominant discourses that refer to Hispanic women. How are these discourses constituted? How are they similar to already constituted organizational discourses? How would these constructions impede the appearance of "the different"? Second, I undertake the question of reconstruction. Following a few recent writings that attempt to bring *cultural specificity* into feminist theorizing, I portray some possible strategies for writing and maintaining these specificities within organizational scholarly discourse.

If the reader detects a certain urgency behind this project, she or he is certainly not mistaken. As indicated above, there is not yet such a thing as "knowledge-about-Hispanic-women" produced in the organizational domain, but its appearance is imminent: There is already a certain "Hispanic Woman" produced in the United States by the social and behavioral sciences that is prone to facilitate—as has been traditionally the case—a crossover into organizational discourse. It is at this point that I am trying to produce an intervention. Deconstructing these discourses, already constituted in "sister disciplines," works toward resisting the appearance of "new" organizational discourses about Hispanic women—or any other "difference"—that, unreflexively, appropriate or codify " 'scholarship' and 'knowledge' . . . by particular analytic categories as they have been articulated in the U.S. and Western Europe" (Mohanty 1991: 51-52). It is in this interest that the chapter is written, as it is also in the interest of representing my own location(s)—and suppressions—as "Hispanic Woman" within the traditions of dominant organizational scholarship.

The Discursive Limits of Management Knowledge

Following more generally from poststructuralist analyses (e.g., Foucault 1977; Derrida 1978, 1982), the position I take here focuses on ways disciplinary *discourses* and *writings* are constituted as *knowledge*. My approach underscores a variety of rhetorical arguments that sustain these textual/discursive constructions. In particular, it underscores the extent to which discourses constituted in other *human sciences* share structural similarities with organizational discourses. More specifically, this analytical approach illustrates that conventional forms of representing Hispanic women in "sister disciplines" are congruent with representational strategies already present in international management discourses. These "congruences," the product of a Western *episteme* (Foucault 1972), define the current *boundaries of knowledge* in the social and behavioral sciences, homogenizing into their discourses any extraneous cultural specificity. From this perspective, then, disciplinary research and theory is *a form of writing,* which mediates the kind of knowledge that is/could be produced: what is said, how it is said, and by whom it is said.

This issue is fundamental but complex. It goes beyond a naive epistemological view that, to do research, one only needs a theory that represents well the *reality* that happens in, say, organizations. It also goes beyond a simple quantitative/qualitative methodological debate. Regardless of the methodology employed in the research site, "methodology" only exists in a text as part of the conventions of writing methodology. Thus writing research and theory is, in itself, the problematic activity rather than a transparent medium of representation. There are too many unexamined assumptions that belong to the dominant scholarly domain already present in the act of writing. More important, it is this limited *written/discursive form* that is presented (published, talked about) *as knowledge.* And this "knowledge" already excludes a multitude of representations that appear nonsensical under the a priori rhetorical logic of the disciplinary discourse. What is this logic and how is it constituted?

I attempt to answer these questions by borrowing from other disciplines (anthropology, literary theory, feminist theory) some approaches—inspired by poststructuralism—for analyzing the limits of writing/inscribing theory and research when trying to portray issues outside the dominant culture (e.g., Clifford and Marcus 1986; Gates 1986; Spivak 1987; Mohanty 1991). These approaches also point at the politics of representation implicit in any disciplinary writing. They make explicit the power/knowledge connection by questioning how certain representations fall inside/outside the discursive limits of various disciplines. They also discuss the consequences of "representational politics" for nondominant cultural groups.

It is here where this chapter offers a contribution. By analyzing the intersections of international management theory and research with texts about Hispanic women in the social and behavioral sciences, I try to make explicit their shared rhetorical conditions. The analyses serve to demonstrate the arbitrary limits that these rhetorics impose upon what could be said about "the other." Further, I argue that this analytical first step must be taken before we—creators of scholarly discourse—are able to notice "the diverse" under their own representational logic. We will not be able to represent any other knowledge until we understand *how* what so far passes as "knowledge" becomes a very limited and interested rhetorical production.

In the following paragraphs, I will discuss a framework for analyzing these *knowledge claims and denials* at the base of their production as writings. This framework is a heuristic to make explicit the cultural rhetoric that sustains most social and behavioral science discourses, including those of organization theory and research. It also underscores how these discursive strategies support a consistent relationship between dominant populations and dominant theorizing, limiting the possibilities for theorizing different relationships and knowledge claims for diverse populations.

More specifically, I am extending a framework (Calás 1989, 1990) developed for analyzing rhetorical formulations in traditional organizational research and theory about other cultural groups. With a few examples of current social and behavioral sciences research that focus on "ethnic women," the analyses show how these writings run parallel to more traditional international management research—an already constituted organizational discourse—where any possible differential "voice" becomes silenced. That is, the analyses illustrate how a current *Western episteme* constructs a more generic *ethnic gendered subject* whose only possible mode of existence depends on its mimetic characteristics, on its homogenization into a "normal cultural subject." Paradoxically, under these conditions, any possible "ethnic/gendered organizational theory and research" that might be constituted must deny its own specificity—that is, suppress any possible contribution to *diverse* organizational knowledge.

After performing these analyses, another mode of writing about "cultural knowledge" is discussed and suggested as a possible *writing* strategy when addressing "Hispanic women."

Understanding the Rhetorics of "Time," "Race," and "Voice"

The four-columns-by-three-rows framework in Table 11.1 consists of four categorizations of management research about other cultures and three modes of rhetorical arguments often used to signify, in Western writings, how "other people" in the world are "different."

I have derived the four research categorizations—*Universalistic, Comparative, Relativistic,* and *Ethnographic*—according to how intensely

Table 11.1. Framework for Rhetorical Analysis

	Epistemological Base			
	Convergence ———			——— *Divergence*
Research Category:	*Universalistic*	*Comparative*	*Relativistic*	*Ethnographic*
Rhetorical Arguments				
Time				
Race				
Voice				

any particular piece of research assumes that disciplinary theory developed in the United States or western Europe can be transferred to any other social/cultural group. In international management, a strong view that standard management theory applies and can be transferred to any culture is supported by the *convergence hypothesis* (e.g., Kerr 1983), which assumes that over time the developed world will be more similar than dissimilar (to the Western world). This hypothesis could be equivalent to an *assimilation view* regarding ethnic populations within a dominant society. On the opposite side, a strong view that economic development will strengthen the idiosyncracies of national cultures supports the *divergence hypothesis,* which posits the need for more adaptive management knowledge. This hypothesis could be equivalent to a *pluralistic view* regarding ethnic populations.

Universalistic international management research would clearly reflect convergence assumptions while *Ethnographic* international management research would assume divergence. *Comparative* and *Relativistic* research would share a middle ground between these two views. These four categories are closely related to Adler's (1984) classification of cross-cultural management research.

I have derived the three modes of rhetorical argumentation—*Time* (Fabian 1983), *Race* (Said 1985; Gates 1986, 1988; Tompkins 1986; JanMohamed 1986), and *Voice* (Lugones and Spelman 1983; Mohanty 1991)—from recent works in anthropology, literary theory, and feminist analyses. These works focus on *how* different human groups are reduced to *objects of study* by the dominant discursive modes of theory construction in the Western world. They show how these reductions exclude the possibility of other representations insofar as the *objects of study* become molded into the prior understandings of dominant theorizing discourses and practices. As will be shown, these three modes of argumentation and their heuristic value change as they move under the assumptions of each research category. The change in arguments serves to highlight the limits of each category as to the "knowledge" that can be produced under it.

Universalistic Research

This category holds on to a traditional assumption in Western philosophy, from Socrates to the Enlightenment, that posits the possibility of finding the one, ultimate Truth (e.g., Flax 1987). In organizational research, this means the assumption that there are universally correct managerial approaches. For example, a large portion of the older international management research falls into this category by unproblematically assuming the transferability of U.S. (and perhaps western European) management knowledge, concepts, and practices to other world societies (e.g., Kerr et al. 1960; Harbison and Myers 1960). Some more recent works still proceed under the same assumptions (e.g., Yavas et al. 1985).

Expectations of increasing, cumulative knowledge and of privilege for those closer to reaching the final discovery follow from this view. Non-Western nonphilosophers (later, nonscientists) are not privileged with the capacity for knowledge. Thus research and theory within this category use a rhetoric that emphasizes the separation of those who know from those who don't know as if it were a natural fact.

Time. Physical time is the most often used temporal discourse under universalistic premises. This notion of time puts a seemingly objective distance between the researcher's culture and his or her subjects. It tries to show how "natural" laws and regularities operate in the behavior of other human groups.

Race. In these writings, race usually appears by its absence. It is seldom expressed in any other way than euphemistically, through the concept of "nationality" or "ethnicity." Implicit in this concept, however, is the assumption of biological or "essential difference" that determines the extent to which "the others" are capable of certain thoughts and feelings.

Voice. The idea of "who can speak the Truth" is at stake here. The notion of literacy and its relationship to knowledge becomes central. "Literacy" implies more than just knowing how to read and write. It implies the capability of research subjects to express themselves in the dominant mode, and it also implies that the researcher is able to determine the kind of knowledge possessed by the subject. Nonliterate societies are not expected to know, and therefore cannot even represent themselves. They need the outside researcher to represent them.

To illustrate the limits under this research category, and the rhetorics that constitute these limits, I will quote from a paper on labor force participation of Puerto Rican women in the New York City area. This study (Falcón et al. 1990) followed from other studies that indicated that this particular ethnic/sex group had lower levels of labor force participation (the assumed universal category) than other groups of women in the United States. The study attempted to document this condition and also to identify some possible causes. The authors write:

> Women's labor force participation rates are more sensitive than men's to household composition effects . . . Interplay between family responsibilities and economic need complicates the processes influencing the participation of women in the labor market. (Falcón et al. 1990: 110)
>
> Many of the women interviewed listed their main activity as keeping house. Six out of every ten island-born women were keeping house. Among the mainland-born, it was four out of every ten. Mainland-born women were more likely to be employed, looking for work if not employed, and in school than their island-born counterparts. Older women were more likely to be employed than those in the early childbearing years (20-24).
>
> Despite nativity or age differentials educational differences were consistent across activity categories. Employed women were more highly educated than those in any other category. This latter finding suggests

> some strong effects of education on the propensity to be in the labor force and much more on the likelihood of being employed. . . .
>
> Not surprisingly, this preliminary analysis suggests associations among age, education, and labor force related activities. Undoubtedly, differences in types of employment activity, educational levels, and levels of participation suggest that Puerto Rican women are not a homogeneous group. (p. 111)
>
> Our findings for Puerto Rican women and those of other researchers on Hispanic women in general . . . suggest that the former are not very different from the latter in terms of the factors which affect their labor force behavior. Those who have the skills (i.e., education, English usage) and household arrangements (no children under 5, not being a female-head) conducive to labor force participation, are likely to participate. . . .
>
> Any effort to remedy the situation should probably focus upon improvement in education and language skills. (p. 113)

Now, let's analyze these paragraphs with the aid of the rhetorical strategies identified above. First, we should remember that in this case the strategies work to sustain the *Universalistic* position of *one standard, one truth for all* (e.g., as if "labor force participation" were a neutral category that could be applied equally to all human beings).

Race appears as the primary device for defining the study itself. To be able to articulate these research questions/problems, within-group (i.e., Puerto Rican women) differences or similarities need to be posed but also contrasted to a more general category (Hispanic groups). We notice, however, that throughout the paragraphs the "contrast" is only a device for homogenization because the "measurements" never considered any issue that may be context specific for this population. In fact, the disclaimer that "Puerto Rican women are not a homogeneous group" notwithstanding, both the design of the study and the analyses of the data lead the authors to conclude: "Our findings for Puerto Rican women and . . . Hispanic women in general suggest that the former are not very different from the latter."

Voice contributes strongly to creating these "knowledge effects." It appears immediately in the assumption that measures standardized in other populations (labor force participation, household composition effects) are equally valid for this one, particularly as they include the "generalized humanity" (i.e., men/women). Under the scientific mantle of surveys/interviews, it is sufficient for the researchers that the subjects are capable of answering their questions. They assume that the meanings of these answers pertain to a universal standard of knowledge regarding the work life of any population. Education and language skills are presented as clear culprits in the deficiencies of this group (low labor force participation) and facilitate the proposal of an easily achievable prescription (more education/skills).

Time completes the rhetorical possibilities under these discursive strategies. The "natural fact" of age, both that of the survey participants and that of their children, helps to "fill in the blanks" in a picture of "Puerto Rican Women" as a problem population, prone to be on welfare unless it participates in the labor force.

Notice also how the combination of these rhetorical strategies maintains the "natural" and permanent inferior position of the ethnic group as they are expected to assimilate into the dominant culture. This combination paints a picture of the "social costs" embedded in any attempt by the studied population to voice their own specificity (e.g., keeping house). Thus "Puerto Rican Women" have been constructed, and devalued—put in their place—in this research through assumed desirable ("true") standards of "labor force participation" where the dominant voices in research, business, and government coalesce.

Comparative Research

Most work under this category (e.g., Adler's ethnocentric and comparative work) stems from philosophical views that appeared later in the Enlightenment period (e.g., Young-Bruehl 1987). In its most basic form (e.g., Hegelian), the comparative approach holds on to the assumption that human beings are limited to knowing only that which they are historically/culturally ready to know. This notion gives way to the acceptance of cultural diversity but with an evolutionary expectation. Comparative studies approach their subjects with an a priori, superior standard of Truth already present in Western rationality, which, given time, would be accessible to all. This type of work constitutes the bulk of cross-cultural management research.

On the surface, this research does not posit the superiority of any one culture over another—all can have "equal opportunity" once they develop. But the evolutionary perspective glosses over the incongruence between the values of any particular society and the underlying cultural values of the research approach. That is, the standards of comparison, such as worker's attitudes and orientations, are meaningful categories of comparison insofar as the social and institutional basis of such categories are at least culturally equivalent (e.g., Inzerilli and Laurent 1983), but the comparison would not be meaningful otherwise.

Notice here that this view contrasts sharply with the Universalistic view because the comparative approaches propose the distance between "the West and the rest" as a problem of social development rather than of natural laws of superiority and inferiority.

Time. Temporal concepts under these ideas are manifested as typological time, where time is used not as a physical measure but as intervals between socioculturally meaningful events. For example, classifications such as traditional versus modern societies, peasant versus industrial, rural versus urban, are manifestations of typological time.

Race. Freedom and development often appear as ways to mark racial differences in these discourses. There is an assumption of "a general humanity" but, concurrently, humanity is separated by the fact that "the others" may or may not have reached the level of the more advanced. The mere act of producing such remarks is a form of creating the separation.

Voice. Here, what "the others say" is given some credence. Those sayings, however, must be filtered through the superior standard of producing Truth, so that their level of "development" can be assessed. Emphasis on educational approaches may or may not appear here, but the assessment of "knowledge" is at least implicit.

The following example illustrates typical comparative research pertaining to ethnic groups. This experimental study (Ayers-Nachamkin et al. 1982) compared Anglo males and females with Chicano males and females regarding their use of power in managerial roles. The researchers hypothesized that males in both groups were more likely to attribute power to themselves and to their own internal conditions, while females would attribute their power to external circumstances and behave accordingly. The results were somewhat unexpected:

> The Chicano female data, however, more nearly resembled that of male subjects. Far from demonstrating any role conflict in this situation, the Chicano female described herself fully as skillful in this role as her male counterpart and was more willing to undertake the task in the future. For whatever reason, the typical feminine sex role simply was not salient for the Chicano female in this study. A possible explanation for the differences between the female populations might be in terms of their actual exposure to the role of business manager or their familiarity with it. When called upon to assume the role herself, the female Chicano may simply be modeling her behavior on that of the *male* manager. Presumably because of the wider exposure to the dominant culture, when the Anglo female assumes the role of business manager she assumes the role of *female* business manager. She may know how women in such a role

> must appear if they are to avoid the potential penalties inherent in these situation. (Ayers-Nachamkin et al. 1982: 469)

With the aid of the framework, the rhetorics that sustain comparative views can be made clear. Race becomes central in the comparative approach. While the emphasis is first placed on difference, the difference is posited as a socialized role rather than a racial issue. That is, the underlying assumption is that Chicanos have the social potential of becoming like Anglos (the generalized humanity) within the appropriate gender category ("the typical feminine sex role," as if it were culturally independent).

Voice as a rhetorical strategy further sustains the "overcoming race" expectation. On first reading, one may be tempted to admire the Chicano female expression (knowledge), where she "described herself fully as skillful in [the manager] role as her male counterpart." But Time comes to the rescue of the researchers, who do not seem to be ready to accept this behavior as a positive expression of the inferior group. They promptly inform us that the reason for such behavior is pure ignorance due to the Chicano female's lack of exposure (Time: traditional versus modern) to the dominant culture but actual exposure to the role of business manager.

The point is made in such a way that the Chicano female's voice becomes totally discredited: her lack of social knowledge and development makes her model "her behavior on that of the *male* manager" while her more knowledgeable Anglo counterpart "assumes the role of *female* business manager. She may know how women in such a role must appear if they are to avoid the potential penalties inherent in the situation." With this final point, the subordinate role of all female (Voice) gets sealed (because she must avoid penalties) while maintaining the superiority of the dominant culture (first white Anglo, then male).

Relativistic Research

These views derive partly from Romanticism and partly from the "humanistic pluralism" ideas of the nineteenth and twentieth centuries. Assumptions under relativism are fairly contiguous to those of the comparative approaches, except that they have a greater tolerance for the possibility that a multiplicity of views can lead to equally valid, if different, notions of Truth.

These approaches have become more fashionable in cross-cultural management research in recent years (e.g., Hofstede 1980, 1987; Adler and Jelinek 1986; Jelinek and Adler 1988) thanks to their claim of "cultural sensitivity." This claim, however, obscures a very important fact: The categories they devise to demonstrate relativism are constructs developed by the dominant culture in the world of organizational research. For example, while Hofstede's work has been very vocal in announcing that U.S. managerial theories may not apply abroad, he does not question the origin of the dimensions he used to arrive at such conclusions or the implications for silencing idiosyncratic "knowledges" when using standardized instrumentation. Even his more recent attempts to incorporate context-specific knowledges (e.g., Hofstede and Bond 1988) are basically an add-on to his original approach. Thus, as relativistic approaches propose that U.S. theories might be culture specific, the next question they should ask is this: What other theories are or should there be? Neither this one nor the other two research approaches discussed above has provided any space for either asking or answering this question.

While one may say that, at an affective level, relativistic approaches sympathize with cultural pluralism, at a cognitive level, relativism hasn't exactly made peace with "epistemological pluralism." If it has sometimes abandoned the path of "scientific knowledge" for more phenomenological approaches, in so doing it has often reached a situation where it needs to "defend" its knowledge basis. By confusing methodological with epistemological issues, this research usually ends up being judged on the standards of comparative approaches. As such, relativistic international organizational research often uses a rhetoric that makes the research acceptable only under comparative standards.

Time. This research often resorts to intersubjective time as a rhetorical strategy. It emphasizes how "we all" are in the same time/space and therefore can communicate with each other, even if we are different. The idea here is to accept that we are not the same but that we are contemporaneous. Implicitly, however, "the West" is bringing the "the rest" to Western time.

Race. Here differences in race (or nationality) are a positive notion. Differences in beliefs and value systems become the focus of attention. "To be different" is acceptable, but the amount of difference is often calibrated through presumably neutral standards—which have been developed in Western theories.

Voice. "The voice of the other" can be very privileged here. Emic and interpretive research approaches may be followed, but this may create a particular problem. After the "native voice" is heard, the problem becomes one of translation, for relativistic approaches hold on to a Romantic notion of communication across cultures. Thus the focus on local voices often gets blurred by the need to agree on equivalent meanings.

To illustrate these points, I will discuss excerpts from an article that tests the universality of Kohlberg's theory of moral reasoning. This article examined possible gender, cultural, and ethnic differences in both theory and methodology in Kohlberg's original model. The author (Cortese 1989) interviewed 70 Mexican American, black American, and white American men and women using a standard interview form and quantitative/statistical scoring. The interviews were later examined through qualitative analysis.

I chose this article as a good example of relativistic rhetoric on two counts. First, it stems from Gilligan's (1982) critique of Kohlberg in her well-known work on the "different voice" of women, a relativistic argument. Gilligan's work has become a staple citation in recent "women-in-management" literature, but these citations often blur Gilligan's major argument. This article is a good example of how the blurring gets done. Second, discourses around "morality in organizations" have become increasingly important as business ethics gain centrality in management education. The ethical arguments behind the Kohlberg/Gilligan controversy are also likely to get lost as they get "translated" into business ethics. This example illustrates how relativistic rhetoric contributes to this problem.

The discussion and concluding section of Cortese's article states:

> Results of the present study supported the hypothesis of structural universality in moral judgement. Responses to questions in the Moral Judgment interview corresponded to the moral judgment stages. Age and gender did not appear to be significant variables. The effects of ethnic-cultural background were inconclusive.
>
> The study also examined the adequacy of Kohlberg's theory as a representation of moral reasoning in women. A care and responsibility orientation to moral judgment was evident in their protocols, as well as in those of some men. Components of morality are ignored by Kohlberg's rational approach; yet they were prominent for many of the women in the present study . . .
>
> Issues of care and communication were evident throughout the interviews in the present study. The women focused on omission, the rejection of duty, or the failure to be responsible to others. Kohlberg dealt only with the cognitive side of moral development. However, morality is more than making judgments. There is moral action and its effects on individuals and interpersonal relationships. . . . The rationalization of moral principles obscures the unique history of individuals. The care and responsibility orientation to morality should not replace the justice orientation; both

contribute to an understanding of moral development processes. (Cortese 1989: 440-41)

These paragraphs amply illustrate the work of Race, Time, and Voice in support of relativistic approaches as well as the difficulties mentioned before. The "sign of difference" (Race) is of primary importance in the design of the study, and so they use it first: "The effects of ethnic-cultural background were inconclusive." With that said, the focus changes to gender differences, which were the original argument in the Kohlberg/Gilligan controversy. It is important to notice that the homogenization of race has occurred only as a result of a *comparative statistical analysis,* which was inconclusive. If the same logic were to be followed, however, gender merited no further qualitative analysis of the protocols because it was not significant—at all—in the quantitative statistical results. Still, it is this paragraph that legitimizes the study. It helps to reduce the argument to one where the data become commensurable under the premises of the original Kohlberg/Gilligan debate over gender—that is, there would be "too many different voices" to be accounted for if ethnic background were also included. Thus Race becomes the background for highlighting the gender argument, making it irrelevant to focus on intersections of race and gender in later qualitative analyses. Throughout this argument, Time in the comparative mode has played an implicit role. Any model of "development" that proposes "stages" results from a rhetoric of "comparative time."

While it could be argued that the "structural universality" of Kohlberg's theory is a methodological artifact—in view of the different results from qualitative analysis of the data—that is not the purpose of Cortese's study. On the contrary, gaining quantitative support for Kohlberg's structure allows for a "romantic" notion that one can follow both Kohlberg's and Gilligan's "different voices." The implicitly comparative argument provided safe grounds for "relativism," once gender was able to *displace* Race as the "sign of difference" (remember that gender differences were not significant in the statistical analyses). At the end, there was no real differential voice to be displayed. The rest of the example allows for intersubjective Time to play its role through "interpersonal relationships." With every gendered body on the same time/space plane, "different voices" can be translated "across cultures" through the possibility of simultaneous care and justice orientations, because "both contribute to an understanding of moral development processes." Once generic male and female voices are made equivalent, any other different—

"underdeveloped?"—ethnic voices become further silenced. The Western voices of Kohlberg and Gilligan, including the trivialization of the latter, occupy all the space available in this homogenizing relativistic rhetoric.

Poststructuralistic Ethnographic Research

Relativism may have given way to ethnographic approaches if it hadn't encountered the problem of "acceptable standards of knowledge." The a priori assumption that there can be an independent standard for judging all knowledges becomes very problematic at the very moment that we start to suspect the equivalence of any category.

Ethnographic research (e.g., Adler's polycentric) is probably the only approach that could provide such space. This kind of work studies each culture in depth and pays careful attention to its historical and social aspects. More important, in its more recent versions—poststructuralist—it pays particular attention to the ways in which knowledge is being created in the research process and by whom—and for whom and for what—it is being created (e.g., Marcus and Fischer 1986; Clifford and Marcus 1986).

To take this latter approach, however, it is necessary to consider that "producing knowledge" is an activity that is not about "truth" but about culture. That is, if one understands the activities of "doing research and theory" and the concept "truth" as institutional and discursive requirements particular to our own academic institutions in this culture, there is no reason for judging "the ways of knowledge" of other peoples in the world under such standards. Poststructuralist philosophies emphasize these issues as a way to bring into the arguments of theory building and research a recognition of the local and political nature of these activities (e.g., Derrida 1988; de Certeau 1986). What are the functions of "Time," "Race," and "Voice" in this case?

Time. The temporal notion of *coevalness* is important here. It is defined as "of the same age, duration, or epoch." Thinking in terms of coevalness means that "we all" share and are a part of the whole time/space *now.* So, what we may be calling "underdeveloped" is of our same time/space as that which we call "developed." They are arbitrary categories that do not pertain to any one real temporal distance. Thus we may want to think twice about how we use temporal labels on the things that we name in our research. In this case, *time/space* is not "distance" but "approximation" between researcher and researched, while both maintain their own historical specificity and differential space.

Race. The notion of race is used here as a visible sign for contestation. One "can see" race, even if there is no definite biological differentiation for what we identify as race. Using race as a sign for contestation means to bring up races for questioning taken-for-granted assumptions about non-Western or nonwhite people. It becomes, for example, a discursive strategy to contend against broad generalizations over nationalities and gender and ethnic groups often present in cross-cultural management research.

Voice. Let's suppose that, after reading the points above, you say that, if you pay attention to those things, you cannot do management research and theory that address issues about other cultural groups anymore. Let's suppose that I say that you are right, that you cannot do it, at least not in the usual way. What is happening here is that we are having an argument about the nature of theory and research as "the voice of knowledge." The implicit questions are these: Is knowledge only produced through what we call theory and research, or are there other forms of producing knowledge? If there are other forms, why don't we "see" them? What discourses/practices exclude these knowledges?

As may be imagined, this type of writing is not particularly widespread in the social and behavioral sciences, but there are already some attempts going in this direction. An example from an economic development text provides a good illustration. It demonstrates the need to abandon Universalistic/Comparative/Relativistic rhetorics if we are to represent the contributions, issues, and conditions of ethnic/gender intersections, without colonizing them under "Western eyes" (Mohanty 1991).

This research (Seligmann 1989) studied the market women in Peru known as *cholas* by locating them in their historical-, political-, geographic-, gender-, and ethnic-specific contexts. The writing produced by these analyses is explicit in its contextualizing strategies. For example:

> When I did my first research in Peru in 1974, I was struck by the forceful, energetic, and at times bawdy market women known as *cholas*. They stood out because they appeared fearless, astute, different, and unpredictable. I could not find a counterpart among Peruvian males. (Seligmann 1989: 694)
>
> Peruvian market women have not been discussed more because of their very nature as brokers who belong to the social category of the chola. The boundaries of this social category are ill-defined in terms of race, class, ethnicity or geographic locus alone. (p. 695)
>
> The capacity of the chola to (a) speak and understand the language and behavior of the peasants, (b) withdraw the services they provide to the

> mestizos, and (c) ally themselves with the indigenous peasantry increases their prospects for successful political resistance to the existing economic and social order. These abilities moderate the tendency for power to flow to the top of the pyramid and become centralized. (p. 717)
>
> Although the meaning of the term chola has changed over time, becoming necessarily a multivalent category, it will only cease to exist when the entire structure of Andean society within a world system changes qualitatively and comprehensively. . . . Meanwhile, we must at least reassess the ideologies of modernization, development, and homogenization that have led to the perception of cholas as transitional beings who will eventually disappear in the process of assimilation. The reality of a global economy that is neither fully proletarianized nor agriculturally self-sufficient has created a position for the cholas as a politically radical and distinct economic and cultural group as well as a socioeconomic and cultural category that Peruvians continue to manipulate for their own purposes. (p. 719)

I have cited at some length Seligmann's writings to underscore the immense difference between poststructuralist rhetoric and the other rhetorics discussed above. Notice the emphasis on constructing *the voice of knowledge* outside the writer's domain. That is, *who* knows and *having* knowledge is displaced in the writing from the author to her subjects. The rhetorical strategies constantly call attention to how the cholas know as well as how appropriate for their own rightful purposes their knowledge is. At the same time, these knowledges are given additional power by distancing the cholas from any category that may have been constituted outside their own cultural specificity—that is, a homogenized "Third World woman" or a generalized "Peruvian woman." This strategy not only resists the colonization of the chola by traditional textual standards but it also permits calling into question, at the end, conventional disciplinary understandings and categorizations.

The second example (Neuhouser 1989) is even more explicit in questioning the privileged categories within traditional disciplinary rhetoric. Following a poststructuralist approach that deconstructs the binary logic embedded in disciplinary writings, the text proceeds to find "the other"—that is, the silent category—that may represent better the specificity of certain Brazilian women. A few paragraphs illustrate this point well:

> Latin American societies often have been characterized as male-dominated machista cultures. . . . However, the notion that machismo defines men as superior to women is an oversimplification. Although men are believed to be more qualified for activities in the public sphere, female superiority is

> acknowledged in the moral sphere. This female counterpart to the male gender ideology of machismo is known as *marianismo*. (Neuhouser 1989: 690)
>
> In rare instances women have been able to use *marianismo* to attain powerful positions in the public sphere of politics. The importance of the ideology of *marianismo,* however, is not so much that it provides a direct resource for women as that it provides a context within which other resources are available and can be used. (p. 691)
>
> In two major "movements" in two different *favelas* women were the leaders in pressuring city government to extend municipal services (water and electricity) into their communities. In both instances, women went door to door within the favelas collecting signatures for petitions that were eventually presented by female delegations to city officials in their downtown offices. (p. 695)
>
> Women's political involvement in Recife cannot be neatly categorized as either class- or gender-based politics. What mobilized these women were "family welfare" issues that represented an intersection of class and gender. . . . Although the *machista* stereotype would exclude women from the political sphere, the material resources acquired within the context of *marianismo* provide strong incentives to disregard such a restriction. (p. 696)

As shown throughout these paragraphs, the right to represent "the other" is a central concern of poststructuralist approaches once the "whose knowledge?" question is formulated. On giving voice to the excluded other, the text proceeds *as if* it were able to bring into the picture that other's own specificity. But notice that making explicit the researcher's concerns—epistemological, methodological, ethical, political, and so on—does not eliminate the rhetorical nature of the text. To the contrary, what it does is to incorporate *explicitly as rhetorics within the text* those elements that traditionally have been kept outside, as limits, in other disciplinary writings. Moreover, rather than pretending that these rhetorics are *truth/knowledge,* standing in a privileged meta level apart from those who contributed to their creation, the writings call attention to the limitations of creating research and theory as if it were knowledge.

I must reiterate, however, that these latter writings—as much as my own text—are still produced by privileged "voices of the West," even if they are "different voices." These texts have been written and published in the privileged spaces of Western scholarship, inspired by a *Western* critique of *Western epistemology.* But it is precisely the reflexivity about these issues embedded in the texts—that is, whose activity is the activity of "knowledge production"? and for whose purposes?—that permits

Table 11.2. Framework for Rhetorical Analysis: Summary of Arguments

	Epistemological Base			
	Convergence ———		———	*Divergence*
Research Category:	*Universalistic*	*Comparative*	*Relativistic*	*Poststructural Ethnographic*
Rhetorical Arguments				
Time	They are behind	Have they progressed?	Difference should not impede to arrive together at the same communication plane	Time/space as arbitrary categories: Who is constructing them?
Race	They are inferior	Eliminate differences once an assessment of similarities indicates such possibility	Differences should not create problems as long as they are understood	Race as the mark of difference and the visible sign to end comparison
Voice	They cannot represent themselves	Evaluation of of other meanings to assess their progress	To come to the same plane it is necessary to translate different meanings	Theorizing? Whose theorizing? For what purposes?
Resulting Knowledge	Convergence hypothesis One best way Developed people do knowledge	Convergence hypothesis implied Contingency views Developed people do knowledge. Others will eventually	Divergence hypothesis Other theories must be developed Attempts to do "other's knowledges" result in comparative strategies	Questions the notion of theory and research as knowledge Focus on the construction of knowledge as a core problem.

opening space for other knowledges. Nonetheless, such a space must be a temporary one, produced by a different "knowledge effect," which does no more than making suspect what "we know," even if allowing for "the unknown" to exist without colonization. The "other" is still unable to represent herself on her own terms.

Table 11.2 summarizes the different arguments in the framework.

Conclusion

Perhaps I do not need to remind the reader that I have stood in a poststructuralist position throughout the writing of this chapter. Through this position, I hope to have contributed in the creation of suspicion over current disciplinary writings, insofar as they pretend to represent "the other." For the same reason, I must resist one more time. I cannot provide a conclusion; the "conclusion" will have to be written by all of us, a community of scholars, in deciding in whose "times," "races," and "voices" we will be inscribing *Hispanic women* in organizational research and theory in years to come.

12

Using the "F" Word: Feminist Theories and the Social Consequences of Organizational Research

MARTA B. CALÁS
LINDA SMIRCICH[1]

By selecting "the Social Consequences of Management" as its theme for the 1989 annual meetings, the Academy of Management, our professional organization, positioned itself to examine issues of ethics and values, and the connections between management practice and the shape that society is taking. Through these activities, we have appointed ourselves observers and critics, functioning as a sort of Academ*(e)y(e),* watching over management practices. A question we would like to raise here is this one: "Who is watching the watchers?" That is, as we examine the social consequences of

AUTHORS' NOTE: An earlier version of this chapter was presented at the August 1989 Academy of Management meeting, Washington, DC and won the Dorothy Harlow *Best Paper Award* in the Women in Management Division. A condensed version was published in the Best Paper Proceedings. Parts of this chapter were originally written in conjunction with the project, "The Relationship of Feminist Theories to Ethical and Value Issues in Organization Science" (National Science Foundation Ethics and Values grant award no. 882066).

management, shouldn't we also focus our attention on the social consequences of our own practices—organizational research and theorizing?

In asking this question, we do not mean to deflect efforts away from the examination of the social consequences of management, because we believe that activity is extremely important. Further, we believe that there is a strong relationship between organizational practices and organizational science, even though many have doubted it. Organizational theories and organizational arrangements construct each other through an interplay of practical interests and scholarship (Benson 1977). Organizational theories reflect the practical concerns of their creators, both the scholar(s) and the organizational participants whose actions are described by the theories. At the same time, these theories—once they are presented as knowledge—guide organizational participants in their efforts to understand and control organizations. In this sense, organizational scientists "make" organizations as much as they study them. And because organizations are important shapers of the texture of our society, we must admit that our work helps make society as well. For these reasons, it is as important to examine the social consequences of our *research approaches* as it is to examine the social consequences of managerial practices. But it may not be easy to do so.

To help us begin to do such reflection over our research activities, we are here taking one possible path: the path already created by feminist scholarship in disciplines related to ours. Interdisciplinary in nature, much feminist scholarship focuses on philosophical and critical issues, presents modes of questioning now alien to our discipline, and illustrates alternative forms of writing that may be possible. Our aim in this chapter is to sketch some ways feminist scholarship can contribute to rewriting organization and management theorizing so that social and ethical consequences are explicitly addressed.

What Do Feminist Perspectives Offer?

The women's movement, passage of Title VII of the Civil Rights Act prohibiting discrimination against employees on the basis of sex, and affirmative action mandates combined to make the late 1960s and 1970s an era of rising expectations for women. In universities, women's studies programs were established in response to the women's movement, and in the Academy of Management, a Status of Women Interest Group was started and then the Women in Management division was formed.

Initially, much of the academic literature on women documented inequalities in society and the workplace and investigated questions of sex differences in various arenas (Freedman and Phillips 1988; Young-Bruehl 1987). In this regard, the women in management literature paralleled the concerns of liberal feminism of the 1960s, sharing its concern for equity.

Feminist theorists have taken a different turn, however, moving beyond the sex differences question, developing feminist scholarship into a major theoretical force that raises questions about the production of knowledge that the women in management literature has not.

In particular, two strands of feminist theorizing provide theoretical grounding for questioning the production of knowledge in the organizational sciences and examining its social consequences. The first is a well-articulated perspective that has been strong in questioning the *values privileged* in traditional social and scientific research. We label it here *women's voice/women's experience*. Second, there are more recent feminist perspectives that point at how all *forms of knowledge* in Western society are discursive structures that *define* our possible *modes of thought*. We label them here *poststructuralist feminism*.

Women's Voice/Women's Experience

Like the women in management literature, the earliest feminist critiques were of institutional arrangements that excluded women from public participation, such as access to the vote and access to higher education. Thus early feminism aimed to facilitate the entrance of women into the world of reason, to allow women to become equals with men in rationality (Young-Bruehl 1987).

Early efforts linking feminism and science focused almost entirely on the absence of women in science and the obstacles responsible for that absence (Rossiter 1982; Keller 1985; Harding 1986). Feminist scholars asked how the historical underrepresentation of women skewed choices of problems and how inadvertent bias influenced the design of research, the interpretation of results, and the construction of theories.

Discussion then moved away from concerns about equity and the consequences of its lack, to a focus on the differences in women's and men's *experiences* and their *alternative ways* of thinking (Belenky et al. 1986; Gilligan 1982; Diamond and Edwards 1977). Feminist writings documented "women's experience" and asserted it to be valid knowledge in its own right. That is, this perspective attempts to demonstrate *the differences between male and female experiences and then position "the different" as another valid form of representing human experience.*

A well-known example of the "women's voice" perspective is Carol Gilligan's *In a Different Voice* (1982). In contrast to Lawrence Kohlberg, who articulated a six-stage *universal* theory of moral development based on a study of males only, Gilligan, in a study of men and women, identified two different systems of moral reasoning that she characterized as moralities of rights and moralities of care.

Gilligan's argument about women's different voice has generated a lot of debate. She is accused of sustaining a stereotypical view of women and being guilty of the same universalizing tendencies that characterized Kohlberg's work. Nevertheless, her work was significant because it called attention to the gendered nature of standards that were supposed to be neutral. Typical of much research practice, Kohlberg called his a theory of moral development, not a theory of moral development of white, privileged males (Minnich 1986). Research into women's experience showed how certain values, more common to male socialization, had come to be accepted as the standard for human beings. Gilligan's work was more evidence showing that the presupposition involved in scientific research—that there are generalizable standards for all humankind—is problematic.

An example of work done under the women's voice perspective with direct parallels to the field of organizational science is Haaken's close reading of Witkin's decades-long (1940s-70s) research on perception (Haaken 1988). This research elaborated the psychological construct "field dependence-independence" and concluded that, "as a general rule," women are more field dependent than men. Field "dependence" has negative connotations in a society that values autonomy and independence. It was clear that field independence represented the "higher" form of development, as Witkin compared field dependence to childlike behavior and an "arrest" in development toward emotional maturity. Haaken argues that it is entirely possible for Witkin to have interpreted field dependence in a positive way. That is, the "inability to separate a stimulus from its embedded context" could mean greater sensitivity to contextual elements in matters of judgment and decision making.

Haaken's analysis of this stream of psychological research shows how gender, politics, and social conditions interweave with the workings of science. One could interpret her as pointing out "biases" that need correcting through better methods. Such an interpretation, however, still holds to a conception of science that idealizes objectivity and value neutrality. Another way to interpret the work of Haaken and others investigating the social and historical basis of knowledge is that they are helping us see the limits of current forms of knowledge production.

Poststructuralist Feminism

Other feminist theories, following postmodernist and poststructuralist concerns, *question the very stability* of such cultural categories as gender, race, and class and *cast doubts on the idea of the validation of knowledge by experience* (Flax 1987; Winkler 1987; Spivak 1987). Poststructuralism appeals to feminists who, rejecting the notion of an essentially "male" or "female" reality or structure, point instead to how these purportedly "natural" oppositions are culturally constituted categories, products, and producers of particular social and material relations.

Their major questions center on modes of signification and the creation of meaning. "Writing," as defined by poststructuralist theory, is the mode of inscribing meaning through symbolic repertoires. Different from symbolic or semiotic approaches, where the analysis of signification focuses on the discovery of "the real meaning," poststructuralism acknowledges the ambiguity of all meaning. Poststructuralists focus on the activities by which nonambiguity and clarity are *claimed* in the search for "true knowledge."

Central to this form of analysis is the deconstruction of binary oppositions in language. Deconstruction demonstrates the ways meanings get constructed by devaluing one side of a linguistic pair (e.g., emotion) and enthroning the other (e.g., reason). Also central to this perspective is the analysis of relationships between discourses and institutional forms as they create a form of power that is supported by knowledge claims.

Poststructuralist theory also questions the construction of the individual as the subject of knowledge. That is, what becomes suspect is the construction of knowledge claims based on the discovery of "the reality" of particular forms of human experience. Poststructuralism points to the ways in which "subjects/individuals" are constructed through matrices of relationships between institutions and discourses. "The real human experience" becomes somewhat determined by historical, institutional arrangements and constantly reproduced by the linguistic forms that sustain them, and so does the "reality" of the researcher.

Feminism, inspired by the theoretical strategies of poststructuralism, focuses on the way the sign "woman," as a gendered subject of knowledge, becomes inscribed as the devalued side of a binary opposition. At the same time, it focuses on the "female body," which as an object of signification has been historically constituted as a particular kind of subject (e.g., Weedon 1987).

The emphasis on writing/inscribing within poststructuralism and poststructuralist feminism is quite different from the naive view that these theories are only concerned with texts and do not recognize the actual conditions in our society. The issue of textuality must be understood to mean that society is a "general text" where cultural conditions become inscribed through our modes of signification. *Writing* in this case refers to the activities that try to "fix" the significance of any social practice. Writing in Western society holds a particular claim to knowledge. To be able to write, to be literate, and to have a written history are all equated with a developed society. Thus writing becomes the metaphor for knowledge, particularly when we write *for publication* and when knowledge and expertise are equated with having been published. Writing—as knowledge—is a preferred mode of constructing the general text of our society.

In summary, while *poststructuralist feminist* works expose the apparently unimpeachable structures of truth and knowledge in society, and help to debunk mythical social constructions that silence and oppress many of society's members, *women's voices,* on the other hand, construct new possible views. Together they stand in constant tension, because poststructuralist feminism prevents women's voices from establishing themselves as "the last word." As acknowledged by Ferguson (1988), the two positions need each other for creating the space that brings society, *constantly,* toward a more just and moral state. This is a never-ending task given the flux in which societies exist.

Rewriting Organizational Knowledge from Feminist Perspectives

We present two examples to illustrate contributions feminist theorizing can make for more socially conscious organizational research and theorizing. We chose these examples—Pfeffer and Davis-Blake (1987) and Schwartz (1986)—because both address social issues in ways that are typical of traditional organizational scholarship. We want to emphasize that we are not pointing to these two papers as instances of bad research, rather we see them as *good examples* of our current forms of knowledge production. They represent how organizational scholarship is expected to look and sound. In the case of the first example, by virtue of its publication in the prestigious *Administrative Science Quarterly,* it may symbolize for many "the best" we can do. It is this notion that we want to hold up for examination. Further, we want to add that we could equally have chosen some of our own earlier work (e.g., Calás et al. 1982; Smircich and Chesser 1981) for this kind of review, for we are also part of the tradition of organizational science knowledge that we now want to question.

Our first example does not recognize explicitly that it is dealing with an issue of profound social consequence. But its content—that, as women enter into traditional work arrangements in greater numbers, the economic value of that work decreases—is an undeniable social issue. Pfeffer and Davis-Blake, in a very carefully controlled statistical analysis, provide documentation of how jobs that are held by higher proportions of women pay less. They argue that the evidence is consistent with an institutional theory explanation that increasing proportions of women act to diminish wages and, reciprocally, that lower salaries tend to be associated with an increase in the proportion of women working in the organization. The authors end the paper there, addressing the strengths of institutional explanations without a hint of reflection upon the social implications of their findings—even though their research data came from universities and even though both of the researchers (one male, one female) are members of an academic field that is becoming increasingly feminized.

The second example indicates that organizational commitment can bring immoral behavior to organizations but leaves the implications of this proposition at the level of "factual explanation." Schwartz argues that committed organizational participants define their individual identities through ego identification with the organization to which they belong. This, in turn, impels organizational members to act against that which threatens organizational survival. He argues that what may seem immoral from the standpoint of the broader social world are normal organizational activities from the standpoint of committed participants—a natural consequence of having a robust organization. The researcher added no moral to his narrative of "organizational morality," even though organizational commitment is widely studied in organizational science and most usually presented as desirable. Let us now rewrite these two examples with the perspectives of, first, women's voices and, then, poststructuralist feminism.

Breaking the Pretense of Silence

In "rewriting" these two examples under the theoretical premises of "women's voices," we call attention to the fact that this organizational literature is written in a univocally patriarchal way. That is, we notice how the avowed "neutrality" of this discourse is *already* male gendered, as the *form* of knowledge promoted by the organizational sciences has its roots in philosophical strands that have equated knowledge with a male-preferred mode of understanding (Young-Bruehl 1987).

In using institutional theory to explain the observed devaluing of a feminized workplace, Pfeffer and Davis-Blake do not go any further than to assess the potency—the explanatory power—of this theoretical framework. By so doing, they are quite consistent with the formats of scholarly journals. But this endpoint is very problematic under a women's voices view for it does not consider the social construction of "market" forces. Immediate questions to be addressed would be the following: What institutional mechanisms devalue women? What theory informs our social institutions such that, despite increasing numbers of women in the workplace, women are not able to positively influence the financial conditions of their workplaces? Because this research casts serious doubt on the oft-voiced view that "things will improve for women as more of them move throughout the hierarchy," what actions can be taken? How can women in organizations become aware of and address this situation? We could also ask: Where is the voice of the female researcher (Davis-Blake) in this research?

While the first example is a "natural" to be reinterpreted through feminist theory, the second one does not seem so obvious. It requires us to consider what women's voices mean to organizational science more generally. The work of Gilligan, Haaken, and others suggests it means questioning the standards not only of moral development or perceptual processes but of all the constructs (constructions) organizational scientists use. We believe, therefore, that it is with nonexplicitly gendered social issues that feminist theories can be of special value.

In the case of Schwartz's paper, the first thing to call attention to is the nonproblematic use of the term *commitment*. What has been the actual contribution to organizations of the concept of commitment? Schwartz takes for granted that organizational commitment is positive and that the concomitant organizational immorality is a necessary evil. But from whose standpoint is commitment positive? In an age of "lean and mean" organizations constantly undergoing restructuring, being uncommitted seems to make sense.

Although the phrase *organizational commitment* could mean what the organization as a whole is committed to (e.g., "Our commitment is to customer satisfaction"), in the language of OB theorists, who have mostly been males, organizational commitment usually means the degree to which individuals are committed (psychologically bound) to their organization's belief systems, procedures, and ways of doing things. This notion parallels closely the pattern of moral reasoning Gilligan found to be associated with males. Her research indicated that males tended to reason their way through moral dilemmas with reference to an abstract conceptual hierarchy of rights, seeking to be impartial and fair. That is, actions are justified according to a system of rules. Women, on the other hand, conceive of themselves as embedded contextually in an interpersonal network where the primary imperative is to be responsible to others and caring to maintain the web of connections. Actions are justified with reference to their impacts on others.

Thus one rewriting of Schwartz notices how OB theory and its construction of commitment may be emanating from a male understanding of the "proper" kind of relations that should exist among persons and organizations. Note that this conception of commitment implies that individuals *should* be committed to organizations. Here individuals are subordinated to the organization. This conception of commitment is tied to a concept of domination and control—culture over nature—associated with male rationality since the philosophies of the Enlightenment (Young-Bruehl 1987).

If one were to follow the women's voice perspective, one could ask: What are women's ways of "committing"? What shapes would "organizations" take if they were based on a morality of care ("committing" to people) rather than a morality of rights ("committing" to rules)? Is it possible to conceive of other types of relationships between persons and organizations that do not have the necessary accomplice of immorality?

Deconstructing Gender Effects

How would poststructuralist feminism elucidate the social consequences of our research and theorizing? Poststructuralist feminism stands in a problematic relationship with the women's voices position. While the women's voices perspective privileges the "female experience" as a way of knowing submerged and undervalued by a patriarchal society, poststructuralist feminism questions the ultimate possibility of sustaining such claims. We must not forget, however, that the women's voices position is a *necessary step* for making a poststructuralist feminist analysis viable. Women's voices revises the "historical text" and forms of subjectivity by inverting the oppositional constructions. The inversions of these oppositions are destabilized by poststructuralist feminism so that it becomes impossible to reinscribe them in their original form.

Let's now rewrite our examples from a poststructuralist feminist perspective. Pfeffer and Davis-Blake used institutional theory to *predict* the economic consequences of the increasing proportions of women in administrative jobs. This was the extent of their interest in the situation and it allowed them the satisfaction that comes to researchers who are successful at prediction, a form of mastery. Our criticism from a women's voices perspective was that they don't use institutional theory to question this situation—which defies the expected positive social consequences of an increased number of females in professional activities. Standing on the neutrality of scientific knowledge, the authors did not notice the gendered nature of the "neutrality of scientific knowledge."

Now, given that poststructuralist feminism focuses on the textual and discursive activities sustaining structures of knowledge, one thing to notice in their text is their rhetorical strategies for sustaining the "truthfulness" of their "neutral discourse." For example, in our particular academic institutional arrangements, quantification is often equated with the "rigorous" and "better" approach to the search for universal laws of organizational reality. In observing this rhetorical strategy from a poststructuralist feminist view, one goes beyond the already old—and somewhat naive—quantitative/qualitative debate to notice the relationship between the institutional form "organizational science" and a discursive strategy that sustains it—quantification. Counting women becomes a particularly seductive rhetorical strategy here. The statistical techne permits the careful organization, localization, classification, and definition of a large number of women's bodies into their proper, devalued, domain. They become the subjects of fixed institutional arrangements through the power of research publications—while the researchers further fix their own expert reputation through the "discovery" of a scientific explanation. From now on, it is possible to invoke this research article as an appropriate explanation of a scientific fact.

Schwartz's work presents a different type of inscription—the constitution of the subaltern. This article offers an interesting situation for poststructuralist feminist rewriting. While the concept of gender is not explicit in the writing, we could say that "gendering" is the rhetoric that sustains the text. His claims of a subject so thoroughly committed to organizational conditions that it loses sight of the moral consequences of its actions bespeaks a feminized labor force, whose submissive nature and lack of rationality will accept the master voice to the point of total acceptance of its will without questioning. At the same time, this text constructs commitment as if it were a wild woman under whose spell organizational members would lose their heads but whose charms are the required object for the potency of organizational performance.

In summary, the *women's voices* approach allows us to understand how *normal* organizational issues can be regarded as normal insofar as we don't question the gender orientation that sustains that normality. By inverting the taken-for-granted assumptions about organizational issues, the women's voices approaches reveal the absence of women's values and concerns in those assumptions. *Poststructuralist feminist* approaches, on the other hand, help us to notice how the signs "woman" and "feminine" function as general limits in our discourses and institutions.

Through poststructuralist feminist approaches, we understand, for example, how the question "What kind of subjects can we be in contemporary organizations?" is answered and inscribed within certain rhetorical strategies. Here the signifier "woman" plays a very important part as a way to convey relationships of domination/subordination and maintain the "normality" of hierarchical structures. The "normal" relationship between organizations as one kind of institution, and organizational research as another institutional arrangement, constantly reconstructs the acceptable patterns of what can be said about organizations in our society; for example, paying attention in research to women's representation in managerial ranks normalizes and legitimizes "the ranks."

Both *women's voices* and *poststructuralist feminism* are concerned with the social and historical construction of our discourses and institutions. But, while the women's voices perspective still expects to effect a radical change in the world, which will come to value women's experiences, poststructuralist feminism is skeptical about these goals. The expectation of making a better world, which women's voices espouses, is questioned by poststructuralist feminism as another attempt to reinscribe a dominant sign in a world that is more complex than what women's voices often believes it to be. From a poststructuralist feminist approach, the work is never done; you have to keep on questioning who you can be as you are today.

Will Others Join Our Strategy?

One may ask, at this point, what has prevented organizational scholars from raising feminist issues in previous years, and how is it different now? Although there is no guarantee that organizational scholarship is now more fertile ground for feminist critiques than it was before, there is no doubt that some things are changing. First, even if timidly, some of the concerns of women's voices are appearing in mainstream organizational research and theorizing (e.g., Smircich 1985b; Grant 1988; Nkomo 1988; Korabik 1988). There is even more attention being given to poststructuralist feminist possibilities (e.g., Martin 1990c; Calás 1988).

Second, the potential opening to feminist theory in organizational science is not unrelated to other institutional developments. The increasing number of women and minorities in the professional ranks of organizational science may have created support in numbers that earlier women in management scholars lacked. While the discipline is still mainly populated by white males, "the different" are less an oddity at this time. Moreover, as more women have become tenured over the years, it has become less problematic for them to do unsafe (critical) work. (But perhaps we should not be so optimistic. Soon, institutional theory may tell us where we stand now.)

Third, the concrete grounding of feminist theories in particular problems of our contemporary Western culture makes this approach especially well suited for an analysis of organizational science's values. Thus it will be fairly easy for organizational scholars to relate to many of the issues already explored by the women's voice approaches, for example, to discuss how universal standards of institutional/organizational behavior may only be universal for individuals who are socialized into traditional white male norms and to explore the moral consequences of such socialization. One must not, however, overly simplify this point. Most, if not all, organizational science stands on constructs that are sustained by an ethos of individualism. Concepts like competition, achievement motivation, leadership, and even group dynamics are legitimated by a taken-for-granted autonomous, acultural, and ahistorical self. Most organizational scholars, no matter how interested in questioning the discipline, will have some trouble grasping an alternative possibility where "the individual," for example, is presented as a cultural and historical construction. This will require organizational scholars to meditate, seriously and intensively, on the possibilities of views contrary to current organizational science wisdom.

We know that there are bound to be some objections to our suggestions. First, unlike managerial practice, which acknowledges its role as a very "interested" party in society (that is, managers are to act with the interests of stockholders uppermost in mind), organizational science in its current state declares itself "disinterested"; it strives to take a value-neutral approach to knowledge and implicitly bars the question of ethics from being asked *about* organizational theories. So the very idea of examining our research practices for their social consequences may be greeted with surprise, disagreement, or hostility. Second, even if there is widespread interest in considering the social and ethical consequences of our approaches to knowledge, why should such inquiry be done from "feminist" perspectives? After all, isn't the very word *feminist* an invitation for trouble. It turns people off; it sound exclusionary; that is, it's something women do but men don't, and it sounds more like politics than scholarship. We realize that these are reactions our proposal is likely to engender. Nevertheless, we decided to stick by our guns—or shall we say our brooms—and do our best to convince you of why what we are proposing makes good sense—all the while still embedded within the constraints of our academic genre, which requires that we only express ourselves in certain ways (strict page limits, *Academy of Management* format).

Our advocacy of feminist perspectives does not stem from pure scholarly reasons—that is, that "more knowledge is good." It is a strategy for making a difference by doing differently. Our rationale goes back to the beginning of this chapter: recognizing that the way scholars do "organizational science" often defines the way society does "organizational practice." Thus having a socially conscious organizational practice may depend first on having a more socially conscious organizational scholarship. As for ourselves, working under the tenets of poststructuralist feminism makes us particularly sensitive to the ways our own text may be an accomplice in sustaining our limiting institutional conditions. We hope that ours is not the last word of a fixed text but an invitation to a dialogue that is still to happen.

Note

1. This chapter is a totally collaborative effort; the authors' names appear in alphabetical order.

13

Re-Visioning Women Manager's Lives

ELLA LOUISE BELL
STELLA M. NKOMO

Given the collection of research on women in management, can any general observations or insights be gleaned about women's status in the workplace, their work styles, and the roles they assume in their both professional and personal lives? We know, for instance, based on the literature, that women managers employed in large-scale, traditional companies face a glass ceiling when they attempt to fulfill their career aspirations (Morrison et al. 1987). There is a growing awareness among researchers that not all women wish to be fast-tracked up through a company's hierarchical ranks. Some women may prefer to balance their work lives with their family lives.

The literature is somewhat confusing about how women behave in managerial roles. Do successful women managers display the same behaviors as male managers in the workplace? There are some researchers who believe differences between women and men in managerial style, especially leadership, are minimal, thereby diminishing the influence of gender (Powell 1990; Dobbins and Platz 1986; Donnell and Hall 1980).

Of course, there are other researchers who argue ardently that men and women differ in the ways they manage people and assume leadership roles (Grant 1988; Rosener 1990).

When taking into account all we have learned about women managers, have only a select group of women been the focal point of our current understanding of women managers? What do we really know about women managers? Or, for that matter, what can we say about the lives of women who also happen to be managers?

The purpose of this chapter is to discuss the deficiencies in the current approaches to the study of women in organizations and to suggest an expanded conceptualization of the way we explore their lives: one that acknowledges the differing experiences of women due to their gender, racial-ethnic, and class identities. And one that takes into account women's lives from a holistic perspective rather than compartmentalizing their lives into rigid and unrelated spheres. In this context, we must begin to recognize the power of the historical forces that influence the roles, status, and opportunities available to women managers. If we are ever to reach a greater understanding of the experience of women in organizations, we must begin to investigate the complex nature of the realities—both the internal (intrapsychic) factors and the external conditions—influencing their lives.

While we have chosen to focus on re-visioning women manager's lives, we also recognize the need for a different, more expansive lens for understanding and interpreting male managers' lives. To study gender implies studying both men and women and the ways in which organizations are gendered phenomenon. The deficiencies we identify in the investigation of female managers that follow in this chapter are probably equally applicable to the ways in which male managers have been studied. For purposes of this chapter, however, we will focus solely on addressing concerns and needs in exploring the lives of women managers.

Theoretical Assumptions in the Study of Women Managers

Research on women in management has become a significant field of study within the last 20 years (Kanter 1977a; Larwood and Wood 1977; Nieva and Gutek 1981; Powell 1988). The first question dominating early research was this: Can women be managers? The basic issue for women was gaining entry into management positions. During the middle to late 1970s, a second question emerged: Do male and female managers differ in their behaviors and actions in organizations? Differentiating between the attitudes and behaviors of men and women in managerial positions was a salient topic found in this literature (Powell 1988; Hennig and Jardim 1977; Terborg 1977; O'Leary 1974; Schein 1973). Emphasis was on comparative research studies, and women managers could only be understood in opposition to men managers (Calás and Smircich 1989b). The third question, which dominates today's research, focuses on upward mobility or, simply stated: Why aren't women managers getting to the top?

Even though it appears on the surface that the researchers have addressed three different questions over time, a close examination of the attempts to answer the questions reveals that our field is mired in a circular pattern of research and writing. In attempting to answer the three questions, researchers have generally relied upon two perspectives or explanations: (a) the gender-centered perspective and (b) the organization-structure perspective (Fagenson 1989). The gender-centered perspective argues that women do not possess the skills or behavioral characteristics to perform competently in managerial leadership roles. Fagenson (1989) explains that, in this context, women are characterized using traditional feminine stereotypes, including being indecisive, passive, and too dependent. Such stereotypes work against women managers in terms of their advancement to executive positions because managers traditionally have been perceived as aggressive, independent, and decisive—sex role characteristics usually associated with men (Schein 1973).

The organization-structure perspective investigates the organization's structural elements, such as job recruitment and entry, job assignment, relationship between formal and informal groups, training, and promotion and reward systems impeding women's entrance and advancement in the workplace (Kanter 1977a; Riger and Galligan 1980; Fagenson 1989).

Inherent problems exist within the both gender-centered and organization-structure perspectives. On the one hand, a major disadvantage of the gender-centered perspective is its dependency on sex role characteristics in "defining" appropriate behaviors of managers. The gender-centered perspective creates simplified, binary categories that mask the complexity of the meaning of gender in organizations. In this approach, an implied hierarchical relationship exists between men and women with one gender (men) dominant and superior, and the other (women) subordinate and inferior (Scott 1988). Perhaps the greatest problem with this approach is its inability to move beyond "blaming the victim." Continued reliance upon this perspective will not lead to enlightened approaches for the eradication of sexism in organizational life.

On the other hand, within the organization perspective, women, as a group, are represented as powerless victims, unable to influence or decisively affect the companies in which they work (Gerson 1985). There is an implicit assumption that the individual and the structure are independent factors and that there is no mutual interaction between the two. By ignoring the salient interactive system dynamics inherent within the organization-structure perspective, we lose critical knowledge about the power women bring into the workplace, the ways in which women's and men's roles are evolving in managerial positions, and whether organizational structures are adapting to increasing numbers of women.

What Is Missing in Our Knowledge of Women Managers?

Despite the appearance of an evolutionary progression of questions about women in management, we have not progressed because of our reliance on two limited perspectives. The dominant question today—"Why aren't women managers getting to the top?"—gets answered by resorting to gender-centered explanations grounded in the deficiencies of women or their sex role characteristics or in superficial structural remedies. As we move into the next decade, we require answers to a very different set of questions, such as the following: Why do top management hierarchies remain white male dominated? How are race, gender, and class identities manifested in organizational life? Is a "mommy track" a correct approach for managing family issues, those that affect both men and women in the workplace? Do organizations need to be redefined to maximize the differing values, perceptions, and characteristics women and people of color offer the work environment? What is the role of women managers in transforming the oppressive features of organizations? Why is career success always defined as "getting to the top"?

As the literature reads today, a woman in management appears out of nowhere, without a history, lacking significant relationships, without a racial identity, and whose only chance to succeed in the work environment depends on her ability to emulate the behaviors and attitudes of men to assimilate into predefined organizational realities. Research on women managers must begin to explore the factors, people, and conditions occurring early on in their lives. That is, what events and significant people in a woman's life history have influenced her attitudes and behaviors toward work? We are missing a clear understanding of how women come to make sense of their lives; one that takes into account the cumulative aspects of their lives. Women's lives do not fit neatly into career theories built largely on male models of success and work.

Problematic to the women in management literature is the hiatus in information, not only about African American women but about other nonwhite women's career experiences. Gerson (1985) points out that research on women, in general, implicitly minimizes differences among them, thereby reinforcing the image of gender uniformity. This situation continues to exist in managerial studies, in spite of research providing evidence that the combined and interactive effects of race, ethnicity, class, and gender have a pervasive impact on the lives women of color (Leggon 1980; Lykes 1983; Giddings 1984; Glenn 1985; Bell 1990). The idea that theories developed on the experiences of white women managers are congruent with the experiences of women of color have yet to be justified. In addition, this idea serves to foster ethnocentric thinking.

There is a need to rethink our approach to investigating the experiences of women managers and the organizations in which they work. A progressive approach might help researchers to move away from the traditionally narrow ways we have come both to understand and to interpret their lives, thereby eventually enabling us to overcome the deficiencies discussed earlier. To fully illuminate the complexities inherent in women manager's lives, three suggestions are offered: (a) understanding identity and the compounded impact of the core identity elements of gender, race, ethnicity, and class; (b) building on the biographical dimensions of the women's lives to create holistic, developmental portrayals of them; and (c) giving consideration to historical forces in the analysis of women manager's career and life experiences.

Identity and the Core Identity Elements

There is a way to avoid the ethnocentric trap in women of management studies, where certain groups of women are relegated to invisibility simply because of their race, ethnicity, or class. Incorporating the concept of identity along with the core identity elements might illuminate our current understanding of women managers. The framework in Figure 13.1 presents our concept of identity, and the four interlocking circles consist of the core identity elements of (a) gender, (b) race, (c) ethnicity, and (d) class. These four elements are interdependent and interactive rather than being hierarchical and static in nature. Taken together, identity and its core elements form a gestalt: One element may become prominent while others remain in the background. Thus the relationships among them are not additive or even reciprocal (Hicks 1981).

Gender, race, ethnicity, and class may not be thought of as having any more salience than other identity elements, such as profession, age, emotional makeup, or physical characteristics. In Western civilization, however, the four core identity elements have significant and far-reaching consequences in women's lives (Spelman 1988; Hill-Collins 1990). Fox-Genovese (1991: 222) ardently argues that "race and gender should, in fact, enjoy privileged positions in our understanding of American culture for they lie at the core of any sense of self."

The Concept of Identity

The meaning of *identity* is often ambivalent in the literature (Baumeister 1986; McAdams 1988; Josselson 1987). Baumeister (1986), in his work on identity, observed that psychologists discuss identity as an element within an individual, a function of personality, while sociologists describe identity as a set of roles one assumes in relation to one's environment. For purposes of this discussion, we prefer a definition of *identity* that "synthesize[s] both parts, the inner self and the outer context" (Baumeister 1986: 247). As McAdams (1988: 4) has suggested, "if identity is like a painting, environmental opportunities are the canvas and colors."

Erikson's (1968) definition of *identity* underscores the complex and somewhat confusing nature of its process. He describes identity as being "located in the core of the individual and yet also in the core of his communal culture" (Erikson 1968: 22). He writes of identity as a process "by which the individual judges himself in the light of what he perceives to be the way in which others judge him" (p. 22). For Erikson, identity is the "whole interplay between the psychological and the social, the developmental and the historical" (p. 23).

Josselson (1987) introduced the influence of gender in her research on identity formation among women. She found that, "in comparison to men, women orient themselves in more complicated ways, balancing many involvements and aspirations, with connections to others paramount; their identities are thus compounded and more difficult to articulate" (Josselson 1987: 8). What some researchers describe as the interactive style of women managers may have a direct relationship to the way women's identities develop and how their identities differ from those of men.

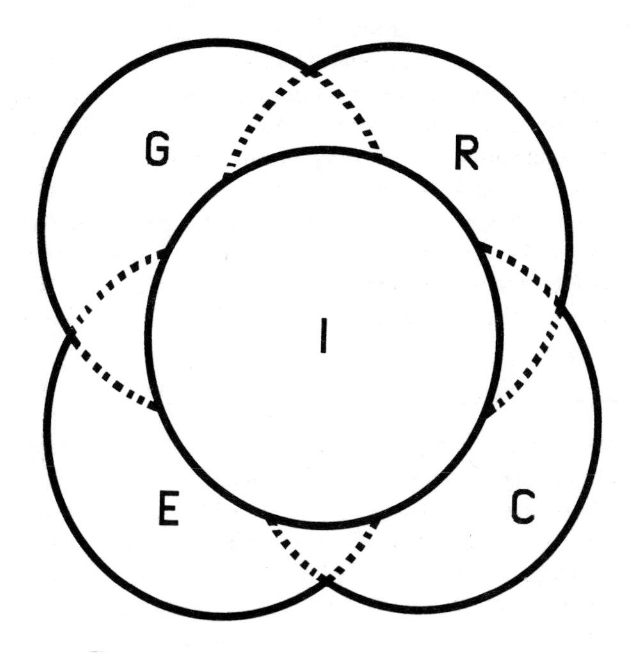

Figure 13.1. Identity and the Core Identity Elements

The Core Identity Elements

Gender forms the first interlocking semicircle shown in Figure 13.1. As a concept, at the most basic level, gender is a classification system denoting ways in which women and men differ. To exist in this society as a human being from birth means to be "gendered" as either female or male (Fox-Genovese 1991). More than merely being a biological classification of the sexes, gender includes the societal orientations, values, and roles distinguishing women from men and the interactions between them. Fox-Genovese (1991: 120), in fact, defines *gender* as "a system of relations—specific relations between women and men." Gender is one of the major bases of domination in our society and a powerful determinant of one's life opportunities (Harding 1986).

Insights have been revealed throughout the last decade that have substantially increased our knowledge of gender differences. There is firm conviction among feminist researchers who espouse differences in the psychological makeup of women and men (Miller 1976; Gilligan 1982). Gilligan, for example, discovered in her work on women that their way of connecting to others stressed emotional relatedness, in contrast to men, who seemed to function by separation and autonomy. Other research has indicated that women's lives develop in more complex patterns than men's lives (Giele 1980; Josselson 1987). And women structure their lives in unique ways to accommodate motherhood and the world of work (Gerson 1985; Freeman 1990).

Race forms the second semicircle found in Figure 13.1, and it is a profound determinant of one's political rights, one's location in the labor market, and one's sense of identity (Omi and Winant 1986). Its immediacy is manifested in everyday life experiences and social interactions (Blauner 1989; Van Dijk 1987). Pinderhughes (1989: 89) believes the concept of race "must be understood intellectually as well as emotionally." On the emotional level, race is a hotly charged concept for everyone in this society (Pinderhughes 1989). Why is the concept of race so volatile? The reasons are extremely complex and interrelated. It is the combination of the historical legacy of slavery in Western civilization, followed by a postslavery period with its significant sociopsychological consequences, and then contemporary living conditions and relationships between people from different racial backgrounds.

Pinderhughes (1989), has observed that people—regardless of their racial affiliation—experience a psychological debilitation when engaging the concept of race, causing most people to feel highly uncomfortable and under stress. One reason for this anxiety is that all too often people confuse the concept of race with racism or even outright bigotry. Given America's moral ideology based on freedom for all individuals, combined with the espoused values against racism as well as other forms of oppression, no one wants to be accused of being a racist and no one wants to be a victim of a racist act.

On the intellectual level, problems with the concept of race are also clearly apparent. In the social sciences, definitions of race are fraught with multiple meanings, causing Gordon Allport (1954: 110) to proclaim in his writing, "The concept of race is badly abused and exaggerated." Early origins of the use of race can be traced to anthropologists, who used the concept to classify groups of people based on physical traits—basically, skin color (Allport 1954).

In Western culture, the concept of race remains powerful, having acquired significant social and political ramifications. Members of the dominant white community have used the concept of race to create a social caste system or stratification hierarchy based on skin color. Pinderhughes (1989: 71) contends, "The status assignment based on skin color identity has evolved into complex social structures that promote a power differential between Whites and various people-of-color." Politically, the concept of race has been used to reinforce already powerful groups, while weakening those groups with less power in this society.

There are a limited number of studies that provide evidence on the interactive effects of race and gender among women manager. Thomas (1989) investigated the formation of developmental work-centered relations among protégés and the influence of race. He found the African American women in his sample reluctant to develop close working relationships with their white male managers because it conjured up in their minds images of black concubines serving white masters. Greenhaus et al. (1990), in their cross-racial study on career development and job satisfaction among managers, reported that African American women experienced lower levels of career satisfaction and felt a greater sense of isolation in contrast to white women.

Ethnicity, the third semicircle, is perceived in the social science literature as being closely related to the concept of race. In fact, Allport (1954: 113) noted, "Most human characteristics ascribed to race are undoubtedly due to cultural diversity and should, therefore, be regarded as ethnic, not racial." Cox (1990) believes there is a tendency to mistake race for ethnicity, especially when it comes to perceiving certain groups. He observes that whites and blacks are perceived as racial groups, while Hispanics and Asians are perceived as ethnic groups. Cox (1990: 6) strongly urges that such perceptions "imply that a group is either biologically or culturally distinct from another, whereas it generally is both." To clarify the combined meaning of *race* and *ethnicity,* Cox coined the term "racio-ethnic."

The concept of ethnicity refers to the shared cultural characteristics of a group that have evolved over a period of time in response to the group's adaptation to conditions in the environment. Many ethnic groups are often implicitly tied to the geographic areas where their ancestral lines can be traced, as, for example, Italian Americans or Greek Americans. Other ethnic groups are identified by their religious affiliations as it is with Jewish Americans. For African Americans, race is the salient factor. Still other ethnic groups are bonded by a common language, as in the situation of Hispanic Americans. In addition to geographic turf, religion, and language, ethnic groups may share other cultural characteristics, including holidays, customs, traditions, a common folklore and mythology, a historical legacy, nonverbal communication styles, and belief systems—just to name a few.

While there are existing studies that explore the combined effects of race and gender among women managers, research that investigates the compounded dynamics among gender, race, and ethnicity within this group are scarce. Little is known about the career experiences of Asian American, Hispanic American, or Native American women. These ethnic groups remain the silent voices.

The fourth and last semicircle in Figure 13.1 is class. Since the original work by Marx (Marx and Engels [1848] 1971), much has been written in the social sciences about class. Contemporary researchers typically have taken two basic approaches to defining class. One approach takes a subjective view of class and asks individuals to identify their class status (Jackman and Jackman 1983). The other approach to class focuses on the objective reality of a stratification system (Acker 1980). This system is usually based on education and occupational position (Kohn 1979). In this discussion, the view used is that a woman's class identity is a function of her family's origin, her occupational background, and her education.

Traditionally, researchers have assumed that women derive their class status from their husbands or fathers. Because of the increasing number of women employed in jobs outside of the household, however, more recent research argues that, to understand a woman's class, it is important to examine beliefs about gender role norms among women. Beeghley and Cochran (1988) found that employed married women who believed in traditional gender role norms tended to use their husband's characteristics in selecting their class identification. Whereas employed married women who believed in egalitarian gender role norms tended to use their husband's characteristics along with their own achievements.

Feminist theories underscore the need not to view class identity in isolation from race and gender (Spelman 1988; Glenn 1985; Hill-Collins 1990). In this vein, class cuts across gender, race, and ethnic identities (e.g., working-class Italian American women, middle-class Asian American woman). Class identification expresses in a symbolic way one's experiences with power and privilege from birth to death (Lockwood 1966). Some of our most profound experiences with power and privilege are enacted within the work environment or in conjunction with it, and these experiences are conditioned by gender and race. Incorporating class in a framework for understanding women in organizations would allow us to better analyze not only cross-gender experiences but also relationships among women.

The Use of Biography

Simply stated, *biography,* for purposes of this chapter, is the story of a woman's life. The story begins with her earliest recollections of childhood and continues through time, each experience building on the achievements, disappointments, struggles, celebrations, and relationships from past events. What a woman comes to understand about the world, her sense of self-worth, her skill level, and the quality of life she comes to expect—all originate early in life. Autobiographies, oral histories, and biographies on women's lives offer testimony to this fact (Lightfoot 1988; Scott 1991; Campbell 1989; Page 1986). Women's stories provide insights on their motives, goals, and capacities as they move through life (Gerson 1985).

We have neglected to understand how women's lives, in their entirety, are influential in their behaviors, feelings, and choices once they are in managerial roles. We haven't told their stories. By incorporating biography into the study of women managers, their lives are illuminated rather than being fragmented into distinct and unrelated spheres (e.g., personal versus professional). When one considers the array of choices and options available to professional women today, a holistic portrayal is critical for discovering the multifaceted roles, connections, and discontinuities inherent in their lives. For instance, women are daughters, wives, mothers, friends, and workers in their communities—all in addition to being managers. Other life dimensions may be very influential in the way a woman manages and organizes her work life.

Life histories of women managers' experiences would broaden our current insights on the interactive layers, roles, and expectations as well as the contexts in which their lives are embedded (Gilligan 1982). Knowledge gathered from these accounts has powerful implications for organizations in terms of sensitizing companies to the needs of women, identifying structural barriers that restrict women's career advancement, and providing strategies for organizational change.

Historical Forces

Thus far, we have advocated for two ways of re-visioning research on women in management. The first one is to encourage the inclusion of the core identity elements in our studies. The second suggestion is the use of biography for creating holistic portrayals of their experiences. The final suggestion we propose is the inclusion of an analysis of the historical forces that can deeply influence women's lives.

The historical reality in which women live their lives cannot be ignored. "Sociological imagination," a term coined by C. Wright Mills, was used to capture the larger historical context that contributes to "the success and the failure of men and women" (Mills 1959: 6). Mills was an ardent believer in exploring the relatedness between biography, social structure, and history in the social sciences (Gerson 1985). History shapes the terrain, the background in which a woman lives; it provides texture in her life. The texture is in constant fluctuation, creating opportunities and resources at times, while at other times diminishing them. Conditions of a historical legacy are inclusive of the subtle to obvious changes occurring in the social norms, beliefs, institutions, and cultural patterns of the society: History leaves an indelible mark on the cultural fabric.

Consider the civil rights movement of the 1960s. During this historical period, unprecedented educational and employment possibilities were made available to African Americans. The civil rights movement helped to usher in the women's movement, enabling women not only to increase their numbers in the work force but to enter nontraditional careers. For first time in history, a greater number of women had the option of becoming career oriented, thereby being able to devote more time and energy to developing their careers (Gerson 1985; Bell 1990). Gerson (1985: 21) points out that "periods of [historical] change increase the likelihood of triggering events that promote and sometimes force individual change." Without the historical legacies of both the civil rights and the women's movements, it would be difficult to imagine what the status and experiences of women managers would be in contemporary society. There is a need for researchers to make greater connections between women managers' experiences and the historical realities of their lives.

Closing Remarks

In this chapter, we discussed several deficiencies with our current approaches to studying women managers and presented three ideas for re-visioning the way in which we examine their lives. We call for a holistic approach that explicitly acknowledges the mutuality of a woman's professional and personal life dimensions. We believe an analysis that incorporates the core elements of gender, race, ethnicity, and class are critical to understanding not only her career world but the other contexts of her life. And we should recognize the role of history in the study of women in management.

The suggestions offered do not imply that all the ideas must be used in a single study but that the components be considered when designing a study and presenting results. We have relied too long on narrow perspectives for understanding women managers that have limited our view of women, the kinds of questions we ask, and the solutions we propose for improving the status of women in organizations.

14

Gendering Organizational Theory

JOAN ACKER

Although early critical analyses of organizational theory (e.g., Acker and Van Houten 1974; Kanter 1977a) led to few immediate further efforts, feminist examination of organizational theory has developed rapidly in the last few years (Ferguson 1984; Calás and Smircich 1989a, 1989b; Hearn and Parkin 1983, 1987; Burrell 1984, 1987; Mills 1988b; Hearn et al. 1989; Acker 1990; Martin 1990a, 1990b). The authors of these critiques are responding to and helping to create the conditions for a fundamental reworking of organizational theories to account for the persistence of male advantage in male organizations and to lay a base for new critical and gendered theories of organizations that can better answer questions about how we humans come to organize our activities as we do in contemporary societies.

The conditions for a new critique began with the rapid proliferation of studies about women and work, conceptualized in theoretical terms of prefeminist social science. For example, studies of women's economic and occupational inequality, sex segregation, and the wage gap document the extent of the problems but give us no convincing explanations for their persistence or for the apparently endless reorganization of gender and permutations of male power. Similarly, the extensive literature on women and management documents difficulties and differences but provides no adequate theory of gendered power imbalance. The need for new theory was implicit in the inadequacies of old theory.

Developments within feminist theory also provide foundations for a new criticism of organizational theory. For example, Dorothy Smith's (1987, 1990) analysis of the textually mediated, abstract, objectified, intellectual relations of managing and ruling suggests avenues into a critique, for complex organizations are central locations of such relations. Organizational theory, as Smith (1987) points out, originates in, or in close relationship with, the groups that manage, organize, and control the society. Concepts, explanations, modes of thought, and relevant questions used by organizational researchers are congruent with the everyday ways of thinking of managers and rulers. Researchers and theorists are part of the relations of ruling.

Feminist theorists are intellectual workers whose consciousness and work are organized within those relations but who also stand outside those relations as women. Smith (1987) argues that a bifurcated consciousness arises in the process of becoming situated both within and outside and that this makes it possible (not inevitable) to see processes that had been hidden. Seeing the previously hidden is difficult, because the very practices of thinking that we use are those created within the relations of ruling. Becoming social scientists involves learning those practices; a critique of organizational theory must also be a critique of our own procedures, many of which we seldom recognize as gendered.

Other feminist theorists, attempting to avoid essentialist and universalizing explanations of women's situations, have looked for ways to think about gender, class, and race using complex, historically situated understandings (e.g., Hill-Collins 1990). The view that all social relations are gendered, for example, seeing class relations as gendered processes (Acker 1988), opens the possibility that many apparently gender-neutral processes are sites of gender production. Organizational processes of different kinds may carry within them patterns of gender difference and subordination.

Feminist work on sex and sexuality, often influenced by Foucault (1979) and other postmodernists, has provided another impetus for new theorizing about organizations. By arguing for connections between sexuality, violence, and power (e.g., MacKinnon 1982), feminists moved sexuality from the domain of intimate relations to the domain of the public organization of control (Burrell 1984, 1987; Hearn and Parkin 1987; Hearn et al. 1989).

Finally, postmodernism, poststructuralism, and especially deconstruction have formulated powerful criticisms of modernist theories, which traditional organizational theories exemplify. Whether or not we see the postmodern critique as a way toward understanding the practical activities of gender subordination, such approaches pose a challenge and stimulus for a thorough examination of all thought we have taken for granted. Some of the most interesting critical feminist works today are deconstructions of organizational theory (e.g., Calás and Smircich 1989a, 1989c; Czarniawska-Joerges 1991).

The theoretical literature emerging from these and other sources is so large and diverse that I cannot attempt to summarize all the ways that thinking about organizations is becoming gendered. Instead, in the remainder of this chapter, I build on an earlier article of mine (Acker 1990) to examine the meaning of "gendered organizations" and to suggest some elements in a process of gendering organizational theory.

Thinking About Gender

In spite of all the writing and talking about gender, the meaning of *gendered processes, gendered practices,* or *gendered organizations* is often ambiguous. Feminists disagree about the meaning of *gender* (Butler 1990). The many forms and permutations of gender make some ambiguity inevitable, even desirable. Disagreement is unsurprising, given that *gender*'s current usage is a recent innovation, emerging from feminists' attempts to give voice to a changing consciousness. I will neither outline the disputes nor try to settle them. Rather, I hope to clarify how I think about gender and how this way of thinking may help us to better understand how organizations function and how structures of subordination are maintained and reproduced.

Gender refers to patterned, socially produced, distinctions between female and male, feminine and masculine. Gender is not something that people are, in some inherent sense, although we may consciously think of ourselves in this way. Rather, for the individual and the collective, it is a daily accomplishment (West and Zimmerman 1987) that occurs in the course of participation in work organizations as well as in many other locations and relations.

In the early days of contemporary feminist development, feminist social scientists made a distinction between gender and sex, with gender as socially constructed and sex as biologically given. Today, that distinction is more and more problematic as we understand the social construction of the body and of sexual acts and relations (Burrell and Hearn 1989). This is not to deny the physical materiality of the body and of sexuality but to emphasize the importance of meaning in the use and comprehension of the body. In the discussion that follows, sexuality is part of the ongoing production of gender. Gender, as patterned differences, usually involves the subordination of women, either concretely or symbolically, and, as Joan Scott (1986) points out, gender is a pervasive symbol of power.

The term *gendered processes* "means that advantage and disadvantage, exploitation and control, action and emotion, meaning and identity, are patterned through and in terms of a distinction between male and female, masculine and feminine" (Acker 1990: 146; see also Scott 1986; Harding 1986; Connell 1987; Flax 1990). Gendered processes are concrete activities, what people do and say, and how they think about these activities, for thinking is also an activity. The daily construction, and sometimes deconstruction, of gender occurs within material and ideological constraints that set the limits of possibility. For example, the boundaries of sex segregation, themselves continually constructed and reconstructed, limit the actions of particular women and men at particular times.

Gendered processes do not occur outside other social processes but are integral parts of these processes—for example, class and race relations—which cannot be fully understood without a comprehension of gender (Connell 1987). At the same time, class and race processes are integral to gender relations. The links between class and race domination and gender are ubiquitous. For example, at the top of the typical Southern California high-tech firm stands the rational, aggressive, controlling white man (occasionally a woman but one who has learned how to operate in the class/gender structure), while at the very bottom there are often women of color working on a production line where they have little control over any aspect of their working lives (Fernandez Kelly and Garcia 1988). Examining how the organization was started and is controlled by these particular men and how these particular women came to be the production workers leads us back into the class/gender/race relations of that time and place. Similarly, if we look at the work processes and organizational controls that keep the firm going, we will see the intertwining of gender, race, and class.

Gendered processes and practices may be open and overt, as when managers choose only men or only women for certain positions or when sexual jokes denigrating women are part of the work culture. On the other hand, gender may be deeply hidden in organizational processes and decisions that appear to have nothing to do with gender. For example, deregulation and internationalization of banking has altered the gender structure of banks in both Sweden (Acker 1991) and Britain (Morgan and Knights 1991). In Sweden, these changes contributed to a growing wage gap between women and men, as women remained in low-wage branch banking and men, chosen more often for the growing international banking departments, were rewarded with disproportionate salary increases. In Britain, deregulation, and the resulting increase in competitiveness in the industry, was an important cause of reorganization in one bank that gave women new tasks at the expense of some men but still protected the privileges of men in traditional managerial positions. To understand the persistence of gender patterns, even as external changes cause internal organizational restructuring, I think we should consider the gender substructure of organizations and the ways that gender is used as an organizational resource, topics discussed below.

Elements in a Theory of Gendered Organizations

Gendered Processes

Gendered organizations can be described in terms of four sets of processes that are components of the same reality, although, for purposes of description, they can be seen as analytically distinct. As outlined above, gendering may occur in gender-explicit or gender-neutral practices; it occurs through concrete organizational activities; and its processes usually have class and racial implications as well. Sexuality, in its diverse forms and meanings, is implicated in each of these processes of gendering organizations.

The first set of processes is the production of gender divisions. Ordinary organizational practices produce the gender patterning of jobs, wages, and hierarchies, power, and subordination (e.g., Kanter 1977a). Managers make conscious decisions that re-create and sometimes alter these patterns (Cohn 1985); unions, where they exist, often collude, whether intentionally or not. For example, while employers can no longer, by law, advertise for female workers for some jobs and male workers for others, many still perceive women as suited for certain work and men as suited for other work. These perceptions help to shape decisions. The introduction of new technology may offer the possibility for the reduction of gender divisions but most often results in a reorganization, not an elimination, of male predominance (e.g., Cockburn 1983, 1985). The depth and character of gender divisions vary dramatically from one society to another and from one time to another. In Britain, for example, when women first began to enter clerical work, separate offices were often set up so that women and men would not have to meet on the job, thus avoiding the possibility of sexual encounters and resulting in extreme gender segregation (Cohn 1985). Whatever the variation, there is overwhelming evidence that hierarchies are gendered and that gender and sexuality have a central role in the reproduction of hierarchy.

Gendering also involves the creation of symbols, images, and forms of consciousness that explicate, justify, and, more rarely, oppose gender divisions. Complex organizations are one of the main locations of the production of such images and forms of consciousness in our societies. Television, films, and advertising are obvious examples, but all organizations are sites of symbolic production. Gender images, always containing implications of sexuality, infuse organizational structure. The top manager or business leader is always strong, decisive, rational, and forceful—and often seductive (Calas and Smircich 1989b). The organization itself is often defined through metaphors of masculinity of a certain sort. Today, organizations are lean, mean, aggressive, goal oriented, efficient, and competitive but rarely empathetic, supportive, kind, and caring. Organizational participants actively create these images in their efforts to construct organizational cultures that contribute to competitive success.

The third set of processes that reproduce gendered organizations are interactions between individuals, women and men, women and women, men and men, in the multiplicity of forms that enact dominance and subordination and create alliances and exclusions. In these interactions, at various levels of hierarchy, policies that create divisions are developed and images of gender are created and affirmed. Sexuality is involved here, too, in overt or hidden ways; links between dominance and sexuality shape interaction and help to maintain hierarchies favoring men (Pringle 1989). Interactions may be between supervisors and subordinates, between coworkers, or between workers and customers, clients, or other outsiders. Interactions are part of the concrete work of organization, and the production of gender is often "inside" the activities that constitute the organization itself.

The fourth dimension of gendering of organizations is the internal mental work of individuals as they consciously construct their understandings of the organization's gendered structure of work and opportunity and the demands for gender-appropriate behaviors and attitudes (e.g., Pringle 1989; Cockburn 1991). This includes creating the correct gendered persona and hiding unacceptable aspects of one's life, such as homosexuality. As Pringle (1989: 176) says, "Sexual games are integral to the play of power at work, and success for women depends on how they negotiate their sexuality." Such internal work helps to reproduce divisions and images even as it ensures individual survival.

Gender and Sexuality as Organizational Resources

Gender, sexuality, and bodies can be thought of as organizational resources, primarily available to management but also used by individuals and groups of workers. Simultaneously, however, gender, sexuality, and bodies are problems for management. Solutions to these problems become resources for control. Both female and male bodies have physical needs on the job. Management often controls lunch and toilet breaks as well as physical movement around the workplace as integral elements in furthering productivity. Numbers of researchers, from Crozier on (Acker and Van Houten 1974), have observed that women workers are more tightly controlled in these ways than men workers. Higher-level employees are often rewarded with fewer bodily constraints and special privileges in regard to physical needs—for example, the executive washroom and dining room.

Reproduction and sexuality are often objects of and resources for control. As Burrell (1984: 98) argues, "Individual organizations inaugurate mechanisms for the control of sexuality at a very early stage in their development." Reproduction and sexuality may disrupt ongoing work and seriously undermine the orderly and rational pursuit of organizational goals. Women's bodies, sexuality, and procreative abilities are used as grounds for exclusion or objectification. On the other hand, men's sexuality dominates most workplaces and reinforces their organizational power (Collinson and Collinson 1989). In addition, talk about sex and male sexual superiority helps construct solidarity and cooperation from the bottom to the top of many organizations, thus promoting organizational stability and control.

Gender is also a resource in organizational change. Hacker (1979) showed how technological transformation at ATT in the 1970s was facilitated by moving women into formerly male jobs slated to be eliminated. Today, in the drive for organizational "flexibility," managements often consciously create part-time jobs, low paid and dead end, to be filled by women (see, e.g., Cockburn 1991). It is gender, and often race, that makes women ideal employees. These are only examples from a multiplicity of processes that suggest the possibilities for research about gender and sexuality in organizational control and change.

The Gendered Substructure of Organization

The more or less obvious manifestations of gender in organizational processes outlined above are built upon, and in turn help to reproduce, a gendered substructure of organization. The gendered substructure lies in the spatial and temporal arrangements of work, in the rules prescribing workplace behavior, and in the relations linking workplaces to living places. These practices and relations, encoded in arrangements and rules, are supported by assumptions that work is separate from the rest of life and that it has first claim on the worker. Many people, particularly women, have difficulty making their daily lives fit these expectations and assumptions. As a consequence, today, there are two types of workers, those, mostly men, who, it is assumed, can adhere to organizational rules, arrangements, and assumptions, and those, mostly women, who, it is assumed, cannot, because of other obligations to family and reproduction.

Organizations depend upon this division, for, in a free market economy, in contrast to a slave economy, they could not exist without some outside organization of reproduction to take care of supplying workers. In this sense, the gender substructure of organization is linked to the family and reproduction. This relationship is not simply a functional link. It is embedded in and re-created daily in ordinary organizational activities, most of which do not appear on the surface to be gendered. In the exploration of some of these processes, it is possible to see how integral to modern organization this gendered substructure is, and how relatively inaccessible to change it remains.

I began this discussion by considering some of the problems posed by the gendered nature of existing, ostensibly gender-neutral, organizational theory and processes. Feminist critics of traditional theory now widely recognize that this body of theory is gendered, that it implicitly assumes that managers and workers are male, with male-stereotypic powers, attitudes, and obligations (e.g., Acker 1990; Calás and Smircich this volume; Martin 1990; Mills 1989).

What is problematic is the discontinuity, even contradiction, between organizational realities obviously structured around gender and ways of thinking and talking about these same realities as though they were gender neutral. What activities or practices produce the facade of gender neutrality and maintain this disjuncture between organizational life and theory?

These questions can provide a point of entry into the underlying processes that maintain gender divisions, images, interactions, and identities.

This analytic strategy is based on Dorothy Smith's *The Conceptual Practices of Power* (1990) in which she argues that concepts that feminists may see as misrepresenting reality—here the concept of gender-neutral structure—indicate something about the social relations they represent. That is, such concepts are not "wrong." On the contrary, they are constructed out of the working knowledge of those who manage and control, thus they say something about processes of power, including the suppression of knowledge about gender. While it is important to "deconstruct" these concepts, revealing hidden meanings, we can, in addition, investigate the concrete activities that produce them.

The break between a gendered reality and gender-neutral thought is maintained, I believe, through the impersonal, objectifying practices of organizing, managing, and controlling large organizations. As Smith (1987) argues, these processes are increasingly textually mediated. Bureaucratic rules and written guides for organizational processes have been around for a long time, but their proliferation continues as rationalization of production and management expands on a global scale. The fact that much of this is now built into computer programs may mystify the process but only increases objectification and the appearance of gender neutrality. The continuing replication of the assumption of gender neutrality is part of the production of texts that can apply to workers, work processes, production, and management as general phenomena. Thus gender neutrality, the suppression of knowledge about gender, is embedded in organizational control processes.

This work of re-creating gender neutrality as part of the construction of general phenomena that can be organized and controlled through the application of documentary processes is evident in job evaluation,1 a textual tool used by management to rationalize wage setting and the construction of organizational hierarchies. Other managerial processes produce assumptions of gender neutrality, but job evaluation provides a particularly good example because it is widely used in every industrial country (International Labour Office 1986).

Job evaluators use documents, or instruments, that describe general aspects of jobs, such as knowledge, skill, complexity, and responsibility, to assess the "value" of particular, concrete jobs in comparison with other particular, concrete jobs. The content of the documents and the way evaluators discuss and interpret them in the course of the job evaluation process provide an illustration of how concrete organizational activities reproduce the assumption of gender neutrality (Acker 1989, 1990).

Job evaluation, as most experts will tell you, evaluates jobs, not the people who do the jobs. Job evaluation consultants and trainers admonish evaluators to consider only the requirements of the job, not the gender or other characteristics of the incumbent. The tasks, skill requirements, and responsibilities of a job can be reliably described and assessed, while people who fill the jobs vary in their knowledge and commitment. Jobs can be rationalized and standardized; people cannot. A job exists separate from those who fill it, as a position in the hierarchy of an organizational chart. It is a reified, objectified category. But the abstract job must contain the assumption of an abstract worker if it is to be more than a set of tasks written on a piece of paper. Such a worker has no obligations outside the demands of the job, which is a bounded, abstract entity. To fit such demands, the abstract worker does not eat, urinate, or procreate, for these activities are not part of the job. Indeed, the abstract worker has no body and thus no gender. Jobs and hierarchies are represented as gender neutral, and every time such a job evaluation system is used, the notion of gender-neutral structure and the behavior based on that notion are re-created within the organization. Gender-neutral organizational theories reflect this gender-neutral rendering of organizational reality.

Real jobs and real workers are, of course, deeply gendered and embodied. The abstract worker transformed into a concrete worker turns out to be a man whose work is his life and whose wife takes care of everything else. Thus the concept of a job is gendered, in spite of its presentation as gender neutral, because only a male worker can begin to meet its implicit demands. Hidden within the concept of a job are assumptions about separations between the public and private spheres and the gendered organization of reproduction and production. Reproduction itself, procreation, sexuality, and caring for children, the ill, and the aged, unless transferred to the public sphere, are outside job and organizational boundaries. Too much involvement in such activities makes a person unsuitable for the organization. Women do not fit the assumptions about the abstract worker. Thus they are less than ideal organization participants, best placed in particular jobs that separate them from "real" workers.

The exclusion of reproduction is, as I argue above, linked to the ideology of the gender-neutral, abstract worker who has no body and no feelings, along with no gender. This abstraction facilitates the idea that the organization and its goals come first before the reproductive needs of individuals and society, such as, for example, the need to preserve and restore the natural environment. The concept of the abstract worker, completely devoted to the job, also supports the idea that strong commitment to the organization over and above commitment to family and community are necessary and normal (Calás and Smircich this volume). As a consequence, management can more easily make the tough decisions, such as those to close factories while opposing all efforts to protect actual, concrete bodies and minds through plant closure legislation.

The theory and practice of gender neutrality covers up, obscures, the underlying gender structure, allowing practices that perpetuate it to continue even as efforts to reduce gender inequality are also under way (e.g., Cockburn 1991). The textual tools of management, as they are employed in everyday organizational life, not only help to create and then obscure gender structures that disadvantage women but are also part of complex processes that daily re-create the subordination of reproduction to production and justify the privileging of production over all other human necessities.

The gender-neutral character of the job and the worker, central to organizational processes and theories discussed above, depends upon the assumption that the worker has no body. This disembodied worker is a manifestation of the universal "citizen" or "individual" fundamental to ideas of democracy and contract. As Carole Pateman (1986: 8) points out, the most fundamental abstraction in the concept of liberal individualism is "the abstraction of the 'individual' from the body. In order for the individual to appear in liberal theory as a universal figure, who represents anyone and everyone, the individual must be disembodied." If the individual had bodily form, it would be clear that he represents one gender and one sex rather than a universal being. The universal individual is "constructed from a male body so that his identity is always masculine" (Pateman 1988: 223). Even with the full rights of citizens, women stand in an ambiguous relation to this universal individual. In a similar way, the concept of the universal worker, so common in talk about work organizations, "excludes and marginalizes women who cannot, almost by definition, achieve the qualities of a real worker because to do so is to become like a man" (Acker 1990: 150).

Summary and Conclusions

A gendered organization theory should produce better answers to questions about both the organization of production and the reproduction of organization (Burrell and Hearn 1989). I have suggested one strategy for developing such a theory, starting with an inventory of gendered processes that necessarily include manifestations of sexuality. In any concrete organization, these processes occur in complex interrelations. Gendered processes are often resources in organizational control and transformation. Underlying these processes, and intimately connected to them, is a gendered substructure of organization that links the more surface gender arrangements with the gender relations in other parts of the society. Ostensibly gender neutral, everyday activities of organizing and managing large organizations reproduce the gendered substructure within the organization itself and within the wider society. I think that this is the most important part of the process to comprehend, because it is hidden within abstract, objectifying, textually mediated relations and is difficult to make visible. The fiction of the universal worker obscures the gendered effects of these ostensibly gender-neutral processes and helps to banish gender from theorizing about the fundamental character of complex organizations. Gender, sexuality, reproduction, and emotionality of women are outside organizational boundaries, continually and actively consigned to that social space by ongoing organizational practices. Complex organizations play an important role, therefore, in defining gender and women's disadvantage for the whole society.

What are the practical implications of analyses, such as mine, in which ordinary organizational practices and thinking about those practices are grounded in the prior exclusion of women? The implications are not a return to an imaginary, utopian past where production is small scale and reproduction and production are fully integrated in daily life. Nor are the implications an Orwellian future where sexuality, procreation, and child raising would be integrated in superorganizations where all of life is paternalistically regulated.

Instead, we might think about alternative possibilities, some short term and others long term. Short-term, new strategies to transform parts of large organizations from the inside are possible.2 One way to do this is to take control of, or at least to influence and use, the textual tools of management. This is what comparable worth activists aim to do, as they attempt to affect the construction and use of job evaluation instruments to increase the value placed on women's jobs. Comparable worth experience shows that this is difficult and time consuming but not impossible (Acker 1989; Blum 1991). Many other practices could be similarly altered, but union organization controlled by women is the essential condition for doing such things. In the meantime, individual women can become experts in using and manipulating organizational texts; superior knowledge of rules and procedures can often facilitate change.

Managements and management consultants are attempting to transform structure in many organizations, to reduce hierarchy and increase employees' responsibility for and participation in decision making. While efficiency, increased productivity, and competitiveness are management goals, these changes could also lead to new consciousness of the possibilities for more democratic work organization. Lower-level workers, such as routine computer operators or production workers, who are likely to be women, are probably not those who will benefit from the new management technology. But their exclusion could also be the grounds for questioning and consciousness-raising.

Long-term strategies will have to challenge the privileging of the "economy" over life and raise questions about the rationality of such things as organizational and work commitment (see also Calás and Smircich this volume) as well as the legitimacy of organizations' claims for the priority of their goals over other broader goals. The gendered structure of organizations will only be completely changed with a fundamental reorganization of both production and reproduction. The long term is very long term and impossible to specify, but this should not lead us to abandon the search for other ways of organizing complex collective human activities.

Notes

1. The following discussion of job evaluation is based on Acker (1989).
2. This has been suggested by Beatrice Halsaa, Hildur Ve, and Cynthia Cockburn, who are proposing an international feminist activist/researcher conference on the topic.

References

Abbey, A. 1982. "Sex Differences in Attribution for Friendly Behavior: Do Males Misperceive Females' Friendliness?" *Journal of Personality and Social Psychology* 42:830-38.

Abercrombie, N., S. Hill, and B. Turner. 1982. *The Dominant Ideology Thesis.* London: Heinemann.

Acker, J. 1980. "Women and Stratification: A Review of Recent Literature." *Contemporary Sociology* 9:25-34.

———. 1982. "Introduction to Women, Work and Economic Democracy." *Economic and Industrial Democracy* 3(4):i-viii.

———. 1987. "Sex Bias in Job Evaluation: A Comparable Worth Issue." In *Ingredients for Women's Employment Policy,* edited by Christine Bose and Glenna Spitze. Albany: SUNY Press.

———. 1988. "Class, Gender, and the Relations of Distribution." *Signs: Journal of Women in Culture and Society* 13:473-97.

———. 1989. *Doing Comparable Worth: Gender, Class and Pay Equity.* Philadelphia: Temple University Press.

———. 1990. "Hierarchies, Jobs, Bodies: A Theory of Gendered Organizations." *Gender & Society* 4:139-58.

———. 1991. "Thinking About Wages: The Gendered Wage Gap in Swedish Banks." *Gender & Society* 5:390-407.

Acker, J. and D. R. Van Houten. 1974. "Differential Recruitment and Control: The Sex Structuring of Organizations." *Administrative Science Quarterly* 19(2):152-63.

Adler, N. J. 1984. "Understanding the Ways of Understanding." Pp. 31-67 in *Comparative Management: Essays in Contemporary Thought.* Vol. 1, edited by R. Farmer. Greenwich, CT: JAI.

———. 1987. "Pacific Basin Managers: A 'Gaijin,' Not a Woman." *Resource Management* 26(2):169-91.

Adler, N. J. and D. N. Izraeli. 1988. *Women in Management Worldwide.* Armonk, NY: Sharpe.

Adler, N. J. and M. Jelinek. 1986. "Is 'Organization Culture' Culture Bound?" *Human Resources Management* 25:73-90.

Agger, B. 1979. "Work and Authority in Marcuse and Habermas." *Human Studies*, July, pp. 191-208.

Alexander, S. 1976. "Women's Work in Nineteenth-Century London." Pp. 59-111 in *The Rights and Wrongs of Women,* edited by J. Mitchell and A. Oakley. Harmondsworth, UK: Penguin.

Allen, F. R. and C. Kraft. 1982. *The Organizational Unconsciousness: How to Create the Corporate Culture You Want and Need.* Englewood Cliffs, NJ: Prentice-Hall.

Allen, V. 1975. *Social Analysis.* London: Longman.

Allport, G. W. 1954. *The Nature of Prejudice.* Reading, MA: Addison-Wesley.

Althusser, L. 1969. *For Marx,* translated by B. R. Brewster. London: Allen Lane.

———. 1971. *Lenin and Philosophy and Other Essays.* London: New Left.

Alvesson, M. 1984. "Questioning Rationality and Ideology: On Critical Organization Theory." *International Studies of Man and Organization* 14(1):61-69.

Archibald, K. 1970. *Sex and the Public Service.* Ottawa: Queen's Printer.

Armstrong, P. and H. Armstrong. [1978] 1984. *The Double Ghetto.* Toronto: McClelland and Stewart.

———. 1983. *A Working Majority: What Women Must Do for Pay.* Ottawa: CACSW.

———. 1990. *Theorizing Women's Work.* Toronto: Garamond.

Ayers-Nachamkin, B., C. H. Cann, and R. Reed. 1982. "Sex and Ethnic Differences in the Use of Paper." *Journal of Applied Psychology* 67:464-71.

Baker, H. G. 1953. *Rich's of Atlanta: The Story of a Store Since 1867.* Atlanta: University of Georgia, School of Business Administration, Division of Research.

Bales, R. F. and P. E. Slater. [1955] 1975. "Role Differentiation in Small Decision Making Groups." In *Family, Socialization and Interaction Process,* edited by T. Parsons and R. F. Bales. New York: Free Press.

Ball, D. W. 1967. "An Abortion Clinic Ethnography." *Social Problems* 14:293-301.

Balsamo, A. 1985. "Beyond Female as Variable: Construction a Feminist Perspective on Organizational Analysis." Paper presented at the Critical Perspectives in Organizational Analysis Conference, Baruch College, CUNY, September 5-7.

Bannon, S. 1975. "The Women's Bureau Is 21." *Labour Gazette* 75:629-32.

Barker, J. and H. Downing. 1980. "Word Processing and the Transformation of the Patriarchal Relations of Control in the Office." *Capital and Class* 10:64-99.

Barrett, M. 1980. *Women's Oppression Today.* London: Verso.

Barrett, M. and M. McIntosh. 1982. *The Anti-Social Family.* London: Verso Editions, NLB.

Barron, R. D. and G. M. Norris. 1976. "Sexual Divisions and the Dual Labour Market." Pp. 47-69 in *Dependence and Exploitation in Work and Marriage,* edited by D. L. Barker and S. Allen. London: Longman.

Bass, B. M., J. Krusell, and R. A. Alexander. 1971. "Male Managers' Attitudes Toward Working Women." *American Behavioral Scientist* 15:221-36.

Bataille, G. 1962. *Death and Sensuality.* New York: Basic Books.

Baumeister, R. 1986. *Identity, Cultural Change and Struggle for Self.* New York: Oxford University Press.

Bede. 1907. *Bede's Ecclesiastical History of England,* edited by J. A. Giles. London: Bell.

Beechey, V. 1979. "On Patriarchy." *Feminist Review* 3:66-83.

Beeghley, L. and J. Cochran. 1988. "Class Identification and Gender Role Norms Among Employed Married Women." *Journal of Marriage and Family* 50:719-29.
Belenky, M. F., B. M. Clinchy, N. R. Goldberger, and J. M. Tarule. 1986. *Women's Ways of Knowing.* New York: Basic Books.
Bell, E. 1986. "The Power Within: Bicultural Life Structures and Stress Among Black Women." Ph.D. dissertation, Case Western Reserve University.
———. 1989a. "Racial and Ethnic Diversity: The Void in Organizational Behavior Courses." *The Organizational Behavior Teaching Review* 13(4):56-67.
———. 1989b. "The Mammy and the Snow Queen." Paper presented at the Research in Women in Management Conference, Kingston, September.
———. 1990. "The Bicultural Life Experience of Career-Oriented Black Women." *Journal of Organizational Behavior* 11:459-77.
Bell, E., T. Denton, and S. Nkomo. 1992. "Women of Color in Management: Towards an Inclusive Analysis." In *Women and Work.* vol. 4, edited by L. Larwood and B. Gutek. Newbury Park, CA: Sage.
Beller, A. H. 1984. "Trends in Occupational Segregation by Sex and Race." In *Sex-Segregation in the Workplace: Trends, Explanations, Remedies*, edited by B. Reskin. Washington, DC: National Academic Press.
———. 1985. "Changes in the Sex Composition of U.S. Occupations, 1960-1981." *Journal of Human Resources* 20:235-50.
Bem, S. L. 1974. "The Measurement of Psychological Androgyny." *Journal of Consulting and Clinical Psychology* 42:155-62.
———. 1981. "Gender Schema Theory: A Cognitive Account of Sex-Typing." *Psychological Review* 88:354-64.
Bendix, R. 1956. *Work and Authority in Industry.* New York: John Wiley.
Beneria, L. and M. Rolda. 1987. *The Crossroads of Class and Gender.* Chicago: University of Chicago Press.
Benet, M. K. 1972. *The Secretarial Ghetto.* New York: McGraw-Hill.
Benson, J. K. 1977. "Organizations: A Dialectical View." *Administrative Science Quarterly* 22:1-21.
Benson, S. P. 1986. *Counter Cultures: Saleswomen, Managers, and Customers in American Department Stores. 1890-1940.* Urbana: University of Illinois Press.
Bergmann, B. R. and W. Darity. 1980. "Social Relations in the Workplace and Employer Discrimination." In *Proceedings of the 33rd Annual Meeting of the Industrial Relations Research Association.*
Berlew, D. E. and D. T. Hall. 1966. "The Socialisation of Managers: Effects of Expectations on Performance." *Administrative Science Quarterly* 11(2):207-24.
Bernstein, R. 1988. "History Convention Reflects Change from Traditional to Gender Studies." *New York Times,* January 9.
Beyer, J. and T. T. M. Lodahl. 1976. "A Comparative Study of Patterns of Influence in United States and English Universities." *Administrative Science Quarterly* 21:104-29.
Beyer, J., and H. M. Trice. 1979. "A Re-examination of the Relationship Between Size and Various Components of Organizational Complexity." *Administrative Science Quarterly* 24:48-64.
Beynon, H. 1974. *Working for Ford.* Harmondsworth, UK: Penguin.
Beynon, H. and R. M. Blackburn. 1972. *Perceptions of Work: Perceptions Within a Factory.* London: Cambridge University Press.

Bidwell, C. and R. Vreeland. 1964. "Authority and Control in Client-Serving Organizations." *Sociological Quarterly* 4:231-42.

Biggart, N. W. 1977. "The Creative-Destructive Process of Organizational Change: The Case of the Post Office." *Administrative Science Quarterly* 22:410-26.

Bilton, T., K. Bonnett, P. Jones, M. Stanworth, K. Sheard, and A. Webster. 1983. *Introductory Sociology*. London: Macmillan.

Bittner, E. 1967. "The Police on Skid-Row: A Study of Peace Keeping." *American Sociological Review* 32: 699-715.

Blackburn, R. M. and A. Stewart. 1977. "Women, Work and the Class Structure." *New Society* 41:436-37.

Bland, L., C. Brunsdon, D. Hobson, and J. Winship. 1978. "Women 'Inside and Outside' the Relations of Production." In *Women Take Issue* (Women's Studies Group, Centre for Contemporary Cultural Studies, University of Birmingham). London: Hutchinson.

Blau, J. R. 1979. "Expertise and Power in Professional Organization." *Sociology of Work and Occupations* 6:103-23.

Blau, J. R and W. McKinley. 1979. "Ideas, Complexity and Innovation." *Administrative Science Quarterly* 24:200-219.

Blau, P. M., C. M. Falbe, W. McKinley, and P. K. Tracy. 1976. "Technology and Organization in Manufacturing." *Administrative Science Quarterly* 21:20-40.

Blau, P. and W. R. Scott. 1963. *Formal Organizations*. London: Routledge & Kegan Paul.

Blauner, B. 1989. *Black Lives, White Lives: Three Decades of Race Relations in America*. Berkeley: University of California Press.

Blauner, R. 1967. *Alienation and Freedom*. Chicago: University of Chicago Press.

Blum, L. M. 1991. *Between Feminism and Labor: The Significance of the Comparable Worth Movement*. Berkeley: University of California Press.

Blum, L. and V. Smith. 1988. "Women's Mobility in the Corporation: A Critique of the Politics of Optimism." *Signs: Journal of Women in Culture and Society* 13(2):528-45.

Boss, P. and B. Thorne. 1989. "Family Sociology and Family Therapy: A Feminist Linkage." In *Women in Families: A Framework for Family Therapy*, edited by M. McGoldrick, C. M. Anderson, and F. Walsh. New York: Norton.

Bougon, M. 1981. "Uncovering Cognitive Maps: The Self-Q Technique." Pp. 173-88 in *Beyond Method*, edited by G. Morgan. Beverly Hills, CA: Sage.

Bradford, D. L., A. G. Sargent, and M. S. Sprague. 1975. "Executive Man and Woman: The Issue of Sexuality." *In Bringing Women into Management*, edited by F. E. Gordon and M. H. Strober. New York: McGraw-Hill.

Brake, M., ed. 1982. *Human Sexual Relations*. Harmondsworth: Penguin.

Braverman, H. 1974. *Labor and Monopoly Capital*. New York: Monthly Review Press.

Brewer, M. B. and R. M. Kramer. 1985. "The Psychology of Intergroup Attitudes and Behavior." *Annual Review of Psychology* 36:219-43.

British Sociological Association. n.d. *Sociology Without Sexism: A Sourcebook*. London: Author.

Bronfenbrenner, U. 1979. *The Ecology of Human Development*. Cambridge: Harvard University Press.

Broverman, I., et al. 1972. "Sex-Role Stereotypes: A Current Appraisal." *Journal of Social Issues* 28:59-78.

Brown, L. K. 1979. "Women and Business Management." *Signs: Journal of Women in Culture and Society* 5:266-87.

Brown, P. 1954. "Bureaucracy in a Government Laboratory." *Social Forces* 32:259-68.

Brown, P. and C. Shepherd. 1956. "Factionalism and Change in a Research Laboratory." *Social Problems* 3:235-43.

Bruegel, I. 1979. "Women as a Reserve Army of Labour: A Note on Recent British Experience." *Feminist Review* 3:12-23.

Bryman, A. 1984. "Leadership and Corporate Culture: Harmony and Disharmony." *Personnel Review* 13(2):19-24.

Bucher, R. 1970. "Social Process and Power in a Medical School." Pp. 3-48 in *Power in Organization*, edited by M. Zald. Nashville, TN: Vanderbilt University Press.

Bucher, R. and J. Stelling. 1969. "Characteristics of Professional Organizations." *Journal of Health and Social Behaviour* 10:3-15.

———. 1972. "Autonomy and Monitoring on Hospital Wards." *Sociological Quarterly* 13:431-46.

Burawoy, M. 1982. *Manufacturing Consent*. Chicago: University of Chicago.

Burns, T. and G. M. Stalker. 1961. *The Management of Innovation*. London: Tavistock.

Burrell, G. 1980. "Radical Organization Theory." In *The International Yearbook of Organization Studies 1979*, edited by D. Dunkerley and G. Salaman. London: Routledge & Kegan Paul.

———. 1984. "Sex and Organizational Analysis." *Organization Studies* 5(2):97-118.

———. 1987. "No Accounting for Sexuality." *Accounting, Organizations, and Society* 12:89-101.

Burrell, G. and J. Hearn. 1989. "The Sexuality of Organization." In *The Sexuality of Organization*, edited by J. Hearn, D. L. Sheppard, P. Tancred-Sheriff, and G. Burrell. London: Sage.

Burrell, G. and G. Morgan. 1979. *Sociological Paradigms and Organizational Analysis*. London: Heinemann.

Burstyn, V. 1983a. "Economy, Sexuality, Politics: Engels and the Sexual Division of Labour." *Socialist Studies/Etudes Socialistes: A Canadian Annual*, pp. 19-39.

———. 1983b. "Masculine Dominance and the State." In *Socialist Register*, edited by R. Miliband and J. Saville. London: Merlin.

Burton, C. 1985. *Subordination: Feminism and Social Theory*. Sydney: Allen and Unwin.

———. 1987. "Merit and Gender: Organizations and the Mobilization of Masculine Bias." *Australian Journal of Social Issues* 22(2):424-35.

Butler, J. 1990. *Gender Trouble: Feminism and the Subversion of Identity*. New York: Routledge.

Calás, M. B. 1988. "Gendering Leadership: The Differ(e/a)nce That Matters." Paper presented at the annual meetings of the Academy of Management, Anaheim, CA, August.

———. 1989. "'Time,' 'Race,' and 'Voice': The Lack in Global Management." Paper presented at the annual meeting of the Eastern Academy of Management, Portland, ME, May.

———. 1990. "'Time,' 'Race,' and 'Voice': A Framework for 'Rewriting' International Organizational Knowledge." Unpublished manuscript.

Calás, M. B., M. Colón de Toro, and J. M. Romaguera. 1982. "The Relationship of Cognitive Style Maps to the Preference for Experiential Learning of Undergraduate Students." Pp. 54-58 in *Developments in Business Simulation and Experiential Exercises*. Normal: Illinois State University.

Calás, M. B. and R. Jacques. 1988. "Diversity or Conformity? Research by Women on Women in Organizations." Paper presented at the annual conference on Women and Organizations, Long Beach, CA, August.

Calás, M. B. and L. Smircich. 1989a. "Voicing Seduction to Silence Leadership." Paper presented at the Fourth International Conference on Organizational Symbolism and Corporate Culture, Fountainbleau, France.

———. 1989b. "Using the 'F' Word: Feminist Theories and the Social Consequences of Organizational Research." Pp. 355-59 in *Academy of Management Best Papers Proceedings.* Washington, DC: Academy of Management.

———. 1992. "Re-writing Gender into Organization Theorizing: Directions from Feminist Perspectives." In *Re-thinking Organization: New Directions in Organizational Research and Analysis,* edited by M. I. Reed and M. D. Hughes. London: Sage.

Calás, M. B. and J. I. Velez-Arocho. 1979. "Hispanic Participation in High Managerial Positions in National and Multinational Firms in Puerto Rico." In *Proceedings of the Second Symposium for Hispanic Business and Economy.*

Campbell, B. 1973. "Under Fire: Advisory Council on the Status of Women." *Labour Gazette* 73:663-68.

Campbell, B. M. 1989. *Sweet Summer: Growing Up With and Without Dad.* New York: Ballantine.

Canadian Advisory Council on the Status of Women. 1983. *As Things Stand: Ten Years of Recommendations.* Ottawa: CACSW.

Caplow, T. 1954. *The Sociology of Work.* Westport, CT: Greenwood.

Carey, A. 1967. "The Hawthorne Studies: A Radical Criticism." *American Sociological Review* 32:403-16.

Castaneda, C. 1970. *The Teachings of Don Juan: A Yacqui Way of Knowledge.* Harmondsworth, UK: Penguin.

Catrice-Lorey, A. 1966. "Social Security and Its Relations with Beneficiaries: The Problem of Bureaucracy in Social Administration." *International Social Security Review* 19:286-97.

Chandler, A. D., Jr. 1962. *Strategy and Structure: Chapters in the History of the American Industrial Enterprise.* Cambridge: MIT Press.

Charlton, V. 1977. "A Lesson in Day Care." In *Women in the Community,* edited by Marjorie Mayo. London: Routledge & Kegan Paul.

Chatov, R. 1981. "Cooperation Between Government and Business." Pp. 487-502 in *Handbook of Organizational Design.* Vol. 1, edited by P. C. Nystrom and W. H. Starbuck. New York: Oxford University Press.

Checkland, P. 1981. *Systems Thinking, Systems Practice.* New York: John Wiley.

Cheney, J. 1987. "Eco-Feminism and Deep Ecology." *Environmental Ethics* 9:115-45.

Chesler, J. 1973. "Innovative Governance Structures in Secondary Schools." *Journal of Applied Behavioural Science* 9:261-80.

Child, J. 1964. "Quaker Employers and Industrial Relations." *Sociological Review* 12:293-305.

———. 1972. "Organizational Structure, Environment and Performance: The Role of Strategic Choice." *Sociology* 6:1-22.

Chodorow, N. 1971. "Being and Doing: A Cross-Cultural Examination of the Socialization of Males and Females." Pp. 259-91 in *Woman in Sexist Society,* edited by V. Gornick and B. Moran. New York: Basic Books.

———. 1978. *The Reproduction of Mothering: Psychoanalysis and the Sociology of Gender.* Berkeley: University of California Press.
Ciani, M. and B. Romberger. 1991. "Belonging in the Corporation: Oral Histories of Male and Female White, Black, and Hispanic Managers." Paper presented at the annual meeting of the Academy of Management, Miami, August.
Clarke, L. and T. Lawson. 1985. *Gender: An Introduction.* Slough: University Tutorial Press.
Clegg, S. 1975. *Power, Rule and Domination.* London: Routledge & Kegan Paul.
———. 1981. "Organization and Control." *Administrative Science Quarterly* 26:545-62.
Clegg, S. and D. Dunkerley, eds. 1977. *Critical Issues in Organizations.* London: Routledge & Kegan Paul.
———. 1980. *Organization, Class and Control.* London: Routledge & Kegan Paul.
Cleugh, J. 1963. *Love Locked Out.* London: Hamlyn.
Clifford, J. and G. F. Marcus, eds. 1986. *Writing Culture.* Berkeley: University of California Press.
Coch, L. and J. R. P. French. 1948. "Overcoming Resistance to Change." *Human Relations* 1:512-32.
Cockburn, C. 1981. "The Material of Male Power." *Feminist Review* 9:51.
———. 1983. *Brothers: Male Dominance and Technological Change.* London: Pluto.
———. 1985. *Machinery of Dominance.* London: Pluto.
———. 1991. *In the Way of Women: Men's Resistance to Sex Equality in Organizations.* Ithaca: ILR Press.
Cohen, A. and B. A. Gutek. 1985. "Dimensions of Perceptions of Social-Sexual Behavior in a Work Setting." *Sex Roles* 13:317-27.
Cohen, G. 1979. "Symbiotic Relations: Male Decision-Makers—Female Support Groups in Britain and the United States." *Women's Studies International Quarterly* 2:391-406.
Cohen, S. and L. Taylor. 1976. *Escape Attempts.* London: Allen Lane.
Cohn, S. 1985. *The Process of Occupational Sex-Typing.* Philadelphia: Temple University Press.
Collins, E. G. C. and T. B. Blodgett. 1981. "Sexual Harassment: Some See It, Some Won't." *Harvard Business Review* 59(2):76-95.
Collins, P. H. 1989. "The Social Construction of Black Feminist Thought." *Signs: Journal of Women in Culture and Society* 14:745-73.
———. 1990. *Black Feminist Thought.* Boston: Unwin Hyman.
Collinson, D. L. and M. Collinson. 1989. "Sexuality in the Workplace: The Domination of Men's Sexuality." In *The Sexuality of Organization,* edited by J. Hearn, D. L. Sheppard, P. Tancred-Sheriff, and G. Burrell. London: Sage.
Connell, R. W. 1987. *Gender and Power.* Stanford, CA: Stanford University Press.
Constantinople, A. 1973. "Masculinity-Femininity: An Exception to a Famous Dictum." *Psychological Bulletin* 80:389-407.
Constas, H. 1958. "Max Weber's Two Conceptions of Bureaucracy." *American Journal of Sociology* 63:400-409.
Cook, K. 1977. "Exchange and Power in Networks of Inter-organizational Relations." *Sociological Quarterly* 18:62-82.
Cook, M. and G. Wilson, eds. 1979. *Love and Attraction.* Oxford: Pergamon.
Cooper, C. and M. Davidson. 1982. *High Pressure: Working Lives of Women Managers.* London: Fontana.
Cooper, R. 1982. *Canetti's Sting* (Research Paper). Lancaster, UK: University of Lancaster, Department of Behaviour in Organisations.
Coote, A. and B. Campbell. 1982. *Sweet Freedom.* London: Pan.

Cortese, A. J. 1989. "The Interpersonal Approach to Morality: A Gender and Cultural Analysis." *Journal of Social Psychology* 129:429-41.

Coser, R. L. 1958. "Authority and Decision-Making in a Hospital: A Comparative Analysis." *American Sociological Review* 23:56-63.

———. 1963. "Alienation and Social Structure: Case Analysis of a Hospital." Pp. 231-65 in *The Hospital in Modern Society,* edited by E. Freidson. Glencoe, IL: Free Press.

Cox, D. 1979. "Review of Sociological Paradigms and Organizational Analysis: Gibson Burrell and Gareth Morgan." *Reviewing Sociology* 1:3-5.

Cox, T., Jr. 1990. "Problems with Research by Organizational Scholars on Issues of Race and Ethnicity." *Journal of Applied Behavioral Science* 26(1):5-23.

Cox, T., Jr., and S. Nkomo. 1988. "Race as a Variable in OB/HRM Research: A Review and Analysis of the Literature." Paper presented at the Career Division Workshop of the Academy of Management Meeting, Anaheim, CA.

———. 1990. "Invisible Men and Women: A Status Report on Race as a Variable in Organization Behavior Research." *Journal of Organizational Behavior* 11:419-36.

Cressey, P. and J. MacInnes. 1980. "Voting for Ford: Industrial Democracy and the Control of Labour." *Capital and Class* 11:5-33.

Crine, S. 1979. *The Hidden Army.* London: Low Pay Unit.

Crino, M. D., M. L. White, and G. L. DeSanctis. 1983. "Female Participation Rates and the Occupational Prestige of the Professions: Are They Inversely Related?" *Journal of Vocational Behavior* 22:243-55.

Crompton, R. and G. Jones. 1984. *White-Collar Proletariate.* London: Macmillan.

Crozier, M. 1964. *The Bureaucratic Phenomenon.* Chicago: University of Chicago Press.

———. [1965] 1971. *The World of the Office Worker.* Chicago: University of Chicago Press. (first published by Edition du Seuil, Paris)

Cunnison, S. 1966. *Wages and Work Allocation.* London: Tavistock.

Czarniawska-Joerges, B. 1991. "Gender, Power, Organizations: An Interruptive Interpretation." Paper presented at the New Theory in Organizations Conference at Keele, England.

Danet, B. 1971. "The Language of Persuasion in Bureaucracy: 'Modern' and 'Traditional' Appeals to the Israeli Customs Authorities." *American Sociological Review* 36:847-59.

———. 1973. "Giving the Underdog a Break: Latent Particularity Among Customs Officials." Pp. 329-37 in *Bureaucracy and the Public,* edited by E. Katz and B. Danet. New York: Basic Books.

Danet, B. and H. Hartman. 1972a. "Coping with Bureaucracy: The Israeli Case." *Social Forces* 51:7-22.

———. 1972b. "On 'Proteksia': Orientations Toward the Use of Personal Influence in Israeli Bureaucracy." *Journal of Comparative Administration* 3:405-34.

Daniels, A. K. 1969. "The Captive Professional: Bureaucratic Limitations in the Practice of Military Psychiatry." *Journal of Health and Social Behaviour* 10:255-65.

Darbel, A. and D. Schnapper. 1969. *Les agents du système administratif.* Paris: Mouton.

———. 1972. *Le système administratif.* Paris: Mouton.

———. 1974. "Les structures de l'administration française." *International Review of Administrative Sciences* 40:335-49.

Davies, C. 1972. "Professionals in Organizations, Some Preliminary Observations on Hospital Consultants." *Sociological Review* 20:553-67.

———. 1982. "Sexual Taboos and Social Boundaries." *American Journal of Sociology* 87:1032-63.

Davies, M. 1974. "Women's Place Is at the Typewriter: The Feminization of the Clerical Labor Force." *Radical America* 8:1-28.

Davies, R. 1975. *Women and Work.* London: Arrow.

Davis, A. Y. 1981. *Woman, Race and Class.* New York: Random House.

Davis, N. J. and R. V. Robinson. 1988. "Class Identification of Men and Women in the 1970's and 1980's." *American Sociological Review* 53:103-12.

Davis, S. 1984. *Managing Corporate Culture.* Cambridge, MA: Ballinger.

Deal, T. E. and A. A. Kennedy. 1982. *Corporate Cultures.* Reading, MA: Addison-Wesley.

Deaux, K. 1985. "Sex and Gender." *Annual Review of Psychology* 36:49-81.

de Certeau, M. 1986. *Heterologies.* Minneapolis: University of Minnesota Press.

Deem, R. 1978. *Women and Schooling.* London: Routledge & Kegan Paul.

Denhardt, R. B. 1981. *In the Shadow of Organization.* Lawrence: Regents Press of Kansas.

Derrida, J. 1978. *Writing and Difference.* Chicago: University of Chicago Press.

———. 1982. *Margins of Philosophy.* Chicago: University of Chicago Press.

———. 1988. "Letter to a Japanese Friend." Pp. 1-5 in *Derrida and Difference,* edited by D. Wood and R. Bernasconi. Evanston, IL: Northwestern University Press.

Devault, M. L. 1990. "Talking and Listening from Women's Standpoint: Feminist Strategies for Interviewing and Analysis." *Social Problems* 37(1):96-116.

Diamond, A. and L. R. Edwards, eds. 1977. *The Authority of Experience: Essays in Feminist Criticism.* Amherst: University of Massachusetts.

Dickson, D. 1974. *Alternative Technology and the Politics of Technical Change.* London: Fontana.

Dill, B. 1979. "The Dialectics of Black Womanhood." *Signs: Journal of Women in Culture and Society* 4(3):543-55.

DiTomaso, N. 1978a. "The Expropriation of the Means of Administration: Class Struggle over the U.S. Department of Labour." *Kapitalistate* 7:81-105.

———. 1978b. "The Organization of Authority in the Capitalist State." *Journal of Political and Military Sociology* 6:189-204.

———. 1980. "The Contributions of Organizational Sociology to Power Structure Research." *Insurgent Sociologist* 9:135-42.

Dobash, R. P. 1983. "Labour and Discipline in Scottish and English Prisons." *Sociology* 17(1):1-27.

Dobbins, G. H. and S. J. Platz. 1986. "Sex Differences in Leadership: How Real Are They?" *Academy of Management Review* 1:118-27.

Donnell, S. M. and J. Hall. 1980. "Men and Women as Managers: A Significant Case of No Significant Difference." *Organizational Dynamics,* p. 71.

Donzelot, J. 1979. *The Policing of Families.* London: Hutchinson.

Doyle, J. A. 1983. *The Male Experience.* Dubuque, IA: William C. Brown.

Dubeck, P. 1979. "Sexism in Recruiting Management Personnel for a Manufacturing Firm." Pp. 88-99 in *Discrimination in Organizations,* edited by R. Alverez et al. London: Jossey-Bass.

DuBois, E. C., G. P. Kelly, E. L. Kennedy, C. W. Korsmeyer, and L. S. Robinson. 1987. *Feminist Scholarship: Kindling in the Groves of Academe.* Urbana: University of Illinois Press.

Dunkerley, D. 1975. *Foreman: Aspects of Task and Structure.* London: Routledge & Kegan Paul.

Dunkerley, D. and G. Salaman, eds. 1980. *The International Yearbook of Organization Studies, 1979.* London: Routledge & Kegan Paul.
———. 1981. *The International Yearbook of Organization Studies, 1980.* London: Routledge & Kegan Paul.
Eckstein, S. 1976. "The Irony of Organization: Resource and Regulatory." *British Journal of Sociology* 27:150-64.
Edwards, P. and H. Scullion. 1982. *The Social Organisation of Industrial Conflict.* Oxford: Basil Blackwell.
Edwards, R. 1979. *Contested Terrain.* New York: Basic Books.
Eerkes, C. E. 1934. "The Employee: A Preferred Customer." In *Joint Management Proceedings.* New York: National Retail Dry Goods Association.
Ehrlich, C. 1978. *Socialism, Anarchism, and Feminism.* Baltimore: Research Group One. (reprinted by Black Bear, London)
Eichler, M. 1980. *The Double Standard.* New York: St. Martin.
Eisenstein, H. 1985. "The Gender of Bureaucracy: Reflections on Feminism and the State." In *Women, Social Science and Public Policy.* Sydney: Allen and Unwin.
Eisenstein, Z. 1981. *The Radical Future of Liberal Feminism.* New York: Longman.
———. 1984. *Feminism and Sexual Equality: Crisis in Liberal America.* New York: Monthly Review Press.
Elger, T. 1979. "Valorisation and 'De-skilling': A Critique of Braverman." *Capital and Class* 7(Spring):59-99.
Elias, N. 1978. *The Civilising Process.* Oxford: Basil Blackwell.
Elshtain, J. B. 1981. *Public Man, Private Woman.* Oxford: Robertson.
Emerson, J. 1970. "Behavior in Private Places: Sustaining Definitions of Reality in Gynaecological Examinations." In *Recent Sociology.* Vol. 2, edited by H. P. Freitze. New York: Macmillan.
Engel, G. V. 1969. "The Effect of Bureaucracy on the Professional Autonomy of the Physician." *Journal of Health and Social Behaviour* 10:30-41.
Epstein, C. 1970. *Women's Place.* Berkeley: University of California Press.
Erikson, E. 1950. *Childhood and Society.* New York: Norton.
———. 1968. *Identity, Youth and Crisis* New York: Norton.
Etzioni, A. 1964. *Modern Organizations.* Englewood Cliffs, NJ: Prentice-Hall.
———. 1969. *The Semi-Professions and Their Organizations.* New York: Free Press.
"Expose Employees to Knowledge." 1938. *Department Store Economist* 1:14.
Fabian, J. 1983. *Time and the Other.* New York: Columbia University Press.
Factory Commission. 1833. "Commission on Employment of Children in Factories." *Parliamentary Papers* 20.
Fagenson, E. A. 1989. "At the Heart of Women in Management Research: Theoretical and Methodological Approaches and Their Biases." *Journal of Business Ethics* 9:267-74..
Fairhurst, G. T. and B. K. Snavely. 1983a. "A Test of the Social Isolation of Male Tokens." *Academy of Management Journal* 26:353-61.
———. 1983b. "Majority and Token Minority Group Relationships: Power Acquisition and Communication." *Academy of Management Review* 8:292-300.
Falcón, L. M., D. T. Gurak, and M. G. Powers. 1990. "Labor Force Participation of Puerto Rican Women in Greater New York City." *Sociology and Social Research* 74:110-17.
Farley, L. 1978. *Sexual Shakedown.* London: Melbourne House.
Farnham, C., ed. 1987. *The Impact of Feminist Research in the Academy.* Bloomington: Indiana University Press.

Farquhar, M. 1933. "An Analysis of a Toy Department in a Department Store." M.A. thesis, University of Pittsburgh.
Farrow, L. 1974. *Feminism as Anarchism.* New York: Aurora. (reprinted by Black Bear, London)
Feldberg, R. L. and E. N. Glenn. 1979. "Male and Female: Job Versus Gender Models in the Sociology of Work." *Social Problems* 26(5):524-38.
Fenelon, F. 1977. *Playing for Time.* New York: Atheneum.
Fenn, M. 1976. "Comment." *Journal of Contemporary Business* 5:n.pp..
———. 1978. *Making It in Management.* Englewood Cliffs, NJ: Prentice-Hall.
Fennel, M. L., P. R. Barchas, E. G. Cohen, A. M. McMahon, and P. Hildebrand. 1978. "An Alternative Perspective on Sex Differences in Organizational Settings: The Process of Legitimation." *Sex Roles* 4:589-604.
Ferguson, K. E. 1984. *The Feminist Case Against Bureaucracy.* Philadelphia: Temple University Press.
———. 1988. "Knowledge, Politics and Personhood." Presented at the conference, The Feminine in Public Administration and Policy, Washington, DC, May 7.
Fernandez Kelly, M. P. and A. M. Garcia. 1988. "Invisible Amidst the Glitter: Hispanic Women in the Southern California Electronics Industry." In *The Worth of Women's work,* edited by A. Statham, E. M. Miller, and H. O. Mauksch. Albany: SUNY Press.
Ferraro, G. A. 1984. "Bridging the Wage Gap: Pay Equity and Job Evaluations." *American Psychologist* 39(10):1170.
Findlay, S. 1987. "Facing the State: The Politics of the Women's Movement Reconsidered." In *Feminism and Political Economy: Women's Work, Women's Struggles,* edited by H. J. Maroney and M. Luxton. Toronto: Methuen.
Fine, B. 1979. "Struggles Against Discipline." *Capital and Class* 9:75-96.
Flax, J. 1987. "Postmodernism and Gender Relations in Feminist Theory." *Signs: Journal of Women in Culture and Society* 12:621-43.
———. 1990. *Thinking Fragments: Psychoanalysis, Feminism, and Postmodernism in the Contemporary West.* Berkeley: University of California Press.
Follett, M. P. 1937. "The Process of Control." Pp. 159-69 in *Papers on the Science of Administration,* edited by L. Gulick and L. Urwick. New York: Institute of Public Administration.
Foucault, M. 1972. *The Archeology of Knowledge.* New York: Pantheon.
———. 1973. *The Order of Things.* New York: Vintage.
———. 1977. *Discipline and Punish.* London: Allen Lane.
———. 1979. *The History of Sexuality.* Vol. 1. London: Allen Lane.
Fox-Genovese, E. 1991. *Feminism Without Illusions: A Critique of Individualism.* Chapel Hill: University of North Carolina Press.
Franzway, S., D. Court, and R. W. Connell. 1989. *Staking a Claim: Feminism, Bureaucracy and the State.* Oxford: Polity Press/Basil Blackwell.
Freedman, S. M. and J. S. Phillips. 1988. "The Changing Nature of Research on Women at Work." *Journal of Management* 14 (2): 231-51.
Freeman, J. 1970. "The Tyranny of Structurelessness: Women's Liberation." (pamphlet, reprinted in *Berkeley Journal of Sociology* 1970 and *MS* 1973)
Freeman, S. J. M. 1990. *Managing Lives: Corporate Women and Social Change.* Amherst: University of Massachusetts Press.
French, J. R. P., J. Israel, and D. Aas. 1960. "An Experiment on Participation in a Norwegian Factory." *Human Relations* 13:3-19.

Freud, S. 1948. *Beyond the Pleasure Principle.* London: Hogarth.
Furstenburg, F. 1968. "Structural Changes in the Working Class: A Situational Study of Workers in the Western German Chemical Industry." Pp. 145-74 in *Social Stratification,* edited by J. A. Jackson. London: Cambridge University Press.
Gagnon, J. H. and W. Simon. 1974. *Sexual Conduct: The Human Sources of Human Sexuality.* London: Hutchinson.
Galinsky, M. J. and M. D. Galinsky. 1967. "Organization of Patients and Staff in Three Types of Mental Hospitals." Pp. 233-43 in *Behavioural Science for Social Workers,* edited by E. J. Thomas. New York: Free Press.
Gallos, J. V. 1989. "Exploring Women's Development: Implications for Career Theory, Practice and Research." In *Handbook of Career Theory,* edited by M. B. Arthur, D. T. Hall, and B. S. Lawrence. Cambridge, MA: Cambridge University Press.
Game, A. and R. Pringle. 1983. *Gender at Work.* Sydney, Allen & Unwin.
Gardiner, J. 1977. "Women in the Labour Process and Class Structure." In *Class and Class Structure,* edited by A. Hunt. London: Lawrence and Wishart.
Garnsey, E. 1977. "Women's Work and Theories of Class Stratification." *Sociology* 12:223-43.
Gaskell, P. 1836. *Artisans and Machinery: The Moral and Physical Condition of the Manufacturing Population.* London: Parker.
Gates, H. L., Jr., ed. 1986. *"Race," Writing, and Difference.* Chicago: University of Chicago Press.
———. 1988. *The Signifying Monkey.* New York: Oxford.
Geraghty, T. 1981. *Who Dares Wins.* London: Fontana.
Gerôme, N. 1969. "Sur l'administration académique et son environnement." *Sociologie du Travail* 11:145-63.
Gerson, K. 1985. *Hard Choices: How Women Decide About Work, Career and Motherhood.* Berkeley: University of California Press.
Giallombardo, R. 1966. *Society of Women: A Study of Women's Prison.* New York: John Wiley.
Giddens, A. 1979. *Central Problems in Social Theory.* New York: Macmillan.
———. 1981. *A Contemporary Critique of Historical Materialism.* New York: Macmillan.
Giddings, P. 1984. *When and Where I Enter: The Impact of Black Women on Race and Sex in America.* New York: William Morrow.
Giele, J. 1980. "Crossovers: New Themes in Adult Roles and the Life Cycle." In *Women's Lives: New Theory, Research and Policy,* edited by D. McGuigan. Ann Arbor: University of Michigan, Center for Continuing Education of Women.
———. 1982. "Women's Work and Family Roles." In *Women in the Middle Years,* edited by J. Giele. New York: John Wiley.
Gilbert, A. N. 1976. "Buggery and the British Navy: 1700-1861." *Journal of Social History* 10(1):72-98.
Gilligan, C. 1982. *In a Different Voice: Psychological Theory and Women's Development.* Cambridge, MA: Harvard University Press.
Glenn, E. N. 1985. "Racial Ethnic Women's Labor: The Intersection of Race, Gender and Class Oppression." *Review of Radical Political Economics* 17:86-108.
Glenn, E. N. and R. L. Feldberg. 1977. "Degraded and Deskilled: The Proletarianization of Clerical Work." *Social Problems* 25(1):52-64.
———. 1979. "Women as Mediators in the Labour Process." Paper presented at the 74th Annual Meeting of the American Sociological Association, Boston.

Glennon, L. 1979. *Women and Dualism.* New York: Longman.
———. 1983. "Synthesism: A Case of Feminist Methodology." Pp. 260-71 in *Beyond Method,* edited by G. Morgan. London: Sage.
Goffman, E. 1968. *Asylums.* Harmondsworth, UK: Penguin.
Goldthorpe, J., D. Lockwood, F. Bechhofer, and J. Platt. 1968. *The Affluent Worker: Industrial Attitudes and Behavior.* London: Cambridge University Press.
Gombin, R. 1978. *The Radical Tradition.* London: Methuen.
Goodrich, C. 1975. *The Frontier of Control.* London: Pluto.
Gordon, F. E and M. H. Strober, eds. 1975. *Bringing Women into Management.* New York: McGraw-Hill.
Gordon, L. K. 1975. "Bureaucratic Competence and Success in Dealing with Public Bureaucracies." *Social Problems* 23:196-208.
Goss, M. E. W. 1963. "Patterns of Bureaucracy Among Hospital Staff Physicians." Pp. 170-94 in *The Hospital in Modern Society,* edited by E. Freidson. Glencoe, IL: Free Press.
Gould, M. 1980. "When Women Create an Organization: The Ideological Imperatives of Feminism." In *The International Yearbook of Organization Studies,* edited by D. Dunkerley and G. Salaman. London: Routledge & Kegan Paul.
Gouldner, A. 1971. *The Coming Crisis of Western Sociology.* London: Heinemann.
Grady, K. E. 1977. "Sex as a Social Label: The Illusion of Sex Differences." Ph.D. dissertation, City University of New York.
Grandjean, B. D. and H. H. Bernal. 1979. "Sex and Centralization in a Semi-Profession." *Sociology of Work and Occupations* 6:84.
Grant, J. 1988. "Women as Managers: What They Can Offer Organizations." *Organizational Dynamics,* Spring, pp. 56-63.
———. In preparation. "Gender Representation and the State Bureaucracy: Ontario 1963-1986." Ph.D. dissertation.
Grant, J. and P. Tancred-Sheriff. 1986. "A Feminist Perspective on State Bureaucracy." Paper presented to the conference, L'Etat contemporain: Au coeur de la Societe? Lennoxville, Quebec, June.
Greenhaus, J., S. Parauraman, and W. Wormley. (1990). "Effects of Race on Organizational Experiences, Job Performance Evaluation, and Career Outcomes." *Academy of Management Journal*, 33(1): 64-86.
Greenwood, D. 1984. "The Institutional Inadequacy of the Market in Determining Comparable Worth: Implications for Value Theory." *Journal of Economic Issues* 18(2):457-64.
Greer, G. 1970. *The Female Eunuch.* New York: Bantam Books.
Gross, E. 1968. "Plus ça change...? The Sexual Structure of Occupations over Time." *Social Problems* 16:198-208.
Gutek, B. A. 1981. "Experiences of Sexual Harassment: Results from a Representative Survey." In S. Tangri (Chair), *Sexual Harassment at Work: Evidence, Remedies, and Implications.* Symposium conducted at the convention of the American Psychological Association, Los Angeles.
———. 1985. *Sex and the Workplace: The Impact of Sexual Behavior and Harassment on Women, Men, and Organizations.* San Francisco: Jossey-Bass.
———. 1989. "Sexuality in the Workplace: Key Issues in Social Research and Organizational Practice." In *The Sexuality of Organization,* edited by J. Hearn, D. Sheppard, P. Tancred-Sheriff, and G. Burrell. London: Sage.

Gutek, B. A., A. G. Cohen, and A. M. Konrad. 1986. "Group Proportions and Sex-Role Stereotypes: Explaining Social-Sexual Behavior in the Workplace." Unpublished manuscript, Claremont Graduate School.

Gutek, B. A. and V. Dunwoody-Miller. 1986. "Understanding Sex in the Workplace." In *Women and Work: An Annual Review*. Vol. 2, edited by A. H. Stromberg, L. Larwood, and B. A. Gutek. Beverly Hills, CA: Sage.

Gutek, B. A., L. Larwood, and A. Stromberg. 1986. "Women at Work." Pp. 217-34 in *Review of Industrial/Organizational Psychology*. Vol. 1, edited by C. Cooper and J. Robertson. London: John Wiley.

Gutek, B. A. and B. Morasch. 1982. "Sex-Ratios, Sex Role Spillover, and Sexual Harassment of Women at Work." *Journal of Social Issues* 38(4):55-74.

Gutek, B. A., B. Morasch, and A. G. Cohen. 1983. "Interpreting Social-Sexual Behavior in a Work Setting." *Journal of Vocational Behavior* 22:30-48.

Gutek, B. A. and C. V. Nakamura. 1982. "Gender Roles and Sexuality in the World of Work." In *Changing Boundaries, Gender Roles and Sexual Behavior,* edited by E. R. Allgeier and N. B. McCormick. San Francisco: Mayfield.

Haaken, J. 1988. "Field Dependence Research: A Historical Analysis of a Psychological Construct." *Signs: Journal of Women in Culture and Society 13(2):311-30.*

Habermas, J. 1971. *Towards a Rational Society,* translated by J. J. Shapiro. London: Heinemann.

Hacker, S. L. 1979. "Sex Stratification, Technology and Organizational Change: A Longitudinal Case Study of AT&T." *Social Problems* 26:539-57.

Hage, J., M. Aiken, and C. B. Marrett. 1971. "Organization Structure and Communications." *American Sociological Review* 36:860-71.

Hakim, C. 1979. *Occupational Segregation* (Research Paper No. 9). London: Department of Employment.

Hall, R. 1977. *Organizations: Structure and Process.* Englewood Cliffs, NJ: Prentice-Hall.

Harbison, J. and C. Myers. 1960. *Management in the Industrial World.* New York: John Wiley.

Harding, S. 1986. *The Science Question in Feminism.* Ithaca, NY: Cornell University Press.

Harding, S. and M. Hintikka, eds. 1983. *Discovering Reality: Feminist Perspectives on Epistemology, Metaphysics, Methodology, and Philosophy of Science.* Dordrecht, Holland: D. Reidel.

Hartmann, H. 1976. "Capitalism, Patriarchy and Job Segregation by Sex." *Signs: Journal of Women in Culture and Society* 1(3):137-69.

Harvey, L. 1982. "The Use and Abuse of Kuhnian Paradigms in the Sociology of Knowledge." *Sociology* 16(1):85-101.

Hawkesworth, M. E. 1984. "The Affirmative Action Debate and Conflicting Conceptions of Individuality." *Women's Studies International Forum* 7(5):335-47.

Hearn, J. 1982a. "Notes on Patriarchy, Professionalization and the Semi-Professions." *Sociology* 16(2):184-202.

———. 1982b. "The Professions and the Semi-Professions: The Control of Emotions and the Construction of Masculinity." Paper presented at the British Sociological Association Meeting, Manchester University.

———. 1985a. "Men's Sexuality at Work." In *The Sexuality of Men,* edited by A. Metcalf and M. Humpries. London: Pluto.

———. 1985b. "Sexism, Men's Sexuality and Management: The Seen Yet Unnoticed Case of Men's Sexuality." In *Sexuality, Power, and Organizational Theory*, G. Burrell

(Chair), Symposium conducted at the meeting of the Academy of Management, San Diego.
———. 1985c. "Patriarchy, Professionalism and the Semi-Professions." In *Women and Social Policy,* edited by C. Unger. London: Macmillan.
———. 1987. *The Gender of Oppression: Men, Masculinity and the Critique of Marxism.* Brighton: Wheatsheaf.
———., ed. 1991. "Men, Masculinities and Leadership: Changing Patterns and New Initiates" (Special Issue). *Equal Opportunities International* 8(1).
Hearn, J. and P. W. Parkin. 1983. "Gender and Organizations: A Selective Review and a Critique of a Neglected Area." *Organization Studies* 4(3):219-42.
———. 1984. "'Sex' at 'Work': Methodological and Other Difficulties in the Study of Sexualtiy in Work Organizations." Paper presented at British Sociological Association conference, University of Bradford.
———. 1986-87. "Women, Men and Leadership: A Critical Review of Assumptions, Pratices and Changes in the Industrialized Nations." *International Studies of Management and Organization* 16.
———. 1987. *'Sex' at 'Work': The Power and Paradox of Organizational Sexuality.* Brighton: Wheatsheaf.
———. 1991. "Women, Men and Leadership: A Critical Review of Assumptions, Practices and Changes in the Industrialized Nations." In *Women in Management Worldwide.* 2nd ed., edited by N. J. Adler and D. Izraeli. New York: M. E. Sharpe.
Hearn, J., D. Sheppard, P. Tancred-Sheriff, and G. Burrell, eds. 1989. *The Sexuality of Organization.* London: Sage.
Henning, M. and A. Jardin. 1977. *The Managerial Woman.* Garden City, NY: Anchor/Doubleday.
Hickson, J., D. S. Pugh, and D. C. Pheysey. 1969. "Operations Technology and Organization Structure: An Empirical Reappraisal." *Administrative Science Quarterly* 14:378-97.
Hill, C. 1964. *Society and Puritanism in Pre-revolutionary England.* London: Secker and Warburg.
Hill, S. 1981. *Competition and Control at Work.* London: Heinemann.
Hill-Collins, P. 1989. "The Social Construction of Black Feminist Thought." *Signs: Journal of Women in Culture and Society* 14:745-73.
———. 1990. *Black Feminist Thought: Knowledge, Consciousness, the Politics of Empowerment.* Boston: Unwin Hyman.
Hobsbawm, E. J. 1975. *The Age of Capital.* London: Weidenfeld and Nicolson.
Hofstede, G. 1980. "Motivation, Leadership, and Organization: Do American Theories Apply Abroad?" *Organization Dynamics,* Summer, pp. 42-63.
———. 1987. "The Cultural Relativity of Organizational Practices and Theories." Pp. 115-29 in *International Business Knowledge,* edited by W. A. Dymsza and R. G. Vambery. New York: Praeger.
Hofstede, G. and M. H. Bond. 1988. "Confucius and Economic Growth: New Insights into Culture's Consequences." *Organizational Dynamics,* Spring, pp. 5-21.
Holusha, J. 1991. "Grace Pastiak's Web of Inclusion." *New York Times,* May 5 (sec. 3), p. 1.
Hooks, B. 1981. *Ain't I a Woman: Black Women and Feminism.* Boston: South End.
"How Bloomingdale's Trains for Better Customer Service." 1964. *Stores* 46(11):24-25.
Hower, R. M. 1943. *History of Macy's of New York, 1858-1919: Chapters in the Evolution of the Department Store.* Cambridge, MA: Harvard University Press.

Hurtado, A. 1989. "Relating to Privilege: Seduction and Rejection in the Subordination of White Women and Women of Color." *Signs: Journal of Women in Culture and Society* 14:833-55.

Huston, T. L. and R. M. Cate. 1979. "Social Exchange in Intimate Relationships." In *Love and Attraction,* edited by M. Cook and G. Wilson. Oxford, UK: Pergamon.

I.F.F. Research, Ltd. 1980. "Inquiry into the Employment of Women." *Department of Employment Gazette,* London.

Ignatieff, M. 1978. *A Just Measure of Pain: The Penitentiary in the Industrial Revolution: 1750-1850.* New York: Macmillan.

Illich, I. 1973. *Deschooling Society.* Harmondsworth, UK: Penguin.

International Labour Office. 1986. *Job Evaluation.* Geneva: Author.

Inzerilli, G. and A. Laurent. 1983. "Managerial Views of Organization Structure in France and the USA." *International Studies of Management and Organizations* 13:97-118.

Jacklin, C. N. and E. E. Maccoby. 1975. "Sex Differences and Their Implications for Management." In *Bringing Women into Management,* edited by F. E. Gordon and M. H. Strober. New York: McGraw-Hill.

Jackman, M. R. and Jackman, R. W. 1983. *Class Awareness in the United States.* Berkeley: University of California Press.

Jacobs, J. A. 1983. "The Sex-Segregation of Occupations and the Career Patterns of Women." Ph.D. dissertation, Harvard University, Department of Sociology.

Jacobson, S. W. and R. Jacques. 1989. "Beyond Androgyny: Future Directions for Gender Research." Paper presented at the annual meetings of the Academy of Management, Washington, DC, August.

Jaggar, A. M. 1983. *Feminist Politics and Human Nature.* Totowa, NJ: Rowman and Allanheld.

JanMohamed, A. R. 1986. "The Economy of Manichean Allegory: The Function of Racial Difference in Colonialist Literature." Pp. 78-106 in *"Race," Writing and Difference,* edited by J. L. Gates, Jr. Chicago: University of Chicago Press.

Jay, A. 1967. *Management and Machiavelli.* London: Hodder and Stoughton.

———. 1972. *Corporation Man.* London: Cape.

Jelinek, M. and N. J. Adler. 1988. "Women: World-Class Managers for Global Competition." *Academy of Management Executive* 2:11-19.

Jelinek, M., L. Smircich, and P. Hirsch. 1983. "Introduction: A Code of Many Colors." *Administrative Science Quarterly* 28:331-38.

Jenkins, L. and C. Kramer. 1978. "Small Group Processes: Learning from Women." *Women's Studies International Quarterly* 1:67-84.

Johnson, A. G. and W. F. Whyte. 1977. "The Mondragon System of Worker Production Cooperatives." *Industrial and Labour Relations Review* 31:18-30.

Johnson, W. B. and A. H. Packer. 1987. *Workforce 2000: Work and Workers for the 21st Century.* Indianapolis: Hudson Institute.

Josselson, R. 1987. *Finding Herself: Pathways to Identity Development in Women.* San Francisco: Jossey-Bass.

Judelle, B. 1960. "The Changing Customer, 1910-1916." *Stores* 42(10):14.

Kamata, S. 1983. *Japan in the Passing Lane.* London: Allen and Unwin.

Kanter, R. M. 1972. "The Organization Child: Experience Management in a Nursery School." *Sociology of Education* 45:186-211.

———. 1975a. "Women and the Structure of Organizations." Pp. 35-74 in *Another Voice,* edited by M. Millman and R. M. Kanter. Garden City, NY: Anchor.

———. 1975b. "Women and the Structure of Organizations: Explorations in Theory and Behaviour." *Sociological Inquiry* 45:34-74.

———. 1975c. "Women in Organizations: Sex Roles, Group Dynamics and Change Strategies." Pp. 371-86 in *Beyond Sex Roles,* edited by A. Sargent. St. Paul, MN: West.

———. 1976. "The Impact of Hierarchical Structures on the Work Behaviour of Women and Men." *Social Problems* 23:415-30.

———. 1977a. *Men and Women of the Corporation.* New York: Basic Books.

———. 1977b. "Some Effects of Proportions of Group Life: Skewed Sex-Ratios and Responses to Token Women." *American Journal of Sociology* 82:965-90.

———. 1980. "The Impact of Organisation Structure: Models and Methods for Change." In *Equal Employment Policy for Women,* edited by R. S. Ratner. Philadelphia: Temple University Press.

Kanter, R. M. and B. A. Stein, eds. 1979. *Life in Organizations.* New York: Basic Books.

Kanter, R. M and L. A. Zurcher, Jr. 1973. "Concluding Statement Evaluating Alternatives and Alternative Valuing." *Journal of Applied Behavioral Sciences* 9:381-97.

Katz, E. and B. Danet. 1966. "Petitions and Persuasive Appeals: A Study of Official-Client Relations." *American Sociological Review* 31:811-22.

———., eds. 1973a. *Bureaucracy and the Public.* New York: Basic Books.

———. 1973b. "Communication Between Bureaucracy and the Public: A Review of the Literature." In *Handbook of Communication,* edited by I. D. Pool and W. Schramm. Chicago: Rand McNally.

Keller, E. F. 1985. *Reflections on Gender and Science.* New Haven, CT: Yale University Press.

Keneally, T. 1982. *Schindler's Ark.* London: Coronet.

Kerr, C. 1983. *The Future of Industrial Societies: Convergence or Continuing Divergence.* Cambridge, MA: Harvard University Press.

Kerr, C., J. Dunlop, J. Harbison, and C. Myers. 1960. *Industrialism and Industrial Man.* New York: Oxford. University Press.

Kessler, S., D. J. Ashenden, R. W. Connell, and G. W. Dowsett. 1985. "Gender Relations in Secondary Schooling." *Sociology of Education* 58:46.

Kessler, S. J. and W. McKenna. 1978. *Gender: An Ethnomethodological Approach.* New York: John Wiley.

Keil, I. 1965. "Advice to the Magnates: Management Education in the 13th Century." *Bulletin of the A.T.M.* 17(March):2-8.

Kirby, S. and L. McKenna. 1989. *Experience, Research, Social Change: Methods from the Margins.* Toronto: Garamond.

Kohn, M. 1971. "Bureaucratic Man: A Portrait and an Interpretation." *American Sociological Review* 36:461-74.

Kohn, M. L. 1979. "The Effects of Social Class on Parental Values and Practices." Pp. 45-68 in *The American Family: Dying or Developing*, edited by D. Reiss and H. A. Hoffman. Palo Alto, CA: Mayfield.

Konrad, A. M. and B. A. Gutek. 1986. "Impact of Work Experiences on Attitudes Toward Sexual Harassment." *Administrative Science Quarterly* 31(4).

Korabik, K. 1988. "Is the Ideal Manager Masculine? The Contribution of Femininity to Managerial Effectiveness." Paper presented at the national meeting of the Academy of Management, Anaheim, CA, August.

Korda, M. 1972. *Male Chauvinism! How It Works.* New York: Random House.

———. 1976. *Power.* London: Coronet.

Kornegger, P. 1975. *Anarchism: The Feminist Connection.* Cambridge, MA: Second Wave. (reprinted by Black Bear, London)

Kroeger, N. 1975. "Bureaucracy, Social Exchange and Benefits Received in a Public Assistance Agency." *Social Problems* 23:182-96.

LaDame, M. 1930. *The Filene Store: A Study of Employee's Relation to Management in a Retail Store.* New York: Russell Sage.

Lamphere, L. 1985. "Bringing the Family to Work: Women's Culture on the Shop Floor." *Feminist Studies* 11(3):519-40.

Land, H. 1976. "Women: Supporters or Supported?" Pp. 108-32 in *Sexual Divisions in Society,* edited by D. L. Barker and S. Allen. London: Tavistock.

Landsberger, H. A. 1958. *Hawthorne Revisited.* Ithaca, NY: Cornell University Press.

Langer, E. 1970. "The Women of the Telephone Company." *The New York Review of Books* 14:14-22.

Langland, E. and W. Gove, eds. 1981. *A Feminist Perspective in the Academy: The Difference It Makes.* Chicago: University of Chicago.

Larwood, L. and M. Wood. 1977. *Women in Management.* Lexington, MA: D. C. Heath.

Laslett, B. and J. Brenner. 1989. "Gender and Social Reproduction: Historical Perspectives." *Annual Review of Sociology* 15:381-404.

Laws, J. L. 1975. "The Psychology of Tokens: An Analysis." *Sex Roles* 1:51-67.

———. 1979. *The Second X: Sex Role and Social Role.* New York: Elsevier.

Lazonick, W. 1979. "Industrial Relations and Technical Change: The Case of the Self Acting Mule." *Cambridge Journal of Economics* 3:231-62.

Leapman, M. 1986. "An Off-Screen Soap Opera." *The Observer*, June 15.

Lee, R. and P. Lawrence. 1985. *Organizational Behaviour: Politics at Work.* London: Hutchinson.

Leffingwell, W. H. 1922. "Sizing up Customers from Behind the Counter." *The American Magazine* 94:150.

Leggon, L. 1980. "Black Female Professionals: Dilemmas and Contradictions of Status." Pp. 189-202 in *The Black Woman*, edited by R. Rodgers. Beverly Hills, CA: Sage.

Leigh, Z. 1926. "Shopping Around." *Atlantic Monthly* 138:205.

Levinson, D. J. 1986. "A Conception of Adult Development." *American Psychologist* 41(1):3-13.

Levinson, D., C. N. Darrow, E. B. Klein, M. H. Levinson, and B. McKee. 1978. *Seasons of a Man's Life.* New York: Knopf.

Lewenhak, S. 1980. *Women and Work.* Glasgow: Fontana.

Lightfoot, S. L. 1988. *Balm in Gilead: Journey of a Healer.* Reading, MA: Addison-Wesley.

Lipman-Blumen, J. 1976. "Towards a Homosocial Theory of Sex Roles: An Explanation of the Sex Segregation of Social Institutions." In *Women and the Workplace,* edited by M. Blaxall and B. Reagan. Chicago: University of Chicago Press.

Littler, C. 1982. *The Development of the Labour Process in Capitalist Societies.* London: Heinemann.

Lockwood, D. 1966a. *The Blackcoated Worker: A Study in Class Consciousness.* London: Allen and Unwin.

———. 1966b. "Sources of Variation in Working-Class Images of Society." *Sociological Review* 14:249-67.

Lombard, G. F. F. 1941. "Executive Policies and Employee Satisfactions: A Study of a Small Department in a Large Metropolitan Store." D.C.S. thesis, Harvard University, Graduate School of Business Administration.

———. 1955. *Behavior in a Selling Group: A Case Study of Interpersonal Relations in a Department Store.* Boston: Harvard University, Graduate School of Business Administration, Division of Research.

Lugones, M. C. and E. V. Spelman. 1983. "Have We Got a Theory for You! Feminist Theory, Cultural Imperialism, and the Demand for 'The Woman's Voice.' " *Women's Studies International Forum* 6(6):573-81.

Lupton, T. 1963. *On the Shop Floor.* Oxford, UK: Pergamon.

Luxton, M. 1980. *More than a Labour of Love.* Toronto: Women's Press.

Lykes, B. M. 1983. "Discrimination and Coping in the Lives of Black Women." *Journal of Social Issues* 39(3):79-100.

Mackie, L. and P. Pattullo. 1977. *Women at Work.* London: Tavistock.

MacKinnon, C. 1979. *Sexual Harassment of Working Women.* New Haven, CT: Yale University Press.

———. 1982. "Feminism, Marxism, Method and the State: An Agenda for Theory." *Signs: Journal of Women in Culture and Society* 7:515-44.

———. 1983. "Feminism, Marxism, Method and the State: Toward Feminist Jurisprudence." *Signs: Journal of Women in Culture and Society* 8:635-58.

———. 1989. *Toward a Feminist Theory of the State.* Cambridge, MA: Harvard University Press.

Madden, J. F. 1985. "The Persistence of Pay Differentials: The Economics of Sex Discrimination." Pp. 76-114 in *Women and Work: An Annual Review.* Vol. 1, edited by L. Larwood, A. H. Stromberg, and B. A. Gutek. Beverly Hills, CA: Sage.

Mahon, R. 1977. "Canadian Public Policy: The Unequal Structure of Representation." In *The Canadian State,* edited by L. Panitch. Toronto: University of Toronto Press.

———. 1979. "Regulatory Agencies: Captive Agents or Hegemonic Apparatuses." *Studies in Political Economy* 1:162-200.

———. 1984. *The Politics of Industrial Restructuring: Canadian Textiles.* Toronto: University of Toronto Press.

Major, K. 1985. "Study Assistance in a Commonwealth Department: Different Gender, Different Benefits." Paper presented in the unit, Managing Discrimination, Kuring-gai College of Advanced Education.

March, J. G. and H. A. Simon. 1959. *Organizations.* New York: John Wiley.

Marchack, P. 1979. *In Whose Interests.* Toronto: McClelland and Stewart.

Marcia, J. E. 1980. "Identity in Adolescence." In *Handbook of Adolescent Psychology,* edited by J. Adelson. New York: John Wiley.

Marcus, G. F. and M. M. J. Fischer. 1986. *Anthropology as Cultural Critique.* Chicago: University of Chicago Press.

Marcuse, H. 1966. *Eros and Civilisation,* 2nd ed. London: Routledge & Kegan Paul.

Marglin, S. 1974. "What Do Bosses Do?" *Review of Radical Political Economics* 6:60-112.

Maroney, H. J. 1988. "Contemporary Quebec Feminism: The Interrelation of Political and Ideological Developments in Williams' Organizations, Trade Unions, Political Parties and State Policy 1960-1980." Ph.D. dissertation, McMaster University.

Marrett, C. 1971. "On the Specification of Inter-organizational Dimensions." *Sociology and Social Research* 56:83-89.

———. 1972. "Centralization in Female Organizations: Reassessing the Evidence." *Social Problems* 19:348-57.

Marshall, J. 1989. "Revisioning Career Concepts: A Feminist Invitation." In *Handbook of Career Theory,* edited by M. B. Arthur, D. T. Hall, and B. S. Lawrence. Cambridge, MA: Cambridge University Press.

Martin, J. 1988. "The Suppression of Gender Conflict in Organizations: Deconstructing the Fissure Between Public and Private." Paper presented at the Academy of Management Meeting, Anaheim, CA, August.

———. 1990a. "Deconstructing Organizational Taboos: The Suppression of Gender Conflict in Organizations." *Organizational Science* 1:1-21.

———. 1990b. "Re-reading Weber: Searching for Feminist Alternatives to Bureaucracy." Paper presented at the annual meeting of the Academy of Management, San Francisco.

———. 1990c. "Organizational Taboos: The Suppression of Gender Conflict in Organizations." *Organization Science* 1:334-59.

Martin, J., M. S. Feldman, M. J. Hatch, and S. B. Sitkin. 1983. "The Uniqueness Paradox in Organizational Stories." *Administrative Science Quarterly* 28:438-53.

Martin, P. Y. 1981. "Women, Labour Markets and Employing Organizations: A Critical Analysis." In *The International Yearbook of Organization Studies,* edited by D. Dunkerley and G. Salaman. London: Routledge & Kegan Paul.

Marx, K. and F. Engels. [1848] 1971. "The Communist Manifesto." Pp. 85-125 in *The Birth of the Communist Manifesto,* edited by D. J. Struik. New York: International.

———. 1976. *The German Ideology. Vol. 5, Collected Works.* Moscow: Progress.

Mayes, S. S. 1979. "Women in Positions of Authority: A Case Study of Changing Sex Roles." *Signs: Journal of Women in Culture and Society* 4:556-68.

Mayntz, R. 1964. "The Study of Organizations." *Current Sociology* 13:95-156.

McAdams, D. P. 1988. *Power, Intimacy and the Life Story: Personological Inquiries into Identity.* New York: Guilford.

McDonough, R. and R. Harrison. 1978. "Patriarchy and Relations of Production." Pp. 11-14 in *Feminism and Materialism,* edited by A. Kuhn and A. Wolpe. London: Routledge & Kegan Paul.

McGoldrick, M. 1989. "Women Through the Family Life Cycle." In *Women in Families: A Framework for Family Therapy,* edited by M. McGoldrick, C. M. Anderson, and F. Walsh. New York: Norton.

McIntosh, M. 1978. "The State and the Oppression of Women." In *Feminism and Materialism,* edited by A. Kuhn and A. M. Wolpe. London: Routledge & Kegan Paul.

McLane, H. J. 1980. *Selecting, Developing and Retaining Women Executives.* New York: Van Nostrand.

McNally, F. 1979. *Women for Hire.* London: Macmillan.

Mechanic, D. 1962. "Sources of Power and Lower Participants in Complex Organizations." *Administrative Science Quarterly* 7:439-64.

Meeker, B. F. and P. A. Weitzel-O'Neill. 1977. "Sex Roles and Interpersonal Behavior in Task-Oriented Groups." *American Sociological Review* 42:91-105.

Melossi, D. 1979. "Institutions of Social Control and the Capitalist Organization of Work." In *Capitalism and the Rule of Law,* edited by NDC/CSE. London: Hutchinson.

Melossi, D. and M. Pavarini. 1981. *The Prison Factory.* New York: Macmillan.

Mennerick, L. A. 1975. "Organizational Structuring of Sex Roles in a Nonstereotyped Industry." *Administrative Science Quarterly* 20:570-86.

Metcalfe, H. C. and R. Urwick. 1941. *Dynamic Administration: The Collected Papers of Mary Parker Follett.* New York: Harper & Brothers.

Mighty, J. 1991. "Triple Jeopardy: Employment Equity and Immigrant, Visible Minority Women." Paper presented at the women-in-management session of the Administrative Science Association of Canada Annual Meeting, Niagara, Ontario, June.

Miller, J. B. 1976. *Toward a New Psychology of Women.* Boston: Beacon.

Millett, K. 1969. *Sexual Politics.* London: Rupert Hart Davies.

Mills, A. J. 1988a. "Organizational Acculturation and Gender Discrimination." Pp. 1-22 in *Canadian Issues, Vol. 11, Women and the Workplace,* edited by P. K. Kresl. Montreal: Association of Canadian Studies/International Council for Canadian Studies.

———. 1988b. "Organization, Gender and Culture." *Organization Studies* 9(3):351-69.

———. 1989. "Gender, Sexuality and Organization Theory." In *The Sexuality of Organization,* edited by J. Hearn, D. L. Sheppard, P. Tancred-Sheriff, and G. Burrell. London: Sage.

Mills, A. J. and P. Chiaramonte. 1981. "Organization as Gendered Communication Act." *Canadian Journal of Communications* 16:381-98.

Mills, A. J. and S. J. Murgatroyd. 1991. *Organizational Rules: A Framework for Understanding Organizations.* Milton Keynes: Open University Press.

Mills, A. J. and T. Simmons. Forthcoming. *Reading Organization Theory.* Toronto: Garamond.

Mills, C. W. 1951. *White Collar: The American Middle Class.* London: Oxford University Press.

———. 1959. *The Sociological Imagination.* New York: Oxford University Press.

Milward, B. H. and C. Swanson. 1978. "The Impact of Affirmative Action on Organizational Behaviour." *Policy Studies Journal* 7:201-7.

Minnich, E. K. 1981. "A Feminist Criticism of the Liberal Arts." Pp. 22-38 in *Liberal Education and the New Scholarship on Women Issues and Constraints in Institutional Change*, edited by A. Fuller. Washington, DC: Association of American Colleges.

Minson, K. 1980. "Strategies for Socialists? Foucault's Conception of Power." *Economy and Society* 9(1):1-43.

Mitchell, J. 1966. "Women: The Longest Revolution." *New Left Review* 40:11-37.

Mohanty, C. T. 1991. "Under Western Eyes: Feminist Scholarship and Colonial Discourses." In *Third World Women and the Politics of Feminism,* edited by C. T. Mohanty, A. Russo, and L. Torres. Bloomington: Indiana University Press.

Montgomery, D. 1976. "Workers' Control of Machine Production in the 19th Century." *Labor History* 17:485-509.

Montgomery Hyde, H. 1970. *The Love That Dared Not Speak Its Name.* Boston: Little, Brown.

Moraga, C. and G. Anzaldúa, eds. 1983. *This Bridge Called My Back: Writings by Radical Women of Color.* New York: Kitchen Table: Women of Color Press.

Morgan, D. 1981. "Men, Masculinity and the Process of Sociological Inquiry." Pp. 83-113 in *Doing Feminist Research,* edited by H. Roberts. London: Routledge & Kegan Paul.

Morgan, G. 1980. "Paradigms, Metaphors and Puzzle Solving in Organization Theory." *Administrative Science Quarterly* 25:605-22.

———. 1986. *Images of Organization.* London: Sage.

Morgan, G. 1990. *Organizations in Society.* London: Macmillan.

Morgan, G. and D. Knights. 1991. "Gendering Jobs: Corporate Strategy, Managerial Control and the Dynamics of Job Segregation." *Work, Employment & Society* 5:181-200.

Morgan, N. 1988. *The Equality Game: Women in the Federal Public Service (1908-1987).* Ottawa: Canadian Advisory Council on the Status of Women.

Morouney, K. 1991. "The Social Construction of Leading: Formulating a Critique of the Methodology of Leadership." *Proceedings of the Annual Conference of the Administrative Sciences Association of Canada, Women in Management* 12(11):21-30.

Morris, M. 1982. "A Review of Michel Foucault's 'La Volont de Savoir.' " Pp. 245-74 in *Human Sexual Relations*, edited by M. Brake. Harmondsworth, UK: Penguin.

Morrison, A. M., R. P. White, E. Van Velsor, and the Center for Creative Leadership. 1987. *Breaking the Glass Ceiling: Can Women Reach the Top of America's Largest Corporations.* Reading, MA: Addison-Wesley.

MR. 1982. "Causes and Effects of Occupational Streaming Within the Administrative and Clerical Division of the NSW Public Service." Paper presented in the unit, Individual and Organisation, Kuring-gai College of Advanced Education.

Mumby, D. K. and L. L. Putnam. 1990. "Bounded Rationality as an Organizational Construct: A Feminist Critique." Paper presented at the annual meeting of the Academy of Management, San Francisco.

Mumford, L. 1946. *Technics and Civilisation.* London: Routledge.

Murdock, M. 1990. *The Heroine's Journey: Woman's Quest for Wholeness.* Boston: Shambhala.

National Retail Dry Goods Association. 1942. "A Saleswomen Speaks to Management." *Bulletin of the National Retail Dry Goods Association* 24(12):18.

Nelson, D. 1975. *Managers and Workers: Origins of the New Factory System in the United States, 1880-1920.* Madison: University of Wisconsin Press.

Neuhouser, K. 1989. "Sources of Women's Power and Status Among the Urban Poor in Contemporary Brazil." *Signs: Journal of Women in Culture and Society 14:685-702.*

Newman, W. 1982. "Pay Equity Emerges as a Top Labor Issue in the 1980's." *Monthly Labor Review* 105(4):49-51.

Nieva, V. F. and B. A. Gutek. 1980. "Sex Effects on Evaluation." *Academy of Management Review* 5(2):267-76.

———. 1981. *Women and Work: A Psychological Perspective.* New York: Praeger.

Nisbet, L. 1977. "Affirmative Action: A Liberal Program?" In *Reverse Discrimination,* edited by B. R. Gross. Buffalo, NY: Prometheus.

Nkomo, S. 1988. "Uncharted Journey: Minority Women in Management." Paper presented at the national meeting of the Academy of Management, Anaheim, CA, August.

Noble, T. and B. A. Pym. 1970. "Collegial Authority and the Receding Locus of Power." *British Journal of Sociology* 21:431-45.

Northcraft, G. and J. Martin. 1982. "Double Jeopardy: Resistance to Affirmative Action from Potential Beneficiaries." In *Sex-Role Stereotyping and Affirmative Action Policy,* edited by B. A. Gutek. Los Angeles: UCLA Institute for Industrial Relations.

Oakley, A. 1972. *Sex, Gender and Society.* London: Temple Smith.

O'Brien, M. 1981. *The Politics of Reproduction.* London: Routledge & Kegan Paul.

O'Hagan, A. 1900. "Behind the Scenes in the Big Stores." *Munsey's Magazine* 22:535.

O'Leary, V. 1974. "Some Attitudinal Barriers to Occupational Aspirations in Women." *Psychological Bulletin* 81:809-26.

O'Leary, V. and R. Hansen. 1982. "Typing Hurts Women Helps Men: The Meaning of Effort." In *Women in the Workforce,* edited by H. J. Bernardin. New York: Praeger.

Omi, M. and H. Winant. 1986. *Racial Formation in the United States: From the 1960s to the 1980s.* New York: Routledge & Kegan Paul.

Oppenheimer, V. K. 1968. "The Sex-Labeling of Jobs." *Industrial Relations* 7:219-34.

———. 1970. *The Female Labor Force in the U.S.* (Population Monograph Series No. 5). Berkeley: University of California.

———. 1973. "Demographic Influence on Female Employment and the Status of Women." *American Journal of Sociology* 78:946-61.

"Organizational Analysis: Critique and Innovation." 1977. *Sociological Quarterly* (Special Issue) 18(1).

O'Sullivan, E. 1977. "Interorganizational Cooperation: Is It Effective for Grassroots Organizations?" *Groups and Organization Studies* 2:347-58.

Ott, E. M. 1989. "Effects of the Male-Female Ratio at Work: Policewomen and Male Nurses." *Psychology of Women Quarterly* 13:41-57.

Ouchi, W. 1981. *Theory Z.* Reading, MA: Addison-Wesley.

Overton, P., R. Schneck, and C. B. Hazlett. 1977. "An Empirical Study of the Technology of Nursing Subunits." *Administrative Science Quarterly* 22:200-219.

Page, C., ed. 1986. *A Foot in Each World: Essays and Articles by Leanita McClain.* Evanston, IL: Northwestern University Press.

Parkin, W. 1989. "Private Experiences in the Public Domain: Sexuality and Residential Care Organizations." Pp. 110-24 in *The Sexuality of Organization,* edited by J. Hearn et al. London: Sage.

Parkin, W. and J. Hearn. 1987. "Frauen, Mannen, and Fuhrung." In *Hanwortbuch der Fuhrung,* edited by A. Kieser, G. Reber, and R. Wunderer. Stuttgart: C. D. Poeschel.

Parsons, T. and R. F. Bales, eds. [1955] 1975. *Family, Socialization and Interaction Process.* New York: Free Press.

Parsons, T., R. F. Bales, and E. A. Shils. 1951. *Working Papers in the Theory of Action.* Glencoe, IL: Free Press.

Pascale, R. and A. G. Athos. 1982. *The Art of Japanese Management.* London: Allen Lane.

Pateman, C. 1981. "The Concept of Equality." In *A Just Society? Essays on Equity in Australia,* edited by P. N. Troy. Sydney: George Allen and Unwin.

———. 1983. "The Impact of Feminism on Political Theory." Paper presented to the 53rd ANZAAS Congress, Perth, May.

———. 1986. "Introduction: The Theoretical Subversiveness of Feminism." In *Feminist Challenges,* edited by C. Pateman and E. Gross. Winchester, MA: Allen & Unwin.

———. 1988. *The Sexual Contract.* Cambridge, MA: Polity.

Payne, R. L. and D. C. Pheysey. 1971. "Organization Structure and Sociometric Nominations Amongst Line Managers in Three Contrasted Organizations." *European Journal of Social Psychology* 1:261-84.

Peck, G. R. 1982. "The Labour Process According to Burawoy: Limits of a Non-dialectical Approach." *Insurgent Sociologist* 11(3):81-90.

Peitchinus, S. G. 1989. *Women at Work.* Toronto: McClelland and Stewart.

Perkin, H. 1969. *The Origins of Modern English Society.* London: Routledge & Kegan Paul.

Perrow, C. 1967. "A Framework for the Comparative Analysis of Organizations." *American Sociological Review* 32:194-208.

———. 1970. *Organizational Analysis: A Sociological View.* Belmont, CA: Wadsworth.

———. 1986. *Complex Organizations.* New York: Random House.

Peters, T. J. and R. H. Waterman. 1982. *In Search of Excellence.* New York: Harper & Row.

Pettigrew, A. M. 1979. "On Studying Organizational Cultures." *Administrative Science Quarterly* 24:570-81.

Pfeffer, J. and A. Davis-Blake. 1987. "The Effect of the Proportion of Women on Salaries: The Case of College Administrators." *Administrative Science Quarterly* 32(1):1-24.

Pheysey, D. C., R. L. Payne, and D. S. Pugh. 1971. "Influence of Structure at Organizational and Group Levels." *Administrative Science Quarterly* 16:61-73.

Phillips, A. and B. Taylor. 1980. "Sex and Skill: Notes Towards a Feminist Economics." *Feminist Review* 6:79.

Pinderhughes, E. 1989. *Understanding Race, Ethnicity, and Power: The Key to Efficacy in Clinical Practice.* New York: Free Press.

Pirsig, R. M. 1976. *Zen and the Art of Motorcycle Maintenance.* London: Corgi.

Pleck, J. 1977. "The Work-Family Role System." *Social Problems* 24:417-27.

Pollert, A. 1981. *Girls, Wives, Factory Lives.* London: Macmillan.

Poulantzas, N. 1976. *La Crise de l'Etat.* Paris: Presses Universitaires de France.

———. 1978. *State, Power, Socialism.* London: New Left.

Powell, G. 1988. *Women and Men in Management.* Newbury Park, CA: Sage.

———. 1990. "One More Time: Do Female and Male Managers Differ?" *The Academy of Mangement Executive* 4:68-75.

Pringle, R. 1989. "Bureaucracy, Rationality and Sexuality: The Case of Secretaries." In *The Sexuality of Organization,* edited by J. Hearn, D. L. Sheppard, P. Tancred-Sheriff, and G. Burrell. London: Sage.

Provan, K. J., J. Beyer, and C. Kruytbosch. 1980. "Environmental Linkages and Power in Resource-Dependence Relations Between Organizations." *Administrative Science Quarterly* 25:200-223.

Query, J. M. N. 1973. "Total Push and the Open Total Institution: The Factory-Hospital." *Journal of Applied Behavioral Sciences* 9:294-307.

Quinn, R. E. 1977. "Coping with Cupid: The Formation, Impact, and Management of Romantic Relationships in Organizations." *Administrative Science Quarterly* 22:30-45.

Rader, V. F. 1979. "Client Influence on a New Organization: A Case Study of Federal City College." *Urban Education* 14:31-51.

Reddish, H. 1975. "Written Memorandum of Evidence to the Royal Commission on Trade Union's and Employers' Associations." Pp. 298-301 in *Industrial Relations in the Wider Society*, edited by B. Barratt, E. Rhodes, and J. Beishon. London: Collier/Macmillan.

Reed, M. 1985. *Redirections in Organizational Analysis.* London: Tavistock.

Reich, C. 1962. *The Sexual Revolution.* London: Vision.

———. 1972. *The Greening of America.* Harmondsworth, UK: Penguin.

Reskin, B. 1984. *Sex-Segregation in the Workplace: Trends, Explorations, Remedies.* Washington, DC: National Academy Press.

Rhodes, A. 1984. "Status of Women Councils: Should We Keep Them. Improve Them. Dump Them." *Chatelaine* 57:177-90.

Rich, A. 1980. "Compulsory Heterosexuality and Lesbian Existence." *Signs: Journal of Women in Culture and Society* 5:631-60.

Riger, S. and P. Galligan. 1980. "Women in Management: An Exploration of Competing Paradigms." *American Psychologist* 35:902-10.

Riley, P. 1983. "A Structurationist Account of Political Culture." *Administrative Science Quarterly* 28:414-37.

Robinson, P. A. 1972. *The Sexual Radicals.* London: Paladin.

Roethlisberger, F. J. and W. J. Dickson. 1939. *Management and the Worker.* Cambridge, MA: Harvard University Press.

Rosaldo, M. Z. 1974. "Women, Culture and Society: A Theoretical Overview." Pp. 17-42 in *Women, Culture and Society,* edited by M. Z. Rosaldo and L. Lamphere. Stanford, CA: Stanford University Press.

Rose, G. L. and P. Andiappon. 1978. "Sex Effects on Managerial Hiring Decisions." *Academy of Management Journal* 21:103-12.

Rosen, B. and T. H. Jerdee. 1974. "Influence of Sex Role Stereotypes on Personnel Decisions." *Journal of Applied Psychology* 59:9-14.

Rosenbaum, J. E. 1979. "Tournament Mobility: Career Patterns in a Corporation." *Administrative Science Quarterly* 24:220-41.

———. 1980. "Hierarchical and Individual Effects on Earnings." *Industrial Relations* 19(1):1-14.

———. 1985. "Jobs, Job Status and Women's Gains from Affirmative Action: Implications for Comparable Worth." In *Comparable Worth: New Directions for Research,* edited by H. I. Hartmann. Washington, DC: National Academy Press.

Rosener, J. B. 1990. "Ways Women Lead." *Harvard Business Review,* November-December, pp. 119-25.

Rossiter, M. 1982. *Women Scientists in America: Struggles and Strategies to 1940.* Baltimore, MD: Johns Hopkins University Press.

Roszak, T. 1969. *The Making of a Counter Culture.* New York: Doubleday.

Rothschild-Whitt, J. 1976. "Conditions Facilitating Participatory-Democratic Organizations." *Sociological Inquiry* 46:75-86.

———. 1979. "The Collectivist Organization: An Alternative to Rational Bureaucratic Models." *American Sociological Review* 44:509-27.

Rubenstein, D. 1978. "Love and Work." *Sociological Review* 26:5-25.

Ruble, T. L., R. Cohen, and D. N. Ruble. 1984. "Sex Stereotypes: Occupational Barriers for Women." *American Behavioral Scientist* 27(3):339-56.

Ryan, P. 1981. "Segmentation, Duality and the Internal Labour Market." In *The Dynamics of Labour Market Segmentation,* edited by R. Wilkinson. New York: Academic Press.

Said, E. W. 1985. "Orientalism Reconsidered." *Cultural Critique,* Spring, pp. 89-107.

Salaman, G. 1979. *Work Organisations: Resistance and Control.* London: Longman.

———. 1981. *Class and the Corporation.* Glasgow: Fontana.

Salaman, G. and K. Thompson, eds. 1965. *People and Organization.* Milton Keynes: Open University Press.

"A Saleswoman Speaks to Management." 1942. *Bulletin of the National Retail Dry Goods Association* 24(12):18.

Satow, R. L. 1975. "Value Rationality and Professional Organizations: Weber's Missing Type." *Administrative Science Quarterly* 20:526-31.

Schein, E. H. 1984. "Coming to a New Awareness of Organizational Culture." *Sloan Management Review* 25(Pt. 2):3-16.

Schein, V. 1973. "The Relationship Between Sex Role Stereotypes and Requisite Management Characteristics Among Female Managers." *Journal of Applied Psychology* 57:89-105.

Schrank, H. T. and J. W. Riley. 1976. "Women in Work Organisations." In *Women and the American Economy: A Look to the 1980's,* edited by M. Kreps. Englewood Cliffs, NJ: Prentice-Hall.

Schuler, H. and W. Berger. 1979. "The Impact of Physical Attractiveness on an Employment Decision." In *Love and Attraction,* edited by M. Cook and G. Wilson. Oxford: Pergamon.

Schwartz, F. N. 1989. "Management Women and the New Facts of Life." *Harvard Business Review* 67(1):65-76.

Schwartz, H. S. 1986. "Immoral Actions of Committed Organizational Participants: An Existential Psychoanalytic Perspective." *Proceedings of the Academy of Management,* pp. 321-325.

Scott, J. 1986. "Gender: A Useful Category of Historical Analysis." *American Historical Review* 91:1053-75.

Scott, J. 1988. "Deconstructing Equality vs. Difference: Or, the Uses of Post-Structuralist Theory for Feminism." *Feminist Studies* 14:33-50.

Scott, K. Y. 1991. *The Habit of Surviving: Black Women's Strategies for Life.* New Brunswick, NJ: Rutgers University Press.

Sedley, A. and M. Benn. 1982. *Sexual Harassment at Work.* London: National Council for Civil Liberties.

Seligmann, L. J. 1989. "To Be in Between: The Cholas as Market Women." *Comparative Studies in Society and History* 31:694-721.

Shaw, N. S. 1974. *Forced Labour: Maternity Care in the United States.* Oxford: Pergamon.

Shepela, S. T. and A. T. Viviano. 1984. "Some Psychological Factors Affecting Job Segregation and Wages." In *Comparable Worth and Wage Discrimination: Technical Possibilities and Political Realities,* edited by H. Remick. Philadelphia: Temple University Press.

Sheppard, D. 1981. "Awareness and Decision-Making in Dual-Career Couples." Ph.D. dissertation, York University, Toronto.

———. 1988. "Wheels Within Wheels: Women, Family, Organizations and Management of Boundaries." Paper presented at Women in the Year 2000: Utopian and Dystopian Visions, Indiana University, April.

———. 1989. "Organizations, Power and Sexuality: The Image and Self-Image of Women Managers." Pp. 139-57 in *The Sexuality of Organization,* edited by J. Hearn, D. L. Sheppard, P. Tancred-Sheriff, and G. Burrell. London: Sage.

Sheppard, D. and P. Fothergill. 1984. "Image and Self-Image of Women in Organizations." Paper presented at the Canadian Research Institute for the Advancement of Women Annual Conference, Quebec, November.

Sheridan, A. 1980. *Michel Foucault: The Will to Truth.* London: Tavistock.

Shuval, J. T. 1962. "Ethnic Stereotyping in Israeli Medical Bureaucracies." *Sociology and Social Research* 46:455-65.

Sigelman, L., H. B. Milward, and J. M. Shepard. 1982. "The Salary Differential Between Male and Female Administrators: Equal Pay for Equal Work?" *Academy of Management Journal* 25(3):668.

Silverman, D. 1970. *The Theory of Organizations.* London: Heinemann.

Simmons, G. L. 1975. *A Place for Pleasure: The History of the Brothel.* London: Harwood Smart.

Simpson, R. L. and I. H. Simpson. 1969. "Women and Bureaucracy in the Semi-Professions." Pp. 196-265 in *The Semi-Professions and Their Organization,* edited by A. Etzioni. New York: Free Press.

Siren and Black Rose. 1971. *Anarcho-Feminism.* Chicago: Siren. (reprinted by Black Bear, London)

Smircich, L. 1983a. "Concepts of Culture and Organizational Analysis." *Administrative Science Quarterly* 28:339-58.

———. 1983b. "Studying Organizations as Cultures." Pp. 160-172 in *Beyond Method,* edited by G. Morgan. London: Sage.

———. 1985a. "Is the Concept of Culture a Paradigm for Understanding Organizations and Ourselves?" Pp. 55-72 in *Organizational Culture,* edited by P. J. Frost, L. F. Moore, M. R. Louis, C. C. Lundberg, and J. Martin. London: Sage.

———. 1985b. "Toward a Women Centered Organization Theory." Paper presented at the annual meetings of Academy of Management, San Diego, CA, August.

Smircich, L. and R. J. Chesser. 1981. "Superiors' and Subordinates' Perceptions of Performance: Beyond Disagreement." *Academy of Management Journal* 24(1):198-205.

Smith, C. W., ed. 1983. "The Duality of Social Structures, Structuration and the Intentionality of Human Action." *Journal for the Theory of Social Behaviour* 13(1).

Smith, D. 1975. "Analysis of Ideological Structures and How Women Are Excluded: Considerations for Academic Women." *Canadian Review of Sociology and Anthropology* 12:353-69.

———. 1977. "Women, the Family and Corporate Capitalism." In *Women in Canada.* Rev. ed., edited by M. Stephenson. Don Mills, Ontario: General Publishing.

———. 1987. *The Everyday World as Problematic: A Feminist Sociology.* Toronto: University of Toronto Press.

———. 1990. *The Conceptual Practices of Power: A Feminist Sociology of Knowledge.* Toronto: University of Toronto Press.

Sohn-Rethel, A. 1978. *Intellectual and Manual Labour: A Critique of Epistemology.* New York: Macmillan.

Spelman, E. V. 1988. *Inessential Woman: Problems of Exclusion in Feminist Thought.* Boston: Beacon.

Spencer, L. and A. Dale. 1979. "Integration and Regulation in Organizations: A Contextual Approach." *The Sociological Review* 27:679-702.

Spender, D. 1980. *Man Made Language.* London: Routledge & Kegan Paul.

Spivak, G. C. 1987. *In Other Worlds: Essays in Cultural Politics.* New York: Methuen.

Stacey, M. 1981. "The Division of Labour Revisited or Overcoming the Two Adams." In *Practice and Progress: British Sociology 1950-1980,* edited by P. Abrams, R. Deem, J. Finch, and P. Rock. London: Allen & Unwin.

Stacey, M. and M. Price. 1981. *Women, Power and Politics.* London: Tavistock.

Stanley, L. and S. Wise. 1983. *Breaking Out: Feminist Consciousness and Feminist Research.* London: Routledge & Kegan Paul.

Staw, B. M., ed. 1979. *Research in Organizational Behavior. Vol. 1, An Annual Series of Analytical Essays and Critical Reviews.* Greenwich, CT: JAI.

Staw, B. M. and L. L. Cummings, eds. 1980. *Research in Organizational Behavior. Vol. 2, An Annual Series of Analytical Essays and Critical Reviews.* Greenwich, CT: JAI.

Stead, B. A., ed. 1978. *Women in Management.* Englewood Cliffs, NJ: Prentice-Hall.

Stewart, A. J. 1990. "Discovering the Meanings of Work." In *The Experience and Meaning of Work in Women's Lives,* edited by H. Y. Grossman and N. L. Chester. Hillsdale, NJ: Lawrence Erlbaum.

Stone, L. 1979. *The Family, Sex, and Marriage in England, 1500-1800.* Harmondsworth, UK: Pelican.

Storey, J. 1983. *Managerial Prerogative and the Question of Control.* London: Routledge & Kegan Paul.

Stott, M. 1978. *Organization Woman.* London: Heinemann.

Suchner, R. W. 1979. "Sex Ratios and Occupational Prestige: Three Failures to Replicate a Sexist Bias." *Personality and Social Psychology Bulletin* 5:236-39.

[Tancred-] Sheriff, P. 1976. "Sociology of Public Bureaucracies 1965-1975." *Current Sociology* 24:1-175.

[Tancred-] Sheriff, P. and E. Jane Campbell. 1981. "La place des femmes: Un dossier sur la sociologie des organisations." *Sociologie et Sociétés* 13:113-30.

Tancred-Sheriff, P. 1987. *Organizational Tendencies of Canadian Universities: Nature and Implications* (University of Saskatchewan Sorokin Lectures No. 18). Saskatoon: University of Saskatchewan.

Tancred, P. 1988. "Employment Equity: What Can We Learn from Other Attempts to Disestablish Privilege?" Paper presented at the CRIAW conference, Quebec City, November.

Tancred-Sheriff, P. 1989. "Gender, Sexuality and the Labour Process." In *The Sexuality of Organization,* edited by J. Hearn, D. Sheppard, P. Tancred-Sheriff, and G. Burrell. London: Sage.

Taylor, S. E., S. T. Fiske, N. L. Etcoff, and A. J. Ruderman. 1978. "Categorical and Contextual Bases of Person Memory and Stereotyping." *Journal of Personality and Social Psychology* 35:778-93.

Terbog, J. 1977. "Women in Management: A Research Review." *Journal of Applied Psychology* 62:647-64.

Terreberry, S. 1968. "The Evolution of Organizational Environments." *Administrative Science Quarterly* 12:590-613.

Thomas, D. A. 1989. "Mentoring an Irrationality: The Role of Racial Taboos." *Human Resource Management* 28(2): 279-90.

Thompson, E. P. 1968. *The Making of the English Working Class.* Harmondsworth, UK: Penguin.

Tiger, L. 1969. *Men in Groups.* London: Nelson.

Tompkins, J. 1986. " 'Indians': Textualism, Morality, and the Problem of History." Pp. 59-77 in *"Race," Writing, and Differences,* edited by J. L. Gates. Chicago: University of Chicago Press.

Torrey, J. W. 1976. "The Consequences of Equal Opportunity for Women." *Journal of Contemporary Business* 5:13-27.

Touhey, J. C. 1974a. "Effects of Additional Men on Prestige and Desirability of Occupation Typically Performed by Women." *Journal of Applied Social Psychology* 4:330-35.

———. 1974b. "Effects of Additional Women Professionals on Ratings of Occupational Prestige and Desirability." *Journal of Personality and Social Psychology* 29:86-89.

Townley, B. 1991. "Pygmalion and the Self-Fulfilling Prophecy: A New Myth for a New Age?" Paper presented at the Women in Management Session of the Administrative Sciences Association of Canada Annual Meeting, Niagara, Ontario, June.

Toynbee, P. 1982. "Lesbianism Is a Central Issue." *Guardian* 23:8.

"Training for Better Sales." 1953. *Stores* 35(9):28.

Treiman, D. J. and H. I. Hartmann, eds. 1981. *Women, Work and Wages: Equal Pay for Jobs of Equal Value.* Washington, DC: National Academy Press.

Tronto, J. 1987. "Beyond Gender Difference to a Theory of Care." *Signs: Journal of Women in Culture and Society* 12(4):644-63.

Tudor, B. 1972. "A Specification of Relationships Between Job Complexity and Powerlessness." *American Sociological Review* 37:596-604.

Turner, S. P. 1983. "Studying Organizations Through Levi-Strauss's Structuralism." Pp. 189-201 in *Beyond Method*, edited by G. Morgan. London: Sage.

Twyman, R. W. 1954. *History of Marshall Field & Co., 1852-1906*. Philadelphia: University of Pennsylvania Press.

Valentine, C. E. 1978. "Internal Union Democracy: Does It Help or Hinder the Movement for Industrial Democracy?" *The Insurgent Sociologist* 8:40-51.

Van Dijk, T. 1987. *Communicating Racism: Ethnic Prejudice in Thought and Talk*. Newbury Park, CA: Sage.

Vaught, C. and D. L. Smith. 1980. "Incorporation and Mechanical Solidarity in an Underground Coal Mine." *Sociology of Work and Occupations* 7:159-87.

Veiga, J. 1983. "Mobility Influences During Managerial Career Stages." *Academy of Management Journal* 26(1):64-85.

Vinnicombe, S. 1980. *Secretaries, Management, and Organizations*. London: Heinemann.

Walker, C. R. and R. H. Guest. 1952. *The Man on the Assembly Line*. Cambridge, MA: Harvard University Press.

Wallis, M. 1989. "The Dynamics of Race in Institutions." Paper presented at the Critical Approaches to Organizations session of the Canadian Sociology and Anthropology Association Annual Meeting, Laval University, Quebec City, June.

Ward, D. A. and G. G. Kassebaum. 1965. *Women's Prison: Sex and Social Structure*. London: Weidenfeld and Nicolson.

Weber, M. 1967. *The Protestant Ethic and the Spirit of Capitalism*. London: Unwin.

Weedon, C. 1987. *Feminist Practice and Poststructuralist Theory*. Oxford: Basil Blackwell.

Weeks, J. 1981. *Sex, Politics and Society*. London: Longman.

Weinstein, D. 1977. "Bureaucratic Opposition: The Challenge to Authoritarian Abuses at the Workplace." *Canadian Journal of Political and Social Theory* 1:31-46.

Wells, T. 1973. "The Covert Power of Gender in Organizations." *Journal of Contemporary Business* 2:53-68.

West, C. 1982. "Why Can't a Woman Be More Like a Man?" *Work and Occupations* 9(1):5-30.

West, C. and D. H. Zimmerman. 1987. "Doing Gender." *Gender & Society* 1:125-51.

West, J. 1977. "The Factory Slaves." *New Society* 39:384-85.

———., ed. 1982. *Work, Women, and the Labour Market*. London: Routledge & Kegan Paul.

White, M. C., M. D. Crino, and G. L. DeSanctis. 1981. "Ratings of Prestige and Desirability: Effects of Additional Women Entering Selected Business Occupations." *Personality and Social Psychology Bulletin* 7:588-92.

Whitehead, T. N. 1938. The Industrial Worker. Vol. 1. London: Oxford University Press.

Whittington, C. and R. Holland. 1981. "Social Theory Work: Teaching Sociology to Social Workers." *Social Work Education* 1:19-26.

Whyte, W. F. 1949. "The Social Structure of the Restaurant." *American Journal of Sociology* 54:302-10.

Whyte, W. H. 1952. *The Organisation Man*. Harmondsworth, UK: Penguin.

Wilkins, A. L. 1983. "The Culture Audit: A Tool for Understanding Organizations." *Organizational Dynamics*, Autumn, pp. 24-38.

Willis, P. 1977. *Learning to Labour*. Farnsborough, UK: Saxon House.

Wilson, E. 1977. *Women and the Welfare State*. London: Tavistock.

Winkler, K. J. 1987. "Poststructuralism: An Often-Abstruse French Import Profoundly Affects Research in the United States." *The Chronicle of Higher Education,* November 25, pp. A7-A9.

Wolff, J. 1977. "Women in Organizations." Pp. 7-20 in *Critical Issues in Organizations,* edited by S. Clegg and D. Dunkerley. London: Routledge & Kegan Paul.

Wolpe, A. 1978. "Education and the Sexual Division of Labour." Pp. 290-328 in *Feminism and Materialism,* edited by A. Kuhn and A. Wolpe. London: Routledge & Kegan Paul.

Wood, S., ed. 1982. *The Degradation of Work?* London: Hutchinson.

Woodward, J. 1958. *Management and Technology.* London: Department of Scientific and Industrial Research.

———. 1965. *Industrial Organization: Theory and Practice.* London: Oxford University Press.

———. 1970. *Industrial Organization: Behavior and Control.* London: Oxford University Press.

Yavas, U., E. Kaynak, and M. Dilber. 1985. "The Managerial Climate in Less-Developed Countries." *Management Decision* 23:29-40.

Young-Bruehl, E. 1987. "The Education of Women as Philosophers." *Signs: Journal of Women in Culture and Society* 12(2):207-21.

Zelditch, M. 1955 [1975]. "Role Differentiation in the Nuclear Family: A Comparative Study." In *Family, Socialization and Interaction Process,* edited by T. Parsons and R. F. Bales. New York: Free Press.

Zetterberg, H. L. 1966. "The Secret Ranking." *Journal of Marriage and the Family* 28:134-42.

Zimmer, L. 1988. "Tokenism and Women in the Workplace: The Limits of Gender-Neutral Theory." *Social Problems* 35(1):64-77.

Zimmerman, D. H. 1970. "Record-Keeping and the Intake Process in a Public Welfare Agency." In *On Record: Files and Dossiers in American Life*, edited by S. Wheeler. New York: Russell Sage.

Name Index

Subject Index

About the Contributors

Joan Acker is Professor of Sociology at the University of Oregon. She was Visiting Research Professor at the Swedish Center for Working Life from 1987 to 1990. Recent publications include "Thinking About Wages: The Gendered Wage Gap in Swedish Banks" (*Gender & Society,* 1991), "Hierarchies, Jobs, Bodies: A Theory of Gendered Organizations" (*Gender & Society,* 1990), *Doing Comparable Worth: Gender, Class and Pay Equity* (1989), and "Class, Gender, and the Relations of Distribution" (*Signs,* 1988).

Ella Louise Bell is Visiting Associate Professor at the Sloan School of Management. Her research and publications investigate the life experiences among African American and Euro-American professional women and seek to understand the intersection of race and gender in the contexts of women's lives. Together with colleagues Stella Nkomo and Toni Denton, she has received funding of $134,000 from the Rockefeller and Ford Foundations for the study "Life Journeys of Women Managers in Corporations." She was the Guest Editor for the special edition of the *Journal of Organizational Behavior* (November 1990), which focused on career issues of black professionals. She has been active in the Career, Organizational Development and Women Divisions of the Academy of Management.

Susan Porter Benson taught women's and social history at Bristol Community College from 1968 to 1986. During that time, she also worked as the New England Coordinator for "Threads," an Amalgamated Clothing and Textile Workers Union program, teaching labor history courses to active and retired members—most of them women. She has participated in numerous community projects on the history of wage-earning women. Since 1986, she has taught at the University of Missouri—Columbia. Recent publications include *Counter Cultures: Saleswomen, Managers, and Customers in American Department Stories, 1890-1940* (University of Illinois, 1986) and a contribution to the textbook *Who Built America: Working People and the Nation's Economy, Politics, Culture, and Society* (Pantheon, 1992). Her current research project is "Working-Class Families in the World of Consumption 1880-1960." She is on the editorial board of *Gender and History, The Radical History Review,* and *American Quarterly.*

Gibson Burrell graduated in sociology from the University of Leicester, thereafter completing an M.Phil. (Leicester, 1974) and a Ph.D. (Manchester, 1980). Following a research post at the University of Birmingham, he became Lecturer in Behaviour in Organizations at the University of Lancaster. He has been Professor of Organizational Behavior at the University of Warwick since 1987. His research interests include the development of organization theory using concepts from social theory and philosophy as well as "sexuality in organizations." He is married with three teenage daughters and lives in the geographic center of England.

Clare Burton has been Director of Equal Opportunity in Public Employment for the New South Wales Government in Australia since 1989, on leave from her position as Associate Professor in the Faculty of Business at the University of Technology, Sydney. She has been researching and consulting on Equal Employment Opportunity programs for more than a decade and has written extensively on employment issues relating to women. Her publications include *Subordination: Feminism and Social Theory* (Allen and Unwin, 1985); *Women's Worth: Pay Equity and Job Evaluation in Australia* (Australian Government Publishing Service, 1987); and *The Promise and the Price: The Struggle for Equal Opportunity in Women's Employment* (Allen and Unwin, 1991). She has been active in the feminist movement since the early 1970s and, more recently, has been a member of the National Pay Equity Coalition, which works to promote the principle of equal pay for work of equal value.

Marta B. Calás was born in Cuba. She holds degrees from the University of Puerto Rico (B.B.A.), the University of California at Berkeley (M.B.A.), and the University of Massachusetts at Amherst (Ph.D.). She is currently a faculty member at the University of Massachusetts, where her current work focuses on the limitations of international management scholarship from a cultural analysis perspective. With Linda Smircich, she has cowritten several papers exploring connections among culture, feminism, poststructuralism, postmodernism, and organization and management theory. She is a member of the Board of Directors of the Eastern Academy of Management and of the Europe-based Standing Conference on Organizational Symbolism.

E. Jane Campbell obtained her Ph.D. in sociology from McMaster University in 1981. Since 1980, she has been principal of Campbell Research Associates, a firm specializing in program evaluation, feasibility, and planning studies in the social and health services. During the past decade, she has managed studies for government clients and non-profit organizations, including a number of studies that have focused on issues of special concern to women. In carrying out evaluations of health, social, housing, and criminal justice programs, she has sought to give the service consumers, frequently economically disadvantaged women, a major participating role. She has presented papers at the meetings of the Canadian Sociology and Anthropology Association including "Victims' Responses to the Opportunity to 'Have a Voice in Court' " and "Effects of Women's Self-Employment on the Family."

Aaron Groff Cohen is currently Instructor of Psychology at California State University at Northridge. He received his Ph.D. in applied social psychology from the Claremont Graduate School in 1989. His research interests are in the area of gender roles, including men's roles, work and family issues, and sexual harassment. He has published several articles with Barbara A. Gutek on the topic of gender in the workplace including "Sex Differences in the Career Experiences of Members of Two Divisions of APA" (*American Psychologist,* forthcoming); "Dimensions of Perceptions of Social-Sexual Behavior in a Work Setting" (*Sex Roles,* 1985); "Predicting Social-Sexual Behavior at Work: A Contact Hypothesis" (with Alison M. Konrad, *Academy of Management Journal,* 1990); and "Interpreting Social-Sexual Behavior in a Work Setting" (with Bruce Morasch, *Journal of Vocational Behavior,* 1983).

Judith Grant received her B.A. (Honors) in Sociology from St. Mary's University in 1981 and her M.A. in Sociology from McMaster University in 1983. She has been a sessional lecturer in Sociology at McMaster, Mohawk College, and Memorial University of Newfoundland. She is the author of "Women's Issues and the State: Representation, Reform and Control" (*Resources for Feminist Research,* 1988) and of "Un point de vue féministe sur la bureaucratie étatique" (with Peta Tancred, *Sociologie et Sociétés, 1991).* She has been a volunteer at the local women's shelter and is currently enrolled in the Faculty of Education at Brock University.

Barbara A. Gutek is Professor of Management and Policy and of Psychology at the University of Arizona. She received her Ph.D. from the University of Michigan in 1975, specializing in organizational psychology. Her research focuses on women and work and impacts of computerization on workers and organizations. She is author, coauthor, or editor of nine books including *Women and Work: A Psychological Perspective* (with Veronica F. Nieva, 1981); the series *Women and Work: An Annual Review* (1985, 1986, 1988, coedited with Laurie Larwood and Ann Stromberg); and *Sex and the Workplace: Impact of Sexual Behavior and Harassment on Women, Men, and Organizations* (1985). In 1990-91, she was chair of the Women in Management Division of the Academy of Management.

Jeff Hearn is currently Senior Lecturer in Applied Social Studies at the University of Bradford, England. His interest in the relationship of gender and organizations comes from two main directions: organizational sociology and men's antisexist activities. He has been involved in men's groups since 1978 and was for many years active in child-care campaigns. He studied at Oxford University and Oxford Polytechnic, prior to studying organizations at Leeds University and completing his Ph.D. in social theory at Bradford University. He is author of *Birth and Afterbirth* (Achilles Heel, 1983); coauthor of *"Sex" at "Work"* and author of *The Gender of Oppression* (both Wheatsheaf/St. Martin, 1987); coeditor of *The Sexuality of Organization* (Sage, 1989), of the "Men, Masculinities and Leadership" special issue of *Equal Opportunities International* (MCB University Press, 1989) and of *Men, Masculinities and Social Theory* (Unwin Hyman, 1990); member of the Violence Against Children Study Group for *Taking Child Abuse Seri-*

ously (Unwin Hyman, 1990); and author of *Men in the Public Eye* (Routledge, 1992).

Albert J. Mills is Associate Professor of Organizational Behavior at Athabasca University, Alberta, Canada. His research activities center on the impact of the organization upon people, focusing on organizational change and human liberation. His early images of organization—of frustration, of power disparities, of conflict and of sexually segregated work—were experienced through a series of unskilled jobs and given broader meaning through campaigns for peace. He is currently based at the Netherlands International Institute for Management (Maastricht), where he is engaged in research on the gendering of organizational culture and is involved in the development of international women in management courses. He is the coauthor of two books: *Organizational Rules* (with S. Murgatroyd, 1991) and *Reading Organization Theory* (with T. Simmons, forthcoming). He served on Athabasca University's President's Employment Equity Committee from 1986 to 1990.

Stella M. Nkomo is Associate Professor of Management in the College of Business Administration at the University of North Carolina at Charlotte. Her research and writing focus on race and gender issues in organizations. She has published a number of articles and book chapters on the subject. Along with Ella Bell, she is currently working on a major study of the effects of race and gender on the career and life experiences of black and white women managers. She is currently the Chair-Elect of the Women in Management Division of the Academy of Management and an active member of Women Executives of Charlotte, an organization focusing on supporting and nurturing members' personal and professional growth.

P. Wendy Parkin is a part-time Senior Lecturer in Sociology and Social Work in the School of Human and Health Sciences at Huddersfield Polytechnic, England, combined with a part-time post as a social worker at a Family Center, working in the field of child abuse with Kirklees Metropolitan Council. Throughout her career in social work and teaching, there has been continuous writing and research on issues of gender and sexuality within organizations, including the interconnectedness of various oppressions and, more recently, child abuse. She is coauthor of *"Sex" at "Work"* (Wheatsheaf/St. Martin, 1987) and has contributed to *Women in Management Worldwide* (edited by N. J. Adler, D. N. Izraeli, and M. E.

Sharpe, 1988) and to the *Sexuality of Organization* (edited by J. Hearn, D. L. Sheppard, P. Tancred-Sheriff, and G. Burrell; Sage, 1989). She has also contributed (with B. Clark and M. Richards) to *Taking Child Abuse Seriously* (edited by the Violence Against Children Study Group; Unwin Hyman, 1990). As part of teaching and practice, she is actively involved in the development of equal opportunities policies and practices in her role as convener of the School of Human and Health Sciences Equal Opportunities Issues Group at Huddersfield Polytechnic.

Deborah Sheppard is a sociologist with degrees from McGill, Carleton, and York Universities, Canada. She has taught sociology and organizational behavior at York and at Concordia University in Montreal. She is coeditor (with J. Hearn, P. Tancred-Sheriff, and G. Burrell) of *The Sexuality of Organization* (Sage, 1989). In addition to her continuing work on the relationship between gender and organizational culture, her research has included decision making in dual-earner families, the relationship between gender, work, and family, and the implications of teaching and studying from a perspective of personal and social transformation. She has given many public talks and presentations on issues of particular concern to women. She is a consultant in the Washington, DC, area (with offices at 5521 Mohican Road, Bethesda, MD 20816-2159).

Linda Smircich was born on Long Island, New York. She received a B.A. in Social Science from the State University of New York at Oswego and an M.B.A. and Ph.D. from the School of Management at Syracuse University. She was on the faculty at Pennsylvania State University and is now a faculty member at the University of Massachusetts. From 1986 to 1988, she chaired the Faculty Senate Council on the Status of Women at the university. Currently, she is on the Executive Board of the Women in Management division of the Academy of Management. For the past six years, she has been writing with Marta Calás. Recently, they were awarded a grant from the National Science Foundation for a conference that analyzed the ethics and values of organization theory through feminist theories. They also coorganized and copresented a preconference workshop for the 1991 meetings of the Academy of Management, Women in Management division.

Peta Tancred is Professor of Sociology and Director of the Centre for Research and Teaching on Women at McGill University, Montréal, Canada. Her feminist research interests during the past decade have been firmly rooted in the organizational area; within this domain, she has published on a wide variety of topics including women and computers, employment equity, women and the state, women in universities, women's contribution to the sociology of organizations, and, in collaboration with Jeff Hearn, Deborah Sheppard, and Gibson Burrell, *The Sexuality of Organization.* She is the editor of *Feminist Research: Prospect and Retrospect* (McGill-Queen's, 1988) and has been a member of the publications committee of the Canadian Research Institute for the Advancement of Women. Her efforts on behalf of equity in the university setting were channeled, in part, through her work as the Chair of the Task Force and then of the Standing Committee on the Status of Women for the Ontario Confederation of University Faculty Associations (1984-86). She is a frequent speaker on behalf of women at university and community events and on behalf of women's studies at the national and international levels.

Donald R. Van Houten received his undergraduate degree from Oberlin College and developed his principal interests in the sociologies of work and organizations while getting his Ph.D. at the University of Pittsburgh. After three years teaching at Indiana University, he moved to the University of Oregon in 1968, where feminist and Marxist critiques of the late-1960s and early 1970s caused him to rethink his approaches to work and organizations. He regularly integrates theory and evidence on gender into his courses, research, and publications. Recent papers and articles on Sweden have discussed selective recruitment of women into Swedish jobs in the 1960s, the degree and consequences of sex segregation in autonomous work groups of the 1970s, and the disproportionate number of women in poor-quality jobs in Sweden in the 1980s. He recently completed a five-year term as Dean of the College of Arts and Sciences at the University of Oregon, where he intensified efforts to eradicate sexual harassment and successfully increased the recruitment of women faculty. His current research focuses on privatization in British and U.S. higher education including an analysis of its potentially differential effects on women.